Greater India Society Publication No. 3

SOCIAL LIFE IN ANCIENT INDIA:
STUDIES IN VATSYAYANA'S KAMASUTRA

Greater India Society Publication No. 3

SOCIAL LIFE IN ANCIENT INDIA:
STUDIES IN VATSYAYANA'S KAMASUTRA

BY

HARAN CHANDRA CHAKLADAR,
LECTURER IN ANTHROPOLOGY AND ANCIENT INDIAN HISTORY AND CULTURE, CALCUTTA UNIVERSITY

GYAN

Published by

Gyan Publishing House
5, Ansari Road
Daryaganj, New Delhi-110002
Phone: 011-47034999, 9811692060
E-mail: books@gyanbooks.com

Distribution Network
gyanbooks.com
India, USA, Canada, UK, Australia, France

ISBN : 978-81-212-2128-3 (HB)
First Published, 1929

2nd Impression 2021

Printed at: Gyan Press, Delhi.

Social Life in Ancient India:
Studies in Vatsyayana's
Kamasutra
Author: Haran Chandra Chakladar

Greater India Society Publication No. 3.

SOCIAL LIFE IN ANCIENT INDIA: STUDIES IN VĀTSYĀYANA'S KĀMASŪTRA

BY

HARAN CHANDRA CHAKLADAR

LECTURER IN ANTHROPOLOGY AND ANCIENT INDIAN HISTORY AND CULTURE, CALCUTTA UNIVERSITY.

BRHATTARA BHĀRATA PARISAD

GREATER INDIA SOCIETY

91, Upper Circular Road,

CALCUTTA.

1929

INTRODUCTORY NOTE

Since its inception the Greater India Society has been receiving help and support from students of Indian History and Culture. Eminent scholars, both Indian and European have given a most cordial *accueil* to this research association by offering their valuable works to be published under the auspices of the Society. Dr. R. C. Majumdar's *Champa* is associated with the Society's name. Last year we had the privilege of presenting to the public the standard work on Hindu Law and Custom by Dr. Jolly in an authorised English translation revised by the author. This year we have the pleasure of publishing two works by Prof. Haran Chandra Chakladar which will surely interest all Indologists. Mr. Chakladar is a professor of Sanskrit and History of long experience and now he is in the Department of Ancient Indian History and Culture of the University of Calcutta.

A scholar of the older generation, he has kept abreast of modern research in his subjects of Indian History, Ethnology and Anthropology by a close study of the important contributions made by the scholarly world of England, France, Germany and Italy.

In the present volume he takes up a most fascinating subject—the Life and Society in Ancient India. The work, as presented herewith, though forming part of a general survey of Social Life in Ancient India, is really a complete and comprehensive study of that life as reflected in one of the most important secular documents that have come down to us from the ancient world—the Kāmasūtra of Vātsyāyana, and we are sure that lovers of Indian lore will fully appreciate its value. Prof. Chakladar's second contribution to our Series will be on the Aryan Occupation of Eastern India which is being published simultaneously.

The best thanks of the Society are due to Prof. Chakladar and to his learned friends who helped us in bringing out the two new volumes. Thanks are also due to the Manager of the Calcutta Oriental Press who spared no pain in seeing the books through the press with great attention and promptitude.

CALCUTTA
July 20, 1929.

KALIDAS NAG
Secretary, Greater India Society

FOREWORD

The social life in ancient India has not yet received the same attention as the other aspects of ancient Indian history and culture. Only caste has been studied with some care, and from the legal point of view, some other aspects of social life also. But what Zimmer in his *Altindisches Leben* has done for the early Vedic period, still remains to be done for the subsequent ages of Indian civilisation and culture. However, before a synthetic history embracing the long period, through which Indian society has grown aud developed, is attempted, an intensive study has to be made of the different ages through which it has come. It was with this object that I took up the study of Vātsyāyana's K ā m a s ū t r a which gives a beautifully vivid picture of Indian society in the early centuries of the Christian era. It wonderfully supplements the account we receive from the sacred literatures, Brahmanical, Buddhistic and Jain. Dealing with an avowedly secular matter as it does, it depicts society from an independent point of view, and gives details, especially of the darker features of social life, with a fulness that we naturally miss in the sacred texts.

An indispensable preliminary was an accurate determination of the time when Vātsyāyana wrote his book, especially as in the history of Indian literature there are very few definite dates. I have therefore first of all discussed this question at some length from internal and external evidence. My paper on the date of the Kāmasūtra was first published in the *Journal of the Bihar and Orissa Research Society* in 1919, and again, after a thorough revision, in the *Journal of the Department of Letters* (Vol. IV) of the University of Calcutta. The conclusions arrived at by me have been confirmed by the discussions that my paper has raised, both in India and in Europe, and I have reviewed them towards the end of Chapter I. Prof. A. B. Keith in his recently published *History of Sanskrit Literature*, shows himself inclined to bring down my date by about two centuries, but he has not fully set forth his reasons for thingking so.

Vātsyāyana delineates many local customs—d e ś y o p a c ā r ā ḥ— as he calls them, characterizing the various peoples of India inhabiting the different parts of its wide area. I have, therefore, thought it necessary, while passing in review the customs peculiar to each province or people to fix the location of the countries about which there have been controversies among scholars ; this matter has therefore been treated, with some fulness, in Chapter II of this book. It first appeared in the *Annals of the Bhandarkar Institute* (Vols. VII and VIII).

The rest of my book attempts to give as complete an account as possible of the social life of India as depicted by Vātsyāyana, and I have shown how he sometimes corroborates, and very often supplements, the account derived from other sources, specially from works written about his own time, so as to present a fairly accurate idea of the state of Indian society in the period to which Vātsyāyana belongs. Much of the matter contained in Chapters V and VI appeared in the *Sir Asutosh Mookerjee Silver Jubilee Volumes* (Vol. III, Part I) under the caption *Sidelights on social life in Ancient India : Studies in Vātsyāyana's Kāmasūtra.*

The only contributions on the social life of the age of Vātsyāyana that appeared before my studies, are two papers by Prof. P. Peterson referred to in Chapter VI (P. 172). These are mainly translations with short notes of two out of the sixty-four sections of the Kāmasūtra and cover only a very small part of the ground traversed by me.

H. C. C.

CHAPTER I

DATE OF THE KÂMASŪTRA

Vātsyāyana stands pre-eminent in early Indian literature as an author who brought the analytical power of a keen logician to bear on the science of erotics which, in our modern days, has only lately begun to be studied with the care that it deserves. The science had attracted the serious attention of the Indian savants very early, as far back, perhaps, as the time when the *Śātapatha Brāhmaṇa* was being compiled, and in the centuries that elapsed before Vātsyāyana made his appearance, the various sections of the science were being studied separately and individually. But it was Vātsyāyana who synthesised the whole science and revived the popular interest in this branch of knowledge. Apart from its interest as a work on the science of love, Vātsyāyana's *Kāmasūtra*, at the present day, is of immense importance to us as throwing a flood of light on the manners and customs of his contemporary Indian society. To appreciate the full value, for the social history of India, of the picture that Vātsyāyana presents, we must, in the first place, try to ascertain, as closely as possible, the time when he flourished and for this purpose it will be necessary to trace the history of his science, to ascertain his relation to other departments of Indian literature, and also to analyse critically the few references that may be gleaned from his work, to the political history of India.

Vātsyāyana's Reference to Earlier Works on the Science of Love.

In speaking of the origin of the *Kāmaśāstra*, Vātsyāyana says at the beginning of his work [1] that at first, *Prajāpati*, the 'Lord of Beings,' for the welfare and preservation of his progeny composed a huge encyclopædia in a hundred thousand chapters dealing with the three objects of human life, *viz.*, *Dharma*, *Artha* and *Kāma* [2]; the first two of these subjects were next taken up by *Manu* and *Bṛhaspati* respectively and *Nandī* the attendant of Mahādeva, took up the third which he dealt with in a thousand chapters. This last work was condensed into five hundred chapters by *Śvetaketu*, the son of Uddālaka. The work of Śvetaketu was further abridged into a hundred and fifty chapters and divided into seven sections by *Bābhravya*, a native of the Pañcāla country. Next, *Dattaka*, at the request of the

1. *Vide* Chapter I of the *Kāmasūtra*, pp. 4-7 of the Benares edition. The quotations from the Kāmasūtra have been made throughout from the Benares edition, edited by Pandit Dāmodarlāl Gosvāmī and published in the *Chowkhamba Sanskrit Series* and the references are to the pages of this edition. The Sanskrit text edited by Mahāmahopādhyāya Pandit Durgāprasāda of Jaipur had been published earlier, but the Benares edition is more easily accessible to the public, the Jaipur edition being meant for private circulation alone. There is also a Bengali edition of the text and the commentary with a Bengali translation, published by Babu Maheś Chandra Pal of Calcutta. There is some difference in the arrangement of the chapters ; otherwise the readings are much the same with only occasional variations.

2. This agrees with what is said in the *Mahābhārata*, *Śāntiparva*, Ch 59, with regard to the origin of the sciences. Here we are told that at the request of the gods who were filled with anxiety at the entire absence of discipline among mankind, Prajāpati Brahmā produced from his own intelligence a hundred thousand chapters in which were delineated D h a r m a—the science of religion and duty, A r t h a—the science of politics and economics and K ā m a—the science of love,—

ततोऽध्यायसहस्राणां शतञ्चक्रे स्वबुद्धिजम् ।
यत्र धर्मस्तथैवार्थः कामश्चैवाभिवर्णितः ॥२९॥

But there is no agreement as regards the subsequent development except that in the Mahābhārata also Bṛhaspati is one of the authors of Daṇḍanīti or Arthaśāstra.

courtesans of Pāṭaliputra, wrote a separate treatise dealing with the *Vaiśika* section of Bābhravya. His example was followed by six other writers—*Cārāyaṇa*, *Suvarṇanābha*, *Ghoṭakamukha*, *Gonardīya*, *Goṇikāputra* and *Kucumāra*, each of whom took up a section of Bābhravya and wrote a monograph on it. As the science treated in this fragmentary fashion by numerous writers was about to be mangled and spoiled and as the work of Bābhravya, being huge in bulk, was difficult to be mastered, Vātsyāyana proposes to give an epitome of the whole subject in a single work of moderate dimensions. Towards the end of the Kāmasūtra, again, Vātsyāyana says that having mastered the significance of the *sūtras* of Bābhravya (from his teachers, as one would do in the case of a sacred text or *āgama*) and having pondered over them in his mind, he composed the Kāmasūtra in the approved method.[1] He thus admits that the great work of Bābhravya formed the groundwork of his own book as is also quite evident from the frequent references that he makes to it in every part of his Kāmasūtra : one out of his seven sections, the *Sāmprayogika*, covering about a fourth part of the whole work, is entirely taken from Bābhravya, as he says at the end of that section.[2] There can, therefore, be no doubt that Vātsyāyana had before him the great work of Bābhravya Pāñcāla. The commentator also quotes several verses stating the opinions of the followers of Bābhravya, and about a *sūtra* of Vātsyāyana he observes that it is a verse of

1 बाभ्रवीयांश्च सूत्रार्थान् आगमय्य विमृश्य च ।
वात्स्यायनश्चकारेदं कामसूत्रं यथाविधि ॥

Kāmasūtra. Benares edition, p. 381.

2 एवमेतां चतुःषष्टिं बाभ्रव्येण प्रकीर्तिताम् ।

Benares edition, page 182. Besides, at pp. 68 79, 94. 238., ,, 274, 296, 353, etc., the school of Bābhravya has been referred to.

Bābhravya;[1] he seems, therefore, to have access to some treatise specially belonging to Bābhravya's school.

It may be noted that Vātsyāyana speaks of having treated Bābhravya's book like an *āgama*, a work of holy scripture, indicating that it was considerably ancient. A Bābhravya who is called Pāñcāla by Uvaṭa, the commentator, is mentioned in the *Ṛk-prātiśākhya* as the author of the *Krama-pāṭha* of the Ṛgveda and Professor Weber[2] holds that this Bābhravya Pañcāla, and the Pañcāla people through him, took a leading part in fixing and arranging the text of the Ṛgveda. The Mahābhārata also says that the author of the Kramapāṭha was a Pāñcāla of the Bābhravya gotra and that his proper name was *Gālava*.[3] This connection of the Pañcāla people with the Ṛgveda receives a confirmation from what Vātsyāyana tells us in connection with the sixty-four varieties of *Samprayoga* or connubial intercourse. He says that they belonged to the Pañcāla country and were

1 The Commentary (Ben. edn., p. 279) says, **यथाहुर्बाभ्रवीयाः**—

पुत्रिकां चित्ररूपाणि पशवः शुकसारिकाः ।
सर्वेषां गूढभावानां दूतकर्माणि कुर्वत ॥ इति ।

Besides, the commentator quotes eight verses—*Bābhravīyāḥ Ślokāḥ*—at pp. 37-38. Moreover, he introduces the sūtra **सुरतान्ते सुखं पुंसां**, etc. (p. 81) with the remark **अमुमेवार्थं बाभ्रव्यगीतेन श्लोकेनाह ।**

2. *History of Indian Literature*, translated by J. Mann and T. Zachariæ, Popular Edition, pp. 10 and 34.

3. *Mahābhārata*, *Calcutta* edition, *Śāntiparva*, ch. 342, vv. 102-104 and the Kumbakonam, South Indian Recension, ch. 352, verses 37-38.

वामादेशितमार्गेण मत्प्रसादान्महात्मना ॥
पाञ्चालेन क्रमः प्राप्तस्तस्माद्भूतात् सनातनात् ।
बाभ्रव्यगोत्रः स बभौ प्रथमं क्रमपारगः ॥
नारायणाद्वरं लब्ध्वा प्राप योगमनुत्तमम् ।
क्रमं प्रणीय शिक्षाञ्च प्रणयित्वा स गालवः ॥

collectively called *Catuḥshashṭi*[1]—"the sixty-four"—from analogy with the Ṛgveda. He avers that the *Ṛks* collected in ten *maṇḍalas* are called the *Catuḥshashṭi* (being divided into eight Ashṭakas of eight chapters each) and the same principle holds in the case of the *Samprayogas* too (as they are divided into eight times eight varieties); and besides, because they are both connected with the Pañcāla country, therefore, the Bahvṛcas, the followers of the Ṛgveda, have out of respect given this appellation of *Catuḥshashṭi* to them.[2] It may be noted here that the followers of Bābhravya (Bābhravīyāḥ) are mentioned in the Mahābhāshya (on Pāṇini I. 1) but we cannot be certain whether a Vedic school or a Kāmaśāstra school is there meant. If Bābhravya, the author of the work on the *Kāmaśāstra*, is the same as the great author of the *Kramapāṭha*, then he has to be placed in a very early age indeed. But Bābhravya is merely a *gotra* or family name and it may be doubted whether the science of erotics could have been systematized so early; though it must be admitted that erotics and eugenics, the sciences that the Kāmasūtra embraces in its scope, had received particular attention from the *Ṛshis* at the time of composition of the hymns of the Atharvaveda, many of which deal with philtres and charms to secure love and drive away jealousy, with the means for obtaining good, healthy children and other allied matters.

The Pañcāla country where Bābhravya flourished appears to have been the part of India where the science of erotics was specially cultivated. We have seen how

1 पाञ्चालिकी चतुःषष्टिरपरा ; Ben. ed.. p. 40. संप्रयोगाङ्गं चतुःषष्टिरित्याचक्षते चतुःषष्टिप्रकारत्वात् ; *ibid.* p. 92.

2 ऋचां दशतयीनां च संज्ञितत्वादिहापि तदर्थसंबन्धात् पञ्चालसंबन्धाच्च बह्वृचैरेषा पूजार्थं संज्ञा प्रवर्तितेत्येके ॥ अष्टानामष्टधा विकल्पभेदादष्टावष्टकाश्चतुःषष्टिरिति बाभ्रवीयाः ; *ibid.* pp. 93-94.

great was the debt of Vātsyāyana to Bābhravya Pāñcāla, specially with regard to the section dealing with *Samprayoga*, the subject-matter proper of the *Kāmasūtra*. Some of the most revolting ceremonies in the Aśvamedha sacrifice seem to have originated in the Pañcāla country.[1] The Pañcāla people were evidently credited in ancient times with special knowledge in matters relating to the sexes, and one of them is said to have changed even the natural sex, as we see in the case of Śikhaṇḍin, the son of the Pañcāla king, Drupada.[2] Polyandry as we see it in the case of *Draupadī Pāñcālī*, may be regarded as an ancient institution of the Pañcāla country and the Pāṇḍava brothers, belonging as they did, to the allied tribe of the Kurus, as we see from the common Vedic phrase *Kuru-Pañcāla*, were certainly familiar with it and could have no difficulty in acceding to it ; in fact, the Kurus of Hastināpura and the reigning dynasties in North and South Pañcāla are said, in the Purāṇas, to belong to the same stock and to be descended from the same great ancestor Bharata.[4] In this connection, a statement of Vātsyāyana is very significant. He says that according to the followers of Bābbravya, who belonged to Pañcāla, as we have seen, a woman's chastity may not be respected when she is found to have intimacy with five lovers[5] (in addition to her husband, explains the Commentary) showing that five was considered as the limit beyond which it was not proper for a woman to go ; if she did so, she could be approached with impunity by any one. The Commentary explains that in the case of Draupadī this limit was not passed, as Yudhishṭhira and

1 See *Weber*, op. cit., pp. 114-115.

2 *Mahābhārata*, *Udyoga Parva* chh. 189-194.

3 See Macdonell and Keith, *Vedic Index*. i, pp. 165-169

4 F. E. Pargiter. *North Pañcāla Dynasty*. J. R. A. S. 1918, p. 238.

5 दृष्टपञ्चपुरुषा नागम्या काचिदस्तीति बाभ्रवीयाः, *Kāmasūtra*. Ben. ed., p. 68.

others were all her husbands.[1] The indulgence shown by the Pañcāla people to *five* lovers, appears to be significant. It is difficult to see in it a symbolic meaning as is done by Dahlmann. It is worthy of remark in this connection that Âpastamba from whom, as we shall presently see, Vātsyāyana quotes several aphorisms, refers to the bestowal of a single woman in marriage to a whole family.[3]

Of the predecessors of Bābhravya mentioned by Vātsyāyana, the earlier ones appear to be mythical, but *Śvetaketu*, the son of Uddālaka, is better known He is mentioned in the Mahābhārata as having established a fixity in sexual relations which before him were entirely free and promiscuous like those of the lower animals, the institution of marriage having not yet come into exist ence.[4] This refers to a primitive stage of society, and it is hardly possible, I am afraid, that this *Śvetaketu Auddālaki* could have been the author of the work in five hundred chapters referred to by Vātsyāyana. However, in the *Chāndogyopanishad*, and in the *Śatapatha Brāhmaṇa*[5] in the portion called the *Bṛhadāraṇyakopanishad*, we meet with a Śvetaketu who may be connected with the tradition of the authorship of a work relating to the *Kāmaśāstra*. Here we find three generations of Vedic teachers, Brāhmaṇas of Kurupañcāla—*Aruṇa*,

1 स्वपतिव्यतिरेकेण दृष्टाः पञ्च पुरुषा पतित्वेन यथा सा स्वैरिणी कारणवशात् सर्व्वैरेव गम्या। तथा च पञ्चातीता बन्धकीति पराशरः। द्रौपदी युधिष्ठिरादीनां स्वपतित्वादन्येषामगम्या. कथमेका सत्यनेकपतिरिति चैतिहासिकाः प्रष्टव्याः ; *ibid*, p. 68.

2 *Das Mahābhārata als Epos Und Rechtsbuch*. von J. Dahlmann. S. J., pp. 97-98.

3 कुलाय हि स्त्री प्रदीयत इत्युपदिशन्ति, *Âp. Dharma Sūtra*, II. 27. 3. See also Winternitz, *Notes on the Mahābhārata*. J. R. A. S., 1897, p. 758.

4 *Mahābhārata*. *Âdiparva*, ch. 122. Calcutta Edn.; अनावृता हि सर्वेषां वर्णानामङ्गना भुवि ॥ यथा गावः स्थितास्तात स्वे स्वे वर्णे तथा प्रजाः। ऋषिपुत्रोऽथ तं धर्मं श्वेतकेतुर्न चक्षमे ॥ चकार चैव मर्य्यादामिमां स्त्रीपुंसयोर्भुवि। मानुषेषु महाभागे न त्वेवान्येषु जन्तुषु ॥ See also Kumbakonam edn., ch. 128.

5 *Śatapatha Brāhmaṇa*, x. 6. 1. 1. He is also referred to in two places in the *Taittirīya Saṁhitā*. vi. 1. 9. 2 and 4, 5. 1.

his son *Uddālaka Āruṇi*, and his grandson, *Śvetaketu Auddālaki Āruṇeya.*[1] A story is told in almost the same words in both the Chāndogya as well as the Bṛhadāraṇyaka Upanishads[2] how the young Śvetaketu, after finishing his education, went to the assembly (*samiti* or *parishad*) of the Pañcāla people and was there discomfitted by some questions put to him by Pravāhaṇa Jaivali, a Kshattriya ; he was mortified at thus being nonplussed by a mere Rājanya and complained to his father who also being unable to answer the questions, sought Pravāhaṇa Jaivali himself for being taught in the matters broached by him. Among the matters taught by this Kshattriya of Pañcāla we find a symbolic interpretation of the relations between the sexes.[3] A few chapters later in the *Bṛhadāraṇyakopanishad,*[4] we find the same thing related with further additions including rules for approaching a woman, for dealing with a lover of one's own wife and specially rules for obtaining good progeny, and Uddālaka Âruṇi is there referred to as one of the foremost teachers of this science[5] which represents some of the earliest attempts made in India for the discovery of eugenic laws. These matters were afterwards more fully developed in the Gṛhyasūtras but the beginnings were made in the Upanishads, and, in fact, Âśvalāyana in his Gṛhyasūtra refers to the *upanishad* or the secret lore as the proper source in these things.[6] It is

1 *Chānd. Up.*. V. 3. 1. ; VI. 8. 1. *Śatap. Br. Māndhyandina* Text, x. 3. 4. 1. xi. 4. 1. 1. ; xi. 6. 2. 1 ; xii. 2. 1. 9. etc.

2 *Chānd. Up.* Adhyāya V. Khaṇḍas iii-x specially Khaṇḍas viii and ix ; *Bṛhad Up.* VI. 2. 1 ff.

3 योषा वा अग्निर्गौतम तस्या उपस्थ एव समिल्लोमानि धूमो योनिरर्चिर्यदन्तः करोति तेऽङ्गारा अभिनन्दा विस्फुलिंगास्तस्मिन्नेतस्मिन्नग्नौ देवा रेतो जुह्वति तस्या आहुत्यै पुरुषः संभवति स जीवति यावज्जीवत्यथ यदा म्रियते । *Bṛh. Up.* VI. 2. 13.

4 *Bṛh. Up.*, VI. 4. 3. ff.

5 एतद्ध स्म वै तद्विद्वान् उद्दालक आरुणिराह ; *Bṛh. Up.* VI. 4. 4.

6 उपनिषदि गर्भलम्भनं पुंसवनमनवलोभनं च ; *Âśvalāyana, Gṛhyasūtra* I. 13. 1.

significant that both Pravāhaṇa Jaivali and Uddālaka, of the Upanishad story, belonged to the Pañcāla country where, as we have seen before, the Kāmaśāstra was specially cultivated. From what we have said above, it is evident that Uddālaka considerably advanced the science the rudiments of which he had received from Pravāhaṇa Jaivali, and his son, Śvetaketu, must have carried it still farther as is evident from the body of tradition that has accumulated round his name as the first human founder of the Kāmaśāstra which appears to have been specially studied in his family. There can be no doubt that Śvetaketu and his father were historical personages and lived in a highly cultured age, an age of intense philosophical speculation, as we see from the many stories connected with them in the Brāhmaṇas and the Upanishads and it is not improbable that he had composed an *Upanishad* or secret work in which matters relating to marriage, love and the begetting of children were specially dealt with ; at any rate, a body of eugenic rules of which a few fragments have been preserved in the Bṛhadāraṇyakopanishad, must have come down from him and his family. That Śvetaketu left behind him some such work may be gathered from the fact that a personal statement by him has been quoted by Âpastamba in his *Dharmasūtra* where Śvetaketu is represented as having said that even after his marriage he carried on Vedic studies at his teacher's house for two months every year and thus acquired a greater knowledge of the *Śruti* than before,[1] and we may note that this passage which seems to be a direct quotation from Śvetaketu, has not been traced as yet in any of the Vedic works where he is referred to. Âpastamba further states, in another chapter, that though Śvetaketu was a

1 निवेशे वृत्ते संवत्सरे संवत्सरे द्वौ द्वौ मासौ समाहित आचार्य्यकुले वसेद् भूयः श्रुतिमिच्छन्निति श्वेतकेतुः। एतेन ह्यहं योगेन भूयः पूर्व्वस्मात् कालाच्छ्रुतमकुर्वीति, *Âpastamba Dh. Sūtras* I. 1. 13, 19 and 20.

person belonging to a comparatively recent age, yet he had become a Ṛshi.[1] Coming back to Vātsyāyana we find that the opinions of Auddālaki are referred to by Vātsyāyana in three places[2] in his Kāmasūtra and in one of them he contrasts the opinions of Auddālaki and Bābhravya, thus proving the connection of Auddālaki with the Kāmaśāstra beyond any doubt. It does not, however, necessarily imply that Vātsyāyana had access to Auddālaki's work in five hundred chapters, as in that case he would have made ampler use of it; certain opinions must have been current in Vātsyāyana's time among the teachers of the Kāmaśāstra (whom he frequently refers to as the *Ācāryas*), as having come down from the reputed human founder of the science; or, the legend of Auddālaki and his opinions might have been taken from the work of Bābhravya on whom Vātsyāyana mainly depends.

The monographs written by the successors of Bābhravya,—Dattaka and others—are quoted by Vātsyāyana in the respective chapters of his book. Dattaka's book on the courtesans appears to have been in use in the eighth century A.C. when Dāmodaragupta wrote his ***Kuṭṭanīmatam***[3] and it may have been availed of by the commentator who quotes a *sūtra* of Dattaka where Vātsyāyana has translated

1 श्रुतर्षयस्तु भवन्ति केचित कर्म्मफलशेषेण पुनः सम्भवे श्वेतकेतुः ; *ibid* I, 2, 5 and 3. See *Buhler*. S. B. E. II pp. xxxviii and xliii.

2 कथमेतदुपलभ्यते इति चेत् पुरुषो हि रतिमधिगम्य स्वेच्छया विरमति, न स्त्रियमपेक्षते। नत्वेवं स्त्रीत्यौद्दालकिः ; *Kāmasūtra* Ben. ed., p. 76 ; नासंस्तुता दृष्टाकारयोर्दूत्यमस्तीत्यौद्दालकिः ; *ibid*. p. 273 ; इत्यौद्दालकेरुभयतोयोगाः ; *ibid*, p. 353. The commentator refers (*ibid*, pp. 74, 78) two of Vātsyāyana's sūtras to Auddālaki, evidently from the context.

3 वात्स्यायनमयमवुधं वाभ्रव्यान् दूरेण दत्तकाचार्यान् ।
गणयति मन्मथतन्त्रे पशुतुल्यं राजपुत्रं च ॥
वात्स्यायन-मदनोदय-दत्तक-विटपुत्र-राजपुत्राद्यैः ।
उपदिष्टं यत्किञ्चित्तत्तस्या हृदयदेशमध्यास्ते ॥

—verses 77 and 122 in *Kuṭṭanīmatam* in Kāvyamālā, Gucchaka III.

the substance of it.[1] Of the other writers, *Gonardīya* has been quoted by Mallinātha in his gloss on Kumāra-sambhava, VII, 95, and on Raghuvaṃśa, XIX, 29, 30.

Rājaśekhara in his *Kāvyamīmāṃsā*[2] refers to *Suvarṇa-nābha* as the author of a treatise on a branch of poetics, *viz.*, *Rītinirṇaya* and speaks of *Kucamāra* as having dealt with the *Aupanishadika* section. The latter is evidently the same as Vātsyāyana's *Kucumāra*, the author of a monograph on the *Aupanishadika* portion of the Kāma-śāstra, and most probably one and the same work has been referred to by the two authors, there being nothing extra-ordinary in the fact that the sections dealing with the secrets and mysteries (*upanishad*) of both poetics and erotics should coalesce.[3] Kauṭilya in the Arthaśāstra has quoted[4] *Dīrgha Cārāyaṇa* and *Ghoṭamukha* who, as Professor Jacobi holds,[5] are probably the same persons as the Cārāyaṇa and Ghoṭakamukha of Vātsyāyana ; they would therefore have lived prior to the fourth century B. C. and Dattaka and Bābhravya who preceded them must be thrown back to a much earlier date. Dattaka, of course, could not have lived earlier than the fifth century B.C. when Pāṭaliputra became the capital of Magadha. Goṇi-kāputra is mentioned by Patañjali in the *Mahābhāshya* as a former grammarian[6] and Professor Jacobi is inclined to

1 "भागडसंप्लवे विशिष्टगृहगमिति" दत्तकसूत्रम्, अस्य. स्पष्टार्थं सूत्रान्तरमाह—प्रतिगणिकानामिति : *ibid*, p. 321.

2 *Kāvyamīmāṃsā*, edited by C. D. Dalal and R. A. Shastry, Gaekwad's Oriental Series, p. 1.—रीतिनिर्णयं सुवर्णनाभः, *** औपनिषदिकं कुचमार (समाम्नासीत्) इति ।

3 The *Kuchimāra-tantram* edited by Mathuraprasāda Dīkshita, Lahore, 1922, claims to give the substance of Kucimāra's *Upanishad*. संयोगादिष्टसंभाषादुपपन्नञ्च-तस्वतः । कुचिमारेण तपसा यत्कृतं क्रीडनं पुरा ॥ तत् प्रवक्ष्यामि चित्रार्थं नानार्थपद-मिश्रितम् । श्रूयतां नामतश्चैव कुचोपनिषदं पुनः ॥ Verses 2 and 3, p. 1.

4 'तृणमिति' दीर्घश्चारायणः । 'शोता शाटीति' घोटमुखः , *Arthaśāstra*, ed. R. Shama Sastri, 2nd edition, p. 253.

5 *Sitzung. Konigl. Preus. Akad. d. Wissenschaften*, 1911, pp. 959-963.

6 अथेह कथं भवितव्यं नेताश्वस्य स्रुघ्नमित्याहोस्विन्नेताश्वस्य स्रुघ्नस्येति । उभयथा गोणिकापुत्रः—*Mahābhāshya* on Pāṇini, I. 4. 51.

believe that he is the same person as the Goṇikāputra of Vātsyāyana. But in his case, as also in that of Gonardīya, the identification is rather doubtful as grammar and erotics are not very allied subjects. The works of Bābhravya and Goṇiputraka, who must be the same as our Gonikāputra, as well as that of Vātsyāyana, appear to have been used by Jyotirīśvara Ṭhakkura while composing his *Pañcasāyaka*,[1] a work on erotics which was written in Mithilā by the end of the thirteeth century, the author being considered to be the great-grand-father of the celebrated poet, Vidyāpati who flourished in the middle of the fourteenth century A.C.

The Upper Limit of the Date of Vātsyāyana from the Authors quoted by him

Vātsyāyana has quoted freely from the works of earlier authors not only in his own subject, but in other departments of Sanskrit literature as well. But while he has taken care to mention the authorities whom he cites and discusses when referring to his predecessors in the science of erotics, in the other cases he has not cared to acknowledge his debt by mentioning the sources. Some of them may, however, be indicated, and we shall be enabled thereby to fix a *terminus a quo* for him on literary grounds.

There is a wonderful agreement between Vātsyāyana and the Kalpasūtra of Âpastamba. In Chapter I on the selection of a bride (*Varaṇa-vidhāna-prakaraṇam*) the *Kâmasūtra*

1 दृष्ट्वा मन्मथतन्त्रमीश्वरमतं वात्स्यायनीयं मतं
गोणीपुत्रक-मूलदेवभणितं बाभ्रव्यवाक्यामृतम् ।
श्रीमन्दीश्वर-रन्तिदेवभणितं क्षेमेन्द्रविद्यागमं
तेनाकल्प्यत पञ्चसायक इति प्रीतिप्रदः कामिनाम् ॥

Pañcasāyaka edited by Sadānanda S'āstrî. Lahore, p. 2; see also R. Schmidt, *Beitrage zur Indischen Erotik*, p. 50.

2 Dr. Hoernle. *Comparative Grammar of the Gaudian Languages*, p. xxxv.

has **सुप्तां रुदतीं निष्क्रान्तां वरणे परिवर्जयेत्.**[1] This is exactly the same as that given by Âpastamba in his Gṛhya-Sūtra, 1. 3. 10.[2] The next two *sūtras* show only slight modifications, but making allowance for differences in reading they are exactly identical. Vātsyāyana has[3] :

गुप्तां दत्तां घोनां पृषतामृषभां विनतां विकटां विमुण्डां शुचिदूषितां सांकरिकीं राकां फलिनीं मित्रां स्वनुजां वर्षकरीं च वर्जयेत् ।

नक्षत्राख्यां नदीनाम्नीं वृक्षनाम्नीं च गर्हिताम् ।

लकाररेफोपान्तां च वरणे परिवर्जयेत् ॥

Âpastamba reads[4] :—

दत्तां गुप्तां द्योतामृषभां शरभां विनतां विकटां मुण्डां मण्डूषिकां सांकारिकां रातां पालीं मित्रां स्वनुजां वर्षकारीं च वर्जयेत् ॥ ११ ॥

नक्षत्रनामा नदीनामा वृक्षनामाश्च गर्हिताः ॥ १२ ॥

सर्वाश्च रेफलकारोपान्ता वरणे परिवर्जयेत् ॥ १३ ॥

The next *sūtra* of Vātsyāyana again reads exactly the same as Âpastamba's Gṛhyasūtra, I. 3. 20. **यस्यां मनश्चक्षुषोर्निबन्धस्तस्यामृद्धिर्नेतरामाद्रियेतेत्येके.**[5]

The first *sūtra* of the next chapter of the Kāmasūtra is again the same as in Âpastamba's Gṛhyasūtra, III. 8. 8. The Kāmasūtra has **संगतयोस्त्रिरात्रमधःशय्या ब्रह्मचर्यं क्षारलवणवर्जमाहारः**; Âpastamba reads **त्रिरात्रमुभयोरधःशय्या ब्रह्मचर्यं क्षारलवणवर्जनं च.**[6]

About the sources of the *Dharma* also, Vātsyāyana shows a wonderful agreement with Âpastamba, but this time with his Dharmasūtra. Vātsyāyana after giving a definition of Dharma says that it should be learnt from the Vedas and from the assembly of those who know the

1 Benares edition, p. 187.

2 The *Âpastambîya Gṛhyasūtra*, edited by Dr. M. Winternitz, p. 4.

3 Ben, ed., pp. 187-188.

4 Winternitz, *Ap. Gṛ. Sūtra*, p. 4.

5 *Kāmasūtra*, Ben. ed., p. 188, and Winternitz. Ap. Gr. S., p. 5.

6 *Kāmasūtra*. Ben. ed., p. 191 ; Winternitz, Ap Gr. S., p. 11.

Dharma, [1] just as he says that the Kāmasūtra should be learnt from the books on the subject and the assembly of the citizens.[2] Âpastamba says much the same thing in his Dharmasūtra.[3].

In another chapter, Vātsyāyana quotes a verse referring it simply to the *Smṛti*[4] (*smṛtitaḥ*)——

वत्सः प्रस्नवने मेध्यः श्वा मृगग्रहणे शुचिः ।
शकुनिः फलपाते तु स्त्रीमुखं रतिसंगमे ॥

This verse is found in the Dharmasūtras of *Vasishṭha* [5] and *Baudhāyana* [6] with very slight and immaterial variations. With some further modifications it is found in the Saṃhitās of Manu [7] and Vishṇu [8] also. Its occurrence in almost identical forms in so many works shows that it must have been borrowed from some common and ancient authority on *Dharma*. Again, in a verse in his chapter on marriage, Vātsyāyana shows an agreement in idea with Baudhāyana. Vātsyāyana says that as mutual affection between a couple is the object of all forms of marriage, therefore the *Gāndharva* form which has its basis in love, is easier to celebrate,

1 तं श्रुतेर्धर्मज्ञसमवायाच्च प्रतिपद्येत—Benares Edition, p. 13.

2 तं कामसूत्रान्नागरिकजनसमवायाच्च प्रतिपद्येत, *ibid.* p. 15.

3 *Âpastambîya Dharma Sūtra* edited by Dr. G. Buhler, C. I. E., p. 1 :—

अथातः सामयाचारिकान्धर्मान् व्याख्यास्यामः ॥ धर्मज्ञसमयः प्रमाणम् । वेदाश्च ॥

4 *Kâmasūtra*, Ben. ed., p. 167.

5 *The Vāsiṣṭha Dharma-Śāstram*, edited by Dr. A. A. Fuhrer, ch. 28. 8, p. 77.

6 *The Bodhâyana Dharma Sūtram* edited by L. Srînivāsāchārya. Mysore. 1, 5. 49, p. 57. Bodhāyana reads :

वत्सः प्रस्नवने मेध्यः शकुनिः फलशातने ।
स्त्रियश्च रतिसंसर्गे श्वा मृगग्रहणे शुचिः ॥

7. *Mānava Dharmaśāstra*, edited by Dr. J. Jolly. V. 130.

नित्यमास्यं शुचिः स्त्रीणां शकुनिः फलपातने ।
प्रस्रवे च शुचिर्वत्सः श्वा मृगग्रहणे शुचिः ॥

8 *Vishṇusmṛti*, edited by Dr. J. Jolly, XXIII. 49.

and is free from the technicalities of a long wooing, is the best of all [1] and Baudhāyana refers to this as the opinion of some authorities.[2] This idea we also find in the *Mahābhārata*.[3] From the above, it is clear that Vātsyāyana has embodied in his work at least five *sūtras* from the *Gṛhyasūtra* of Āpastamba, though we cannot feel quite certain with regard to his debt to Baudhāyana. We are not quite sure about the date of these *sūtra* works, but the period to which this Vedic literature belonged, is supposed to have extended to about 500 B.C.[4]

Next, we find that Vātsyāyana has embodied in his book a considerable number of passages from a work whose date is more definitely known, *viz.*, from the *Arthaśāstra* of Kauṭilya [5] which is now generally considered to have been written about 300 B.C., and he has followed the method of Kauṭilya throughout the Kāmasūtra. This has led to the absurd identification of Kauṭilya with Vātsyāyana and a host of other authors in some of the *Koshas* or lexicons.[6]

1 *Kāmasūtra*, Benares edition, 223

व्यूढानां हि विवाहानामनुरागः फलं यतः ।
मध्यमोऽपि हि सद्योगो गान्धर्वस्तेन पूजितः ॥
सुखत्वादबहुक्लेशादपि चावरणादिह ।
अनुरागात्मकत्वाच्च गान्धर्वः प्रवरो मतः ॥

2 *Bodhāyana*, Mysore edition, 1, 11. 16. p. 137.

गान्धर्वमप्येके प्रशंसन्ति सर्वेषां स्नेहानुगतत्वात् ॥

3 विवाहानां हि रम्भोरु गान्धर्वः श्रेष्ठ उच्यते—*Mahābhārata, Âdiparva* ch. 73. verse 4, and ch. 172. v. 19.

4 Winternitz, *Geschichte der indischen Litteratur*, Bd. 1, pp. 246—258.

5 Mr. R. Shāmashastry has brought together a number of parallel passages in the *Artahśāstra* and *Kāmasūtra*; see his *Arthaśāstra*. second edition, pp. xii-xvi.

6 In the *Modern Review*, March, 1918, p. 274, Mr. Srīś Chandra Vasu Vidyārṇava quotes the following verse from the *Abhidhānacintāmaṇi*:—

वात्स्यायनो मल्लनागः कुटिलश्चणकात्मजः ।
द्रामिलः पक्षिलस्वामी विष्णुगुप्तोऽङ्गुलश्च सः ॥

See also, *A Note on the Supposed Identity of Vātsyāyana and Kauṭilya*, by Mr. R. Shamashastry, in the *Journal of the Mythic Society*, Vol vi. pp. 210-216.

Coming down to still later times, we observe that Vātsyāyana quotes from the *Mahābhāshya* of Patañjali. The latter observes with regard to unavoidable faults or defects in grammatical definitions, that simply because certain defects cannot be avoided, one should certainly not desist from formulating rules of interpretation (*paribhāshās*) or from giving a definition, just as one does not refrain from cooking his food merely because there are beggars to ask for a share of it, nor from sowing barley-grains simply for the reason that when the plants grow up there my be deer to destroy the corn. Vātsyāyana says the very same thing in exactly the same language with regard to defects inherent in *Kāma* or desire.[1] This quotation from the Mahābhāshya brings down the upper limit of the date of Vātsyāyana to the second half of the second century B.C,, in round numbers to circa 150 B.C.

Besides the above, there are many references to narrative literature in Vātsyāyana's Kāmasūtra. In one passage,[2] he says that when a girl shows some signs of listening favourably to the proposals of a lover, she should be propitiated by reciting to her such stories as those of *Ahalyā*, *Avimāraka* and *Śakuntalā*. The story of Ahalyā is given in the Rāmāyaṇa about the date of which, however, there is much controversy ; but Ahalyā is also alluded to by Aśvaghosha in *Buddhacarita*. Avimāraka's story forms the subject matter of one of the dramas of Bhāsa whom some scholars have placed

1 न हि दोषाः सन्तीति परिभाषा न कर्त्तव्या लक्षणं वा न प्रणेयम् । न हि भिक्षुकाः सन्तीति स्थाल्यो नाधिश्रीयन्ते । न च मृगाः सन्तीति यवा नोप्यन्ते । *Mahābhāshya* on Pāṇini, I. 1. 39. Vātsyāyana has बोद्धव्यं हि दोषेष्विव, न हि भिक्षुकाः सन्तीति, etc. (Ben ed., p. 25) ; the rest is exactly the same.

2 शृण्वत्यां चाहल्याऽविमारक-शाकुन्तलादीन्यन्यान्यपि लौकिकानि च कथयेत्तद्युक्तानि । Benares edition, p. 271.

3 कामं परमिति ज्ञात्वा देवोऽपि हि पुरंदरः ।
गौतमस्य मुनेः पत्नीमहल्यां चकमे पुरा ॥

Buddhacarita, IV. 72.

about the middle of the first century B. C. while others would assign him to the third century A. C.[1] In any case there could not have been much distance in time between Bhāsa and Vātsyāyana because we find pictured in the works of the dramatist a state of society very closely resembling that depicted in the Kāmasūtra. We cannot be sure, however, that Vātsyāyana derived the story of Avimāraka from the drama because Bhāsa's treatment of it seems to indicate that it was a well-known story like that of Udayana; and, besides, the commentary, Jayamaṅgalā, gives some particulars that are wanting in the drama.

The story of Śakuntalā is referred to by Vātsyāyana in another place also. In his chapter on the courtship of a maiden, he says that the wooer should point out to the girl courted the cases of other maidens like Śakuntalā who situated in the same circumstances as herself obtained husbands of their own free choice and were happy by such union.[2] This refers to the story of the love between Śakuntalā and Dushmanta as we know it from the great drama of Kālidāsa, but Vātsyāyana was certainly not indebted to him for it; it is given very fully in the Mahābhārata.[3] Aśvaghosha in the *Buddhacarita* also narrates how **Viśwāmitra, Śakuntalā's father, was led astray by an Apsaras whom,** however, he calls ***Ghṛtācī*** **instead of** ***Menakā***; in his *Saundarananda-kāvya* **also, the same author speaks of Kaṇva** who brought up **Bharata, the son of Śakuntalā, and** he says further that **the young son of Dushmanta** displayed great skill in

1. Mr. K. P. Jayaswal (J. A. S. B., 1913, p, 265) has advanced the first view, while Prof. D. R. Bhandarkar (*Carmichael Lectures*, 1918, p. 59) supports the second one.

2 याश्चान्या अपि समानजातीयाः कन्याः शकुन्तलाद्याः स्वबुद्ध्या भर्त्तारं प्राप्य संप्रयुक्ता मोदन्ते स्म ताश्चास्या निदर्शयेत्, *Kāmasūtra*, Ben. ed., p. 278.

3. *Ādiparva*, ch. 68 ff.

sporting with the beasts of the forest.[1] In his *Sutrâlankâra* again, Aśvaghosha speaks of Bharata as one of the great kings of India.[2] He was evidently well acquainted with the story of Śakuntalā. The *Kaṭṭhahāri Jâtaka* certainly reminds us of the story of Dushmanta and Śakuntalā.[3] The legend, however, was known in still more ancient times, *viz.*, the period of the composition of the Brāhmaṇa portion of the Vedas. While we observe that Śakuntalā's mother, Menakā, is known as an *apsaras* in both the White and Black Yajurvedas,[4] Śakuntalā herself is spoken of in the Śatapatha Brāhmaṇa[5] as having borne at Nāḍapit[6] the great Bharata who is also called there the son of Duḥshanta, and even the Śatapatha Brāhmaṇa quotes the legend as having been sung in

1 विश्वामित्रो महर्षिश्च विगाढ़ोऽपि महत्तपाः ।
वृशवर्षाण्यरण्यस्थो घृताच्याप्सरसा हृतः ॥

Buddhacarita, IV. 20.

कण्वः शाकुन्तलस्येव भरतस्य तरस्विनः ।

Saundarananda Kāvya, I. 26.

जिज्ञासमाना नागेषु कौशलं श्वापदेषु च ।
अनुचक्रुर्वनस्थस्य दौष्मन्ते र्दवकर्म्मणः ॥ *Ibid*, I. 36.

2 *Sūtrālaṃkâra* traduit en Francois sur la version Chinoise par Edouard Huber, p. 395.

3 Fausboll's *Jātaka*. Vol. 1, No. 7. This bas been pointed out by Signor P. E. Pavolini in the *Giornale della Societa Asiatica Italiona*. Vol. Ventesimo, p. 297. See also note by Mr. R. Chalmers in his English translation of the Frist Volume of the Jātakas, p. 29.

4 मेनका च सहजन्या चाप्सरसौ—*Vājasaneyi-Saṁhitā*, xv. 16; *Taitt. Saṃ.*, 4. 4. 3. 1 Maitrāyaṇī Saṃ., 11. 8. 10.

5 XIII. 5. 4. 11, 13, 14.

एतद् विष्णोः क्रान्तम्। तेनैतेन भरतो दौःषन्तिरीजे तेनेष्ट्वेमां व्यष्टिं व्यानशे येयं भरतानां तदेतद् गाथयाभिगीतमष्टासप्ततिं भरतो दौःषन्तिर्यमुनामनु गङ्गायां वृत्रघ्ने ऽवध्नात् पञ्चपञ्चाशतं हयानिति। अथ तृतीयया। शकुन्तला नाडपित्यप्सरा भरतं दधे परः सहस्रानिन्द्रायाश्वान्मेध्यान् य आहरद्विजित्य पृथिवीं सर्व्वामिति। अथ चतुर्थ्या। महदद्य भरतस्य न पूर्व्वे नापरे जनाः। दिवं मर्त्य इति बाहुभ्यां नोदापुः पञ्च मानवा इति।

6. Harisvāmin, the commentator, explains that the hermitage of Kaṇva where S'akuntalā was nurtured, was called Nāḍapit. See the English translation by J. Eggeling of the *Śatapatha Brāhmana*, Part v, p. 399, foot-note 2.

gathās [1] connected with the great hero who gave his name to the whole continent of *Bhāratavarsha* ; so that the legend appears to belong to the earliest stock of legends of the Indian Aryans.

Besides the above mention of certain well-known stories, there are many references throughout the work of Vātsyāyana to love-stories in general, showing that story-telling was very popular in the days of our author ; and when we are reminded that the enormous mass of narratives in the *Mahāvastu*, *Divyāvadāna* and Aśvaghosha's *Sūtrālankāra* on the one hand, and the *Śānti* and *Anuśāsana Parvas* of the *Mahābhārata* on the other, as well as those in the *Tantrākhyāyika*, were mostly embodied in their present form about the early centuries of the Christian era, we feel inclined to think that it was in this period when narrative literature flourished most in India, that his treatise on love was composed by Vātsyāyana who found the recital of love-stories the readiest means of rousing the tender passion in the hearts of maids and swains.

The Lower Limit of the Date of Vātsyāyana from References to Kāmasūtra in later Literature.

We may now proceed to fix the *terminus ad quem* for the date of Vātsyāyana from an examination of the

1 The *Gāthās* are quoted in a fairly large number in the Brāhmaṇas and the Vedic literature generally, and they are referred to in the earliest portions of the *Ṛgveda* itself (I, 190, 1, etc.). For the most part, these Gāthās contain historical matter singing about the mighty deeds of great heroes in still older times, as we see from the Gāthās quoted above chanting the great achievements of the eponymous hero Bharata. The *Aitareya Brāhmaṇa* (VII. 18) makes a distinction between the *Ṛks* and the Gāthās, saying that the former refer to the Gods and the latter to men. It is no wonder that with the Aryan Indians who placed spiritual concerns far above the temporal from the very earliest times, the literature dealing with the deeds of mere men fell into comparative neglect and was not preserved with the same care as was bestowed upon the *Ṛks*, though occasional verses were preserved in memory and transmitted orally.

references to his work in later literature, and for this purpose we shall take into account only those that will be immediately helpful to us. In the first place we observe that the great Kālidāsa was well acquainted with the Kāmasūtra. In describing the dalliance of the voluptuary Agnivarṇa who reminds us so much of the Kāṇva Devabhūti, Kālidâsa has often followed in Canto XIX of the *Raghuvaṃśa*, the description in the Kāmasūtra, using even its technical expressions, *e. g.*, the word *sandhayaḥ* which is used in verse 16 in the very same sense as that given by Vātsyāyana in his chapter on *Viśīrṇapratisandhāna.* [1] In verse 31, however, there is a more definite and verbal agreement. Vātsyāyana in his chapter on the means of knowing a lover who is growing cold (*Virakta-pratipatti*) gives as one of the indications of such a one **मित्रकृत्यमपदिश्य अन्यत्र शेते.**[2] Kālidāsa in describing Agnivarṇa under similar circumstances uses the very same language—**मित्रकृत्यमपदिश्य पार्श्वतः प्रस्थितं तमनवस्थितं प्रियाः.** Another very striking agreement has been pointed out by Mallinātha and dilated upon by modern scholars. Describing the marriage of Aja and Indumatī, Kālidāsa says that when the two touched each other's hands, the hair on the bridgroom's forearm stood on end and the maiden had her fingers wet with perspiration.[3] Here Mallinātha quotes Vātsyāyana who speaks exactly the same thing happening under the same circumstances.[4] In *Kumārasambhava* VII. 77, however, Kālidāsa has

1 *Kāmasūtra*, Ben. ed., p. 327 ff.

2 This is the reading given by Mallinātha. The *Kāmasūtra* reads **मित्रकार्य्यमपदिश्य,** etc., Ben, ed. p. 323.

3 **आसीद्वरः कण्टकितप्रकोष्ठः स्विन्नाङ्गुलिः संववृते कुमारी ।**

4 **"कन्या तु प्रथमसमागमे स्विन्नाङ्गुलिः स्विन्नमुखी च भवति । पुरुषस्तु रोमाञ्चितो भवति ; एभिरनयोर्भावं परीक्षते ।"** This passage, quoted by Mallinātha, is slightly different from the reading in the printed editions of the Kāmasūtra where we have **स्विन्नकरचरणाङ्गुलिः स्विन्नमुखी च भवति,** Benares edition, p. 266.

reversed this order, saying that it was Hara, the bridegroom, who perspired and the hair stood on end on the bride's hand. [1] But the language is almost the same and we think Kālidāsa's memory did not serve him quite right when he wrote the Kumārasambhava passage and that he improved himself, as Professor Jacobi holds, in the Raghuvaṃśa. The violation in the one case only proves more strongly that Kālidāsa had a knowledge of Vātsyāyana's work and made use of it. Arguing from a similar agreement in another passage of Kālidāsa, Dr. Peterson has come to the definite conclusion that Vātsyāyana is quoted there by the poet. He refers to the following verse (in Act IV) which is considered to be one of the best in his *Abhijñāna Śakuntalam.* [3]

शुश्रूषस्व गुरून् कुरु प्रियसखीवृत्तिं सपत्नीजने
भर्त्तुर्विप्रकृतापि रोषणतया मास्म प्रतीपं गमः ।
भूयिष्ठं भव दक्षिणा परिजने भोगेष्वनुत्सेकिनी
यान्त्येवं गृहिणीपदं युवतयो वामा कुलस्याधयः ॥

Dr. Peterson then goes on to say : "The first, third and fourth precepts here are taken verbally from one *sūtra*, the second occurs elsewhere in our book ; the third we have already had. Scholars must judge : but it seems to me to be almost certain that Kālidāsa is quoting Vātsyāyana, a fact, if it be a fact, which invests our author with great antiquity."[4] It will be observed frm an examination of the corresponding *sūtras* of Vātsyāyana [5] that in

1 रोमोद्गमः प्रादुरभूदुमायाः स्विन्नाङ्गुलिः पुङ्गवकेतुरासीत् ।

2 *Die Epen Kālidāsa's*, p. 155. In this connection see R. Schmidt, *Beitrage Zur Indischen Erotik* 1902 pp. 4-5.

3 *Kālidāsa's Śakuntalā*, the Bengali Recension, edited by Richard Pischel, p. 89.

4 *Journal of the Anthropological Society of Bombay*, 1891, p. 465 ; see also J. B. B. R. A. S., Vol XVIII, pp. 109-110

5 Dr. Peterson here evidently refers to the following sūtras of Vātsyāyana on the duties of a wife : श्वश्रूश्वशुरपरिचर्या तत्पारतन्त्र्यमनुत्तरवादिता, etc, भोगेष्वनुत्सेकः परिजने दाक्षिण्यम् ॥ Benares edition, p. 280. Vātsyāyana devotes the whole of Chapter

the first two lines of the verse quoted above, Kālidāsa has translated the ideas of Vātsyāyana but in the third line he has followed our author verbally. On the authority of this agreement evidently Mahāmahopādhyāya Hara Prasād Śāstri has also expressed the opinion that Kālidāsa's "knowledge of the Kāmaśāstra was very deep indeed."[1] Dushmanta's words in Act V of Śakuntalā—"नागरकवृत्त्या शान्त्वयैनाम्" shows that Kālidāsa has used the word *nāgaraka* there in the full sense imparted to it by Vātsyāyana in his section called *Nāgarakavṛttam*, *viz.*, a city-bred man skilled in speech and love-making. There is moreover, a set of *sūtras* in Vātsyāyana's chapter on *Kanyāvisrambha* which reminds the reader at once of the first act of Kālidāsa's Śakuntalā as will be seen from the translation here given : "When a girl sees that she is sought after by a desirable lover, conversation should be set up through a sympathetic friend (*sakhī*) who has the confidence of both ; then she should smile with head bent down ; when the *sakhī* exaggerates matters, she should take her to task and quarrel with her ; the *sakhī*, however, should say in jest, 'This was said by her ,' even when she has not done so ; then when the *sakhī* is set aside and she is solicited to speak for herself, she should keep silent ; when, however, this is insisted upon, she should mutter sweetly, "O no ! I never say any such thing" in indistinct and half-finished sentences ; and she should, with a smile, cast occasional side-long glances at the lover, etc."[2] From what we have said above, there can be no doubt that the Kāmasūtra was known to Kālidāsa and that he

III of the *Bhāryādhikārika* section to the mutual conduct of co-wives (p. 234ff). Corresponding to the second line of the verse Vātsyāyana has नायकापचारेषु किञ्चित् कलुषिता नात्यर्थं निवदेत् ॥ १८ ॥ साधिक्षेपवचनं त्वेनं मित्रजनमध्यस्थमेकाकिनं वाऽप्युपालभेत न च मूलकारिका स्यात् ॥ Benares edition, p. 227.

1 *Journal of the Bihar and Orissa Research Society*, Vol. II p. 185.

2 *Kāmasūtra*, Ben ed., p. 195.

made verbal quotations from the work. Now Kālidāsa could not have lived later than the middle of the fifth century A.C., because he places the Hūṇas on the banks of the *Vaṅkshū*, the Waksh or Oxus in Bactria,[1] before they had been pushed towards the west or towards the Indian frontier.[2] In all likelihood Kālidāsa lived during

1 The passages of Kālidāsa referred to here are verses 67 and 68 *Raghuvaṃśa*, canto IV, beginning—विनीताध्वश्रमास्तस्य वंक्षुतीरविचेष्टनैः. In the *Journal of the Bihar and Orissa Research Society* (Vol. II, p. 35 ff. and 391 ff.) Mahāmahopādhyāya Haraprasād S'āstrī has sought to place Kālidāsa about the middle of the sixth century A. C. depending on the garbled reading of Mallinātha who reads *Sindhu* instead of *Vaṃkshū* in the line quoted above. With all due deference to the great authority of Pandit S'āstrī, I would venture to differ from him here. There cannot be the shade of a doubt that *Vaṃkshū* is the correct reading here and not *Sindhu*. Vallabhadeva of Kashmir, who lived about five centuries earlier than Mallinātha, reads *Vaṅkshū*, and the unqestioned genuineness and reliability of Vallabha's text as compared with that of Mallinātha has been fully established in the case of the Meghadūta where all those verses that had been accepted by Mallinātha as genuine, but had been rejected as spurious by modern critics like Pandit Īśvarachandra Vidyāsāgara, Gildemeister and Stenzler, are found to be absent from the text of Vallabha, The superiority of Vallabha's text thus established in the case of Meghadūta applies with equal force to the *Raghuvaṃśa*. To an editor like Mallinātha living in the far south in the fourteenth or fifteenth century, *Vaṃkshū* or *Vakshu*, a river in Bactria, was an unfamiliar, outlandish name, and he had no hesitation in substituting for it *Sindhu* which was nearer home, forgetting though that it would have been geographically absurd for Raghu to have marched northwards from the Persian frontier and met the Hūnas on the Indus. It is significant again, as has been shown by Professor K. B. Pathak, who first drew pointed attention to Vallabha's reading (Ind. Ant. 1912, p. 265 ff. and the introduction to his Meghadūta) that Kshīrasvāmin who lived about four centuries earlier than Mallinātha speaks in his commentary on the Amarakosha, of Bactria as the province that is referred to in this passage of Kālidāsa ; this shows that so late as the eleventh century, Bactria through which the river Vaṅkshū or Oxus flows was considered to be the country where Kālidāsa placed the Hūnas. Vaṅkshū is a well-known river in the *Mahābhārata* (*Cf.* Sabhāparva, 51. 26). Moreover, an examination of the variants given in Mr. G. R. Nandargikar's splendid edition of *Raghuvāṃśa* shows that Cāritravardhana, Sumativijaya, Dinakara, Dharmameru and Vijayagaṇi, in fact, most of the great old commentators, follow Vallabha, and adopt the old reading.

2 M. Chavanues has shown from Chinese sources that the Huns had won great power in the basin of the Oxus towards the middle of the fifth century A. C. (*Document sur les Toukiue Occiden aux*, pp. 222-3). We do not know yet exactly when the Hūṇas settled themselves in the Oxus valley. But there can be no doubt that the Hūnas were known in India even before the time mentioned by M. Chavannes. The *Lalitavistara*, thought to tave been written about three hundred

the reigning period of Chandragupta Vikramāditya in the early years of the fifth century A.C.. Varāhamihira who unquestionably lived in the sixth century A.C., has in his *Bṛhat-Saṃhitā* certain chapters, specially two, named *Kāndarpikam* and *Puṃstrī-Samāyoga,*[1] in which he has dealt with matters falling within the sphere of the Kāmaśāstra and in them he seems clearly to have availed himself of Vātsyāyana's work, though he nowhere mentions his name.

The author of the Kāmasūtra is mentioned by name in the *Vāsavadattā* of Subandhu who is supposed to have flourished about the same time as Chandragupta Vikramāditya, *viz.*, at the beginning of the fifth century A C.[2] While describing the Vindhya mountains, Subandhu says: "It was filled with elephants and was fragrant from the perfume of its jungles, just as the Kāmasūtra was written by Mallanāga and contains the delight and enjoyment of mistresses."[3] Thus from the evidence offered by Kālidāsa and Subandhu we can feel definitely certain that the Kāmasūtra was written before 400 A.C.

The name Mallanāga referred to by Subandhu is the proper name of the author of the Kāmasūtra, Vātsyāyana being his *gotra* or family name as pointed out by the commentator and as is corroborated by some of

years after Christ (Dr. Winternitz, *Geschichte der Indischen Litteratur*, Band II, p. 200) mentions *Hūna-Lipi* as one of the scripts learned by the young Siddhârtha (*Lalitavistara* edited by Dr. S. Lefmann, Vol. I. p. 126 ; IA, 1913, p. 266). Besides, Dr. J. J. Modi has shown from an examination of passages in the Avestā that the Huns were known in Persia as a wandering or pillaging nation not later than the seventh century before Christ (*R. G. Bhāndārkar Commemoration Volume*, pp. 71-76). It stands to reason therefore that the Huns should be known to the Indians also, especially since their occupation of the Oxus valley. seeing that Bactria was very well-known to Vātsyāyana and was considered a part of India so late as the sixth century A. C. when Varāhamihira wrote his *Bṛhat-Saṃkitā*.

1 Chapters 76 and 78 of *Bṛhat-Saṃhitā* edited by Dr. H. Kern, Calcutta, 1865.

2 Mahāmahopādhyāya Haraprasād S'āstrī in the J. A. S. B. 1905, p, 253.

3 *Vāsavadattā*, translated dy Dr. Louis H. Gray, p. 69.

the lexicons. [1] Two branches of the *Vatsa-gotra* to which our author belongs are mentioned by Âśvalāyana in his *Śrautasūtra*,[2] and in the history of Sanskrit literature, there are two great representatives, besides our author, of this family : one of them is the great poet Bāṇa, who in one of the introductory verses to his *Kādambarī* speaks of his grandfather as a scion of the Vātsyāyana family,[3] and the other is the author of the *Nyáyabhāshya.* This latter has sometimes been identified with our author as in the verse from Hemacandra's *Abhidhānacintāmaṇi* quoted before[4] ; but we have seen that Hemacandra in the same passage identifies our author also with Kauṭilya, Cāṇakya, or Vishṇugupta who, we definitely know, preceded him by several centuries. The long period that separated these authors from Hemacandra has made him lose the historical perspective and his opinion in this connection does not deserve much consideration. Another argument based on internal evidence may be urged in favour of the identity of the two Vātsyāyanas. The *Kāmasūtra* defines *Kāma* or desire as the consciousness of the enjoyment of appropriate objects through the five organs of sense (and especially through the organ of touch) controlled and directed by the mind associated with the soul.[5] Now, this is exactly the position held with regard to the method of direct perception or *pratyaksha* expounded in the *Nyāyasūtra* as well as in the *Bhāshya*. The Bhāshyakāra

1 वात्स्यातन इति स्वगोत्रनिमित्ता समाख्या। मल्लनाग इति च सांस्कारिकी ; *Kāmasūtra,* Ben. ed., p. 17 ; see also note 5, p. 1.

2 *Âśvalāyana Śrauta Sūtra,* Bibliotheca Indica, XII. 10. 6-7. p. 875.

3 बभूव वात्स्यायनवंशसंभवो द्विजो जगद्गीतगुणोऽग्रणीः सताम्।
अनेकगुप्तार्चितपादपङ्कजः कुबेरनामांश इव स्वयंभुवः ॥

Kādambarī, Introductory verse, 10

4 See footnote 6. p. 15 *ante.*

5 श्रोत्रत्वक्-चक्षुर्जिह्वाघ्राणानामात्मसंयुक्तेन मनसाऽधिष्ठितानां स्वेषु स्वेषु विषयेष्वानुकूल्यतः प्रवृत्तिः कामः। स्पर्शविशेषविषये त्वस्याभिमानिकसुखानुविद्धा [illegible]-प्रतीतिः प्राधान्यात् कामः।—*Kāmasūtra,* Ben. ed.. p. 14.

in his comment on Nyāyasūtras I. 1. 4 and 9, and I. 2, 20-27 makes it sufficiently clear that it is the *Ātman* or soul that receives perception with the help of the mind acting through the senses upon objects.[1] This identity of view of the two Vātsyāyanas with regard to experience or perception is no doubt true, but it will be observed that this view is held also by other schools, for example, the earlier Vedānta. The *Kaṭhopanishad* lays down in unmistakable terms that it is the soul that enjoys things acting through the mind and the senses, and the *Bhagavadgītā* upholds the same doctrine.[2] *Brahmasūtra*, II. 3. 18 (or 19 according to Rāmānuja) also appears to support the Upanishad view as shown by almost all the commentators.[3] It is only Śaṅkara who in his comment on *Brahmasūtra*, II. 3. 29[4] attempts to prove that pleasure and pain are the qualities of *buddhi* or intellect ; but with regard to the *Vyavahārika* or *Saṃsāra* stage with which we are concerned in the Kāmasūtra, there is not much ground of difference even with Śaṅkara. It will be observed, therefore, that the doctrine of perception adumbrated by the Kāmasūtra, does not particularly belong to the *Nyāyabhāshya* but

1 *Vide* the Bhāshya particularly on the following sūtras : इन्द्रियार्थसन्निकर्षोत्पन्नं ज्ञानमव्यपदेश्यमव्यभिचारि व्यवसायात्मकम् प्रत्यक्षम् (1. 1. 4.) and नात्ममनसोः सन्निकर्षाभावे प्रत्यक्षोत्पत्तिः (1. 2. 21). etc ; *cf.* तत्रात्मा सर्वस्य द्रष्टा, सर्वस्य भोक्ता, सर्वज्ञः, सर्वानुभावी. तस्य भोगायतनं शरीरम्। भोगसाधनानीन्द्रियाणि भोक्तव्या इन्द्रियार्थाः, etc., in Vātsyāyana's comment on *Nyāyasūtra*, I. 1. 9.

2 इन्द्रियाणि हयानाहुर्विषयांस्तेषु गोचरान् ।
आत्मेन्द्रियमनोयुक्तं भोक्तेत्याहुर्मनीषिणः ॥ *Kaṭhopanishad*, III. 4.

Similar passages from the Upanishads might easily be multiplied.

श्रोत्रं चक्षुः स्पर्शनं च रसनं घ्राणमेव च ।
अधिष्ठाय मनश्चायं विषयानुपसेवते ॥ *Gītā*, XIV. 9.

3 ज्ञोऽत एव, *Brahmasūtra*, II. 3. 18 ; *vide* Rāmānuja's commentary on the same and also that of *Śrīkaṇṭha*.

4 तस्या बुद्धेर्गुणास्तद्गुणा इच्छा द्वेषः सुखं दुःखमित्येवमादयस्तद्गुणाः, etc. * * * बुद्ध्युपाधिधर्माध्यासनिमित्तं हि कर्तृत्वभोक्तृत्वादिलक्षणं संसारित्वमकर्तुरभोक्तुश्चासंसारिणो नित्यमुक्तस्य सत आत्मनः । *Śaṅkara-Bhāshya* on तद्गुणसारत्वात्तु तद्व्यपदेशः प्राज्ञवत् । *Brahmasūtra*, II. 3. 29.

was very generally held among the philosophical schools at the time that our *Sūtra* was written, and this identity of view does not necessarily imply an identity of authors. Then again, the two Vātsyāyanas appear to have been separated by more than a century. Prof. Jacobi has shown that the *Nyāyasūtras* were composed between 200 and 450 A. C. and that the *Nyāyabhāshya* was also written during the same period,[1] of course, towards the end of it. Mahāmahopādhyāya Dr. Satischandra Vidyābhūshaṇa has proved by a more detailed analysis that the author of the *Nyāyabhāshya* "flourished at about A. D. 400, when Chandragupta II called Vikramāditya was King of Magadha."[2] By this time the author of the Kāmasūtra was, as we have already seen, an authority on erotics and, as we shall show more definitely below, at least a century had passed since he produced his work. Moreover, the styles of composition of the two authors are quite distinct. Then again, the author of the Kāmasūtra belongs most probably, as we shall show hereafter, to Western India while Dr. Vidyābhūshaṇa assigns the writer of the *Nyāyabhāshya* to the Dravida country.[3] From all these considerations, we see that at present there is no valid reason for thinking that the two authors are one and the same.

Coming back to other works in Sanskrit literature referring to Vātsyāyana, we notice that in some editions of the *Pañcatantra* there are two passages in which Vātsyāyana is mentioned by name.[4] However, in the *Tantrākhyāyika* which is considered to be the earliest recension of the Pañcatantra, the name of Vātsyāyana

1 *Journal of the American Oriental Society*, Vol, XXXI, 1911, p. 29.

2 *Indian Antiquary*, 1915, p. 88.

3 *Ibid*, pp. 87-88.

4 *Pañcatantra*, edited by Dr. F. Kielhorn, p. 2, कामशास्त्राणि वात्स्यायनादीनि and p. 38, वात्स्यायनोक्तविधिना निषेव्य ; see Schmidt, *op-cit.*, p. 6.

does not occur, but in enumerating the usual subjects of study it mentions first grammar and then the *Dharma, Artha* and *Kāma Śāstras* in general.[1] The Tantrākhyāyika has been supposed to have been written about 300 A.C.[2] The mention of the *Kāmasūtra* in it shows, at least, that the science of erotics had, in the third century A.C. obtained an equal footing with the sister sciences of *Dharma* and *Artha* as branches of learning that princes were required to acquire. This position it had not attained in 300 B.C., when, as we see from the *Arthaśāstra* of Kauṭilya, though *kāma* had been recognised as one of the subjects of human interest (*trivarga*), it had not as yet a *locus standi* as a science worth study, because it does not find a place in Kauṭilya's list where we find *Dharma, Artha, Itihása, Purāṇa*, and *Ākhyāna* (narratives) but not the *Kāmaśāstra.*[3] In view of the fact, therefore, that it was Vātsyāyana who made popular the science which was almost extinct (*utsanna-prâya*) in his time, the presumption is that the author of Tantrākhyāyika had his Kāmasūtra in mind when he wrote the passage above referred to. What we have said about the Tantrākhyāyika applies with equal force to the *Parva-saṃgraha-parva* which forms the introduction to the Mahābhārata and gives a summary of the whole story; it is certainly later than the main body of the work and may have been composed about the time we are speaking of. It describes the Mahābhārata as a veritable encyclopædia that embraced in its scope the *Arthśástra*, the *Dharmaśāstra* and the

1 ततो धर्म्मार्थकामशास्त्राणि ज्ञेयानि—*The Pañcatantra* edited by Dr. J. Hertel, Harvard O.S., Vol. 14, p. 1.

2 *Das Pañcatantra, seine Geschich e und seine Verbreitung* von J. Hertel, 1914, p. 9; see also Prof. Lanman's introduction to the *Pañchatantra*, Harvard O. S., Vol. 14, p. X.

3 पुराणमितिवृत्तमाख्यायिकोदाहरणं धर्म्मशास्त्रमर्थशास्त्रं चेतीतिहासः ; *Kauṭilya's Arthaśāstra*, edited by R. Shāma Shāstry, p 10.

Kāmaśāstra[1] shewing that the science was well-known at the time this chapter was added to the epic. It is significant in this connection that the Lalitavistara generally assigned to the second or third century A.C.,[2] in its enumeration of the subjects that the young Siddhārtha learnt, does not mention the Kāmaśāstra in general but knows various sections of the science such as *Strīlakshaṇa, Purushalakshaṇa, Vaiśika,* etc., besides many of the *Kalās.*[3] We know that these subjects had been dealt with by Vātsyāyana's predecessors and that there was a monograph on *Vaiśika* by Dattaka of Pāṭaliputra, and it is no wonder that the author of the *Lalitavistara* who here seeks to exhaust all the branches of learning known under the sun, should refer to these subjects though known in his time only to a very few, and on the other hand, it seems to indicate an earlier date for the Lalitavistara than that of the Kāmasūtra, though unquestionably both of them belong to the same period, and nothing can be asserted as certain from only a negative piece of evidence.

We thus see that from the literary data given above, the earlier limit to the composition of the Kāmasūtra may be assigned on the basis of Vātsyāyana's quotations from the *Gṛhya* and *Dharma Sūtras,* the *Arthaśāstra* of Kauṭilya and the *Mahābhāshya* of Patañjali and that the lower limit may be fixed at *circa* 400 A.C. based on the dates of Kālidāsa and Subandhu and, further, that there are strong reasons to believe that it was known in the third century A.C. From the historical data that the Kāmasūtra affords we can come to a more definite determination of Vātsyāyana's date.

1 अर्थशास्त्रमिदं प्रोक्तं धर्म्मशास्त्रमिदं महत् ।
कामशास्त्रमिदं प्रोक्तं व्यासेनामितबुद्धिना ॥
Ādiparva, ch. ii. 383 (Calcutta), 384 (South Indian).

2 Dr. M. Winternitz, *Geschichte der Indischen Litteratur*, Band II, p. 200.

3 *Lalitavistara*, edited by Dr. S. Lefmann, p. 156 ff.

Historical Data about the Date of Vātsyāyana

The well-known passage[1] referring to the Andhra monarch Kuntala Śātakarṇi first pointed out by Sir R.G. Bhandarkar[2] furnishes important data. According to the Puranic list of the Andhra monarchs, Kuntala Svāti or Svātikarṇa is the thirteenth in descent from Simuka, the founder of the family. Sri Malla Śātakarṇi, the third monarch in this list, has been identified by Mr. K.P. Jayaswal with the Sātakani mentioned in the Hāthigumpha inscription of Khāravela and it has been shown by him that an expedition was undertaken by Khāravela in 171 B.C. aganist this Śātakarṇi.[3] Kuntala is separated from him by 168 years according to the Puranic enumeration[4] which is held as substantially correct. Kuntala therefore reigned about the very beginning of the Christian era.[5] Calculating again back from the great Andhra monarch Gautamīputra Śātakarṇi who according to professor D. R. Bhandarkar came to the throne in A.C. 133 [6] and who according to the Puranic list is separated from Kuntala Śātakarṇi by about 123 years, we find that the reigning period of Kuntala falls in the early years of the first century A. C.

1 कर्त्तर्या कुन्तलः शातकर्णिः शातवाहनो महादेवीं मलयवतीम् (जघान), *Kāmasūtra*, Ben. ed., p. 149.

2 *Early History of the Deccan*, p. 31. I beg leave to submit that *Kartarī* here does not mean "a pair of scissors" as translated by Sir R. G. Bhāndārkar, but it is a technical term to denote a kind of stroke dealt by a man with one or both of his hands at a woman's head at the parting of the hair (*Sīmanta*). Vātsyāyana says that these strokes are in vogue among the people of the south (*Dākshiṇātyānām*) and he condemns them as they sometimes proved fatal. The case of Kuntala S'ātakarṇi is an example in point. See *Kāmasūtra*, Ben. ed., pp. 147-9.

3 *J. B. O. R. S.*, Vol. III, pages 441, 442.

4 Pargiter, *Dynasties of the Kali Age*, pp. 38-40.

5 Mr. Ramaprasad Chanda would place *Sātakani* of Khāravela about B. C. 75-20. Kuntala then would belong to the end of the first century A. C. (Memoirs of the Arch. Sur. of Ind. No. 1, p. 1!, 1919).

6 *Dekkan of the Sātavāhana Period*, Ind. Ant., 1918, p. 73.

This is then the upper limit of the composition of the Kāmasūtra which was therefore written between the first and the fifth centuries after Christ. We may next attempt to come to a closer approximation.

Vātsyāyana mentions the *Ābhīras* and the Andhras as ruling side by side at the same time in the South-West of India. He speaks of an Âbhīra Koṭṭarāja,[1] a king of Koṭṭa in Gujerat, who was killed by a washerman employed by his brother. Then, again, in his chapter on the conduct of women confined in harems, Vātsyāyana describes the sexual abuses practised in the seraglio of the Âbhîra kings among others. Now, King Īśvarasena, son of the Âbhîra Śivadatta, is mentioned as a ruling sovereign in one of the Nasik inscriptions and is thought to have reigned in the third century A.C.[3] Besides, Mahākshatrapa Īśvaradatta is considered on very reasonable grounds to have been an Âbhîra, and his coins show that he reigned some time between *circa* 236 and 239 A.C.[4] About a century later, in the early years of the fourth century A.C. (*circa* 336 A.C.), the Âbhîras were met by Samudragupta.[5] The period when the Âbhîras most flourished, therefore, was the third century A.C. on epigraphic and numismatic grounds. The Andhra rulers are also referred to by Vātsyāyana but certainly as mere local kings. In his chapter on *Īśvarakāmita*, or "The Lust of Rulers," Vātsyāyana describes

1 आभीरं हि कोट्टराजं परभवनगतं भ्रातृप्रयुक्तो रजको जघान *Kāmasūtra*, Ben. ed., p. 287. Vātsyāyana here mentions a Kāśīrāja Jayatsena about whom very little is known.

2 क्षत्रियसंज्ञकैरन्तःपुररक्षिभिरेवार्थं साधयन्त्याभीरकानाम् । *Ibid*, p. 294.

3 *Archæological Survey of Western India*, IV, p. 103. See also Professor D. R. Bhāndārkar's paper on the Gurjaras, *J. B. B. R. A. S.*. Vol. xxi, p. 430.

4 *The Western Kshatrapas* by Pandit Bhagwānlal Indraji, J. R. A. S. 1890, p. 657 ff. See also *Catalogue of the Coins of the Andhra Dynasty* by E. P. Rapson, pp. cxxxiii ff. Prof. D. R Bhāndārkar assigns Īśvaradatta to A. C. 188—90 (Arch. Sur. Ind., An. Rep., 1913-14, p. 230).

5 J. F. Fleet, *Gupta Inscriptions*, p. 8.

various forms of sexual abuse practised by kings and it is significant that all the rulers here mentioned are referred to by the names of the people they ruled over and belong to the South-Western India, *viz.*, the Kings of the Aparāntakas, the Vaidarbhas, the Saurāshṭrakas, the Vātsagulmakas and the Andhras.[1] The Andhra monarchs here referred to evidently ruled over the Andhra people proper, and the social customs and practices of the Andhra people are described in various other parts of the book also.[2] There is no reference in the Kāmasūtra to the position of the Andhras as sovereigns exercising suzerain sway. The time, therefore, described by Vātsyāyana is that when the line of the great Andhra emperors had come to an end and the country was split up into a number of small kingdoms, among which the most considerable were those ruled over by the *Andhra-bhṛtyas*, or dynasties sprung up from the officers of the imperial Andhras. Among them the Purāṇas mention the Âbhîras, the Gardabhinas, the Śakas and also some Andhras[3] who evidently ruled over a limited territory at the time referred to. The time when Vātsyāyana flourished is therefore the period when these later Andhra kings and the Âbhîras ruled simultaneously over different parts of Western India, that is, subsequent to *circa* 225 A.C.,[4] when the line of the great Andhras disappeared and before the beginning of the fourth century A.C.,

1 *Kāmasūtra*, Ben. ed., pp. 287-288.

2 *Ibid*, pp. 126, 135, 287, etc.

3 Pargiter, *Dynasties of the Kali Age*, p. 45 ; the Mātsya, Vāyu, and Brahmāṇḍa Purāṇas read—

अन्ध्राणां संस्थिते राज्ये तेषां भृत्यान्वया नृपाः ।
सप्तैवान्ध्रा भविष्यन्ति दशाभीरास्तथा नृपाः ।
सप्त गर्दभिनश्चापि शकाश्चाष्टादशैव तु ।

4 Dr. V. A. Smith, *Early History of India*, 3rd ed. p. 212 Prof. D. R. Bhāndārkar, *Dekkan of Śātavāhana Period* (Ind, Ant. 1918, p. 85), also holds that "the *Śātavāhana* power came to an end in the first half of the third century A. D."

when the Guptas of whom there is no mention in the Kāmasūtra, were again uniting northern India under a common sway. From this the conclusion is inevitable that the Kāmasūtra was composed about the middle of the third century A.C. and this agrees with the conclusion arrived at from an examination of the literary data.

Recent Discussions on the Date

Since the above remarks about the date of the *Kāmasūtra* were placed before the public in the *Journal of the Department of Letters* of the University of Calcutta (Vol. IV), several scholars in India and Europe have expressed their opinion on the same subject. Of these, Prof. A. Banerji Sastri has examined the question in the *Journal of the Bihar and Orissa Research Society*[1] and has arrived at almost the same conclusion as myself on mostly the same arguments, the only dfference being that Prof. Sastri would place Vātsyāyana to "approximately the end of the third century A.D." while I have placed him about the middle. Prof. Sastri, moreover, differs from me in thinking that Bhāsa's drama, *Avimāraka*, was known to Vātsyāyana,[2] while I have expressed my doubts about it.[3]

Banerji-Sastri—end of Third Century A.C.

Prof. Jolly in the introduction to his edition of the Arthaśāstra has sought to prove that the Arthaśāstra was composed in the third century after Christ and the Kāmasūtra which was modelled upon it, in the fourth century A.C.[4] Every one of the arguments of Jolly with regard to the date of the Arthaśāstra has been critically examined by Mr. K. P. Jayaswal in his recently published work on *Hindu Polity*[5]

Jolly—4th Century A.C.

1 Vol ix. Part I, p. 49 ff.
2 *Ibid.*. p. 57.
3 See *ante*, p. 17.
4 *Arthaśāstra of Kauṭilya*, a New Edition, Vol. I. Lahore, 1923, pp. 21-29.
5 *Hindu Polity*, A Constitutional History of India in Hindu Times, Calcutta 1924, Appendix C, pp. 203-14.

5

and has been shown to be untenable, and the 4th century B.C. has been proved to be the only probable date for that work. His theory therefore with regard to the date of Vātsyāyana naturally falls to the ground.

Applying to this date Prof. Jolly's dictum that the Kāmasūtra and the Arthaśāstra could not have been separated by more than a century at most[1] we would arrive at a date which is absurd for the Kāmasūtra. Jolly does not consider the political evidence as very conclusive and holds that "it will be necessary to confine oneself to the literary data in fixing the age of the Kāmasūtra" (p. 29); and the evidence offered by the literary data is this according to him: "If both Kālidāsa and Subandhu are rightly referred to the fifth century A.D., the Kāmasūtra might be placed in the fourth century.'[2] This theory twice applied here by Jolly that whenever there are two authors of whom one shows evidence of his debt to the other, they cannot be separated by more than a century, is one that will hardly hold good in the history of literature of any country in the world. There is no earthly reason why Kālidāsa and Vātsyāyana cannot be separated by two centuries and Kauṭilya and Vātsyāyana by six centuries. Kālidāsa, when he had occasion to refer to the Kāmaśāstra, found Vātsyāyana's book to be the standard work on the subject and naturally borrowed from it, and Vātsyāyana too, when he set himself to write the Kāmasūtra, a work on a secular subject in a country where most of the literature was religious, had naturally his eyes turned to this masterly work which like his was 'thoroughly realistic and worldly'[3], and withal manifested 'a rare unity of plan and structure'[4], and which even now

1 Jolly, op. cit., p. 29.
2 *Ibid.* p, 28.
3 *Ibid.*, p 3.
4 *Ibid.*, p. 5.

we have no hesitation in declaring 'the most precious work in the whole range of Sanskrit literature.'[1] During the many centuries that intervened between the two auothrs, Kauṭilya's work had not been superseded but still dominated the field as it continued to dominate for many centuries longer. Is it any wonder then that Vātsyāyana should take this work on an allied subject as his model and borrow its method and style ?

I, however, agree with Prof. Jolly (p. 26) in holding that the abstention from meat which Vātsyāyana refers to while defining *Dharma*[2] is only a theory, or rather an ideal which, as Vātsyāyana says, people would learn from the *Śāstra* or the works on that subject and it did not represent the actual state of things in his time. A glimpse at real life which we have in his section on *Samprayoga* shows that meat diet was in vogue, and both amongst men and women. Vātsyāyana advises a lover to please his mistress when she feels rather tired or exhausted, with such relishes as roasted or dried meat as well as gruel and extracts of meat of various kinds. One of them is called by Vātsyāyana *accha-rasaka-yūṣam* and the commentary explains that it was a fresh extract of meat (*māṃsa-niryūham*), and another called *amla-yavāgū* is said to be prepared by boiling with meat (māṃsa-siddhā).[3] The doctrine of *ahiṃsā* and the eating of meat have existed in India side by side since the earliest Vedic times and no conclusion can be arrived at with regard to the date of a work simply from the mention or non-mention of the doctrine of *ahiṃsā* in it. Even in the Ṛgveda, the cow was recognised as *aghnyā* and the ox as *aghnya* (not to be slaughtered), while in

1 *Ibid.*, p. 1.

2 मांसभक्षणादिभ्यः शास्त्रादेव निवारणं धर्मः । *Kāmasūtra.*, p. 12.

3 अच्छरसकयूषमम्लयवागुं भृष्टमांसोपदंशानि पानकानि चूतफलानि शुष्कमांसं etc. *Ibid.*, p. 174.

4 Macdonell. *Vedic Mythology*, p. 150.

the *Vinaya Piṭaka* itself we are told that oxen in plenty were slaughtered by Sīha, the Licchavi Commander-in-Chief to feed the Buddha and his attending bhikṣus.[1] A newly converted minister at Benares placed twelve hundred and fifty dishes of meat (māṃsa-pāṭi) before the bhikṣus including the Buddha himself.[2] The mere fact, therefore, that a work prohibits meat-eating is not sufficient reason to dub it as post-Buddhistic.

What has been said above with regard to Prof. Jolly's theory about the date of the Kāmasūtra applies with equal force to what Prof. M. Winternitz has observed on the same subject in the third volume of his *History of Indian Literature* where he has arrived at the same conclusion as Dr. Jolly and on the very same grounds, though independently. Thus the Professor observes : "That it (the *Kāmasūtra*) is later than the Kauṭilīya-Arthaśāstra cannot be doubted. But it can hardly be much later ; for the great similarity between the two books makes it clear that the Kāmasūtra is separated from Kauṭilya only by a short interval. If we place the latter, say, in the third century after Christ, then the Kāmasūtra of Vātsyāyana is to be placed somewhere in the fourth. But it is nothing more than a guess." Here it will be seen that Winternitz also has nothing more to fix the date than the mere guess that Kauṭilya and Vātsyāyana cannot be separated by more than a century. As in the case of Jolly, Winternitz's failure to establish the third century for Kauṭilya necessarily leads to the rejection of the fourth century for Vātsyāyana.

Winternitz—Fourth Century A.C.

Mahāmahopādhyāya Haraprasad Sastri in his

1 *Mahāvagga*, vi. 31, 12 ; vi. 33, 3.
2 *Ibid*. vi. 25, 3.
3 Translated from *Geschichte der Indischen Litteratur* von Dr. M. Winternitz, III Band, p. 540.

MM. H. P. Sastri—First Century A.C.

Magadhan Literature has, on the other hand, sought to push back the date of the Kāmasūtra to the first century A.C., his argument being that "Vātsyāyana flourished at a time when the memory of the scandal (of Kuntala Śātakarṇi) was fresh. So he may be placed in the first century A.D.; for, the public memory is far short and in one or two generations, people forget these scandals."[1] Here the Mahāmahopādhyāya, unlike Jolly, considers the political data as the deciding factor, but accepting his conclusion we are met by the difficulty that in the first century A.C., we have no evidence of Âbhîra monarchs ruling side by side with the Andhras. Both according to epigraphic as well as Pauranic evidence, the Âbhîras rose to power in the third century A.C., so that the date of Vātsyāyana who is no less acquainted with the scandals of the Âbhîra court than with those among the Andhras, cannot be placed in the first century A.C. Moreover, we have ample evidence to show that court scandals are referred to by Indian writers many centuries after they took place. Vātsyāyana himself refers to the scandal of Dāṇḍakya, the Bhoja[2] who must have lived many centuries prior to the composition of the Kāmasūtra. Viśākhadatta in his *Mudrārākṣasa* refers to court intrigues and scandals many centuries older than his time. The *Bṛhat Saṃhitā* refers to scandals like that of king Vidūratha who was killed by his queen with a sharp instrument hid in her hair and to a Kāśīrāja who was similarly killed with a poisoned anklet[3] and there is nothing to show that they lived about the same time as *Varāha-mihira*. Aśvaghoṣa in the fourth chapter of his *Buddhacarita* relates scandals most of which were far

1 *Māgadhan Literature*, by MM. Haraprasad Sastri, Calcutta 1923, p. 84.

2 *Kāmasūtra*, p. 24.

3 *Bṛhat Saṁhitā*, Ch. 78, 1.

removed in date from his. We are therefore unable to see eye to eye with MM. Haraprasad Sastri with regard to the date fixed by him for the Kāmasūtra.

Some other points in MM. Sastri's work call for comment. He identifies Śvetaketu,[1] the mythical reformer of primitive society, who according to an account in the Mahābhārata set up the institution of marriage, with Śvetaketu Āruṇeya, the highly cultured philosopher of the Upanishads. The *Ṛgveda* shows a well-organised family life with the institution of marriage fully developed amongst the Indo-Aryans, and therefore, the age when that institution grew and developed must have preceded the Ṛgvedic era by a very long period and the age of Śvetaketu Āruṇeya—an age of intense metaphysical speculation when the Upaniṣadic literature grew, could certainly not be identical with it. Then there is not the least justification for MM. Sastri's statement that "Auddālaki wrote more on union or Samprayoga than on other subjects. He divided that subject into ten major heads. So his work was called Daśatayī"[2] These are all statements unauthorised by Vātsyāyana who on the other hand asserts that Śvetaketu's huge work in five hundred chapters dealt with the whole of the Kāmaśāstra and that it was Bābhravya who divided and arranged the contents of Śvetaketu's work into seven *adhikaraṇas* or sections; in fact, of the three passages in the Kāmasūtra where Vātsyāyana quotes Auddālaki, one belongs to the Samprayoga section, another to the Pāradārika, and the third to the Vaiśika section.[3] The third of these is the longest quotation from Auddālaki where a whole group of sūtras is spoken of by Vātsyāyana as the opinion of Auddālaki as distinguished from the theory of Bābhravya, so that

1 *Magadhan Literature*, p. 78.
2 *Ibid.*, p. 79.
3 See *ante*, p. 7 ff. and p. 10, note 2.

there is no justification for the conjecture that Auddālaki's work dealt with the one topic of Samprayoga alone. It was rather Bābhravya, the Pāñcāla who specially shone in his delineation of the sixty-four Samprayoga-kalās. For the other statements that Auddālaki's work was called Daśatayī or that he divided Samprayoga into ten sections, there is absolutely no foundation. Vātsyāyana says that the Ṛgveda was called Daśatayī and not Auddālaki's work and in the whole chapter where this topic is dealt with there is no reference to Auddālaki at all.

B. Bhattacharya —Vātsyāyana before Bharata

Prof. Batuknath Bhattacharya in his paper headed "A Brief Survey of the Sāhityaśāstra" in the *Journal of the Department of Letters* of the University of Calcutta, has incidentally discussed the date of the Kāmasūtra.[1] He has not hazarded any definite opinion on the date but has expressed his difference with the conclusion arrived at by me, mainly on two grounds. In the first place, he observes, "It is hard to believe that it (the Kāmasūtra) could have been composed later than the Nāṭya-Śāstra, considering the style in which it is written—a style distinctly aphoristic in nature and reminiscent of the sūtra period (600-200 B.C.)." Vātsyāyana's mention of Kuntala Śātakarṇi precludes any possibility of his composing the sūtras on erotics in the so-called sūtra period of Max Müller, and while comparing the Kāmasūtra with the Nāṭyaśāstra it should be borne in mind that the latter, though passing as the product of *one* author who is more or less mythical, bears on its face the evidence of the handiwork of different ages, that, in fact, we have before us, as Prof. Winternitz observes, "a compilation of various older and later texts." The same scholar also remarks that "the original work

1 See Vol. ix, pp. 110-113.

was probably a Sūtra-text, as indeed the oldest scientific works as a rule were composed in the Sūtra style."[2] The Nāṭyaśāstra has been variously assigned by scholars from the first to the sixth or seventh century A.C.,[3] so that it is not unlikely that some portions of the Nāṭyaśāstra were older than the Kāmasūtra while others were much younger.

The particular point on which, however, Prof. Bhattacharya sets up a comparison between the two works viz., the classification of men and women into different categories, proves nothing, as the different authors have proceeded to classify them from different points of view. Vātsyāyana divides men into Śaśa, Vṛṣa and Aśva and women into Mṛgī, Baḍavā and Hastinī from their different capacities for *samprayoga*, while Bharata's classification of women into 24 varieties[4] is based on æsthetic, intellectual and moral standards. No comparison lies between the two authors in this respect and the more elaborate classification of Bharata does not necessarily imply a later date. We find the same threefold classification of males and females in the *Anaṅgaraṅga*, a work on erotics composed in the late 15th or early 16th century A.C. when the Lodi Emperors were ruling at Delhi.[5]

Next, Prof. Bhattacharya remarks, "It seems a little remarkable that Vātsyāyana should not have mentioned any of his predecessors more contiguous to his own date but should have looked so far back as to the 4th century B.C. This would argue a certain break in the continuity of the study." There was indeed such a break in the continuity of the study of the science of Erotics, as Vātsyāyana himself asserts that the Kāmaśāstra was very near extinction (*utsannakalpam-abhūt*) before he took it up, so much so, that he had to fall back upon the ancient and little-read text of Bābhravya to compile his work; he does not think much of the monographs of Dattaka and others which he holds were rather fragmentary and scrappy (*khaṇḍaśaḥ praṇītam*).[6]

2 *Ges. d. Ind. Lit.* iii, 8. See also *Studies in the History of Sanskrit Poetics* by Sushil Kumar De, M.A., D. Litt., vol. I, pp. 23-36.
3 Winternitz, *op. cit.*, p. 8, n. 3.
4 *Kāmasūtra*, p. 71 and *Nāṭyaśāstra*, xxii, 96-142.
5 *Anaṅga-raṅga*. trans. by Burton and Arbuthnot, Paris. 1908. p. xvi. See S. K. De, *op. cit.*, p. 342.
6 *Kāmasūtra*, pp. 7 and 381. See also *ante*, p. 3 ff.

CHAPTER II

THE GEOGRAPHY OF VÂTSYÂYANA

Vātsyāyana in enumerating the special customs and practices in different parts of India mentions many of its countries and peoples. He appears to have been familiar with all parts of the Indian continent. Of the five great divisions of India since the Vedic times he mentions three, *viz.* the *Prācya* country, the *Madhyadeśa* and the *Dākṣiṇātya* or the *Dakṣiṇāpatha.* In the Vedic age, as we know from a well known passage in the *Aitareya Brāhmaṇa* (viii. 14), the whole of India is shown to consist of five great *Diks* or divisions, the *Prācī Dik* with its Samrāṭ rulers, the *Dakṣiṇā Dik* with its *Bhoja* sovereigns, the *Pratīcī* and *Udīcī Diks* with their *Svarāṭ* and *Virāṭ* rulers, and the *Dhruvā Madhyamā Dik* with its kings called *Rājās.* This partition of India into five *Diks,* that is quarters or divisions, is found to be a familiar practice in the *Atharva-Veda* and both the *Kṛṣṇa* and *Śukla* recensions of the *Yajurveda* Saṃhitā.[1] In later times we find the *Dik* often changed into *Deśa,* as for example, the *Prācī Dik* and the *Madhyamā-Dik* are called the *Prācya-Deśa* and the *Madhya-Deśa* respectively. This traditional division of India into *Diks* or *Deśas* is found throughout in Indian literature : it is found in the Vedic works, the Epics and the Purāṇas, the astronomical works like those of Parāśara add Varāhamihira, and in the *Kāvyamīmāṃsā* of Rājaśekhara[2] written about the

V. knows all parts of India

1 *Atharva-veda* iii. 27 ; iv. 40 ; xii. 3 ; xv. 2 · 6 etc. *Taittirîya Saṁhitā* iv. 4. 12; *Kāṭhaka Saṁhitā*, xxii. 14 ; *Maitrāyaṇî* Saṁhitā iii. 16. 4 ; *Vājasaneyi Saṁhitā* xv. 10—14 etc. etc. This question has been fully dealt with in my paper on "Aryan Occupation of Eastern India," pp. 45—78.

2 Gaekwad's Oriental Series, No. I, p. 93 ff,

6

beginning of the tenth century we find the same five-fold division of the Indian continent. This system of general division of India was also adopted by some of the Chinese travellers.

Madhydeśa or Central Division

A few places in the Central Division of India are referred to by Vātsyāyana in his work and the general name Madhyadeśa also has been employed by him in one passage where he says that in the Madhyadeśa, there being a preponderance of *Āryas*, that is, of persons of decent character who were pure in their habits, the ladies in that region disliked unclean practices like kissing, pressing the nails and biting by the other sex.[1] This Madhyadeśa is no doubt the same as the *Madhyamā Dik* of Vedic literature; and may be considered to have the same limits as the Madhyadeśa of Manu who defines it as the country between the Himavat and the Vindhya mountains, to the west of Prayāga and to the east of Vinaśana, that is, of the spot where the river Sarasvatī disappears[2]; but more probably, it is the region between the Ganges and the Jumna, that is, the land of the *Āryas* according to one of the views pointed out by Vasiṣṭha and Baudhāyana in their *Dharmasūtras.*[3] The commentary, *Jayamaṅgalā* is inclined to adopt this definition of the boundaries of the Madhyadeśa, because, as it says, this is mainly intended by the author of the Kāma-Śāstra.[4]

The word *Ārya* used here by Vātsyāyana is not an ethnical designation but it is applied to a person who, as

1 मध्यदेश्या आर्यप्रायाः शुच्युपचाराश्चुम्बननखदन्तपदद्वेषिण्यः। *Kāmasūtra*, Ben. ed., p, 125.

2 *Manu* II. 21. Translation, Buehler. S. B. E. XXV. p. 33.

3 *Vasiṣṭha*, i. 12; *Baudhāyana*, i. 2, 10.

4 'गङ्गायमुनयोरित्येके' इति वसिष्ठः। अयमेव शास्त्रकृतां प्राधान्येनाभिप्रेतः। *Jayamaṅgalā* *Ṭīkā* on Kāmasūtra, Ben. ed., p. 125.

Vātsyāyana says, is pure in habits (*śucyupacāra*) ; in the example given by him the Ârya ladies of the Madhyadeśa did not like such practices as kissing or biting, apparently because of their aversion to contamination by spittle from another's mouth, that is, to what is known as *ucchiṣṭa*. It is evident, therefore, that *Ārya* in Vātsyāyana means the same thing as in Vasiṣṭha and Baudhāyana, that is, a *Śiṣṭa* or a person of decent habits and character, as will be seen from a reference to their respective *Dharmasūtras*.[1] There can, therefore, be no doubt that the *Āryāvarta* of these latter authors was not the land of the Âryans, but the land of the *Śiṣṭas* whose manners and customs, habits and practices were decent and pure according to the Dharma literature. In the *Mahābhāṣya* Patañjali also explains Âryāvarta as the land of the Śiṣṭas.[2]

In V.'s time Eastern India is more decent than Madhyadeśa

It is worthy of remark, however, that in Vātsyāyana's time decent conduct was more in evidence in Eastern India, among people whom he calls *Prācyas* than among some of the peoples of the Madhyadeśa, and these Prācyas he places among the *Śiṣṭas*. Thus in his chapter on *Auparisṭaka*, a very filthy practice, Vātsyāyana observes, "The people of Eastern India do not resort to women who practise the Auparisṭaka. The people of Ahicchatra resort to such women but do nothing with them, so far as the mouth is concerned. The people of Sāketa do with them every kind of mouth (abuses), while the people of Nagara do not practise this, but do every other thing. The people of the Śūrasena country, on the sothern bank of the Jumna, do everything without any hesitation, for they say that women being naturally unclean, no one can be certain about their character,

1 *Vasiṣṭha*, i. 6 and *Baudhāyana*. i. 5.

2 See *Mahābhāṣya* on Pāṇini vi. 3. 109 and ii. 4, 10. For a fuller discussion. see my *Aryan Occupation of Eastern India*, pp. 14—19.

their purity, their conduct, their practices, their confidences, or their speech. They are not, however, on this account to be abandoned, because religious law, on the authority of which they are reckoned pure, lays down that the udder of a cow is clean at the time of milking. Again a dog is clean when he seizes a deer in hunting. A bird is clean when it causes a fruit to fall from a tree by pecking at it. And the mouth of a woman is clean for kissing and such like things."[1] Vātsyāyana finally sums up by saying that in all these matters connected with love, one should be guided by the custom of one's own country and one's own personal inclination in as much as while on the one hand, the holy texts (*S m ṛ t i*) allowed some latitude in such things, on the other hand, however, they were against the practice of the śiṣṭas (*ś i ṣ ṭ a-v i p r a t i p a t t e ḥ*)[2]. Here the commentary explains that the śiṣṭas spoken of in this passage are the Prācyas, the Âhicchatrikas and the Nāgarakas,[3] and the context shows that he is right.

Of the various peoples mentioned in the above passage from the Kāmasūtra, the Âhicchatrikas and the Śaurasenas were natives of the Madhyadeśa and the Nāgarakas also belonged probably to that region for reasons that will be shown below. Of these, Ahicchatra, identified with modern Ramnagar in the Bareilly district,[4] was the capital of the northern division of the Pañcāla country according to the

Ahicchatra

1 '*The Kāma-Sūtra of Vātsyāyana*' translated and published by the Kāma Śāstra Society of London and Benares, reprint 1883, p. 71.

2 शिष्टविप्रतिपत्तेः स्मृतिवाक्यस्य च सावकाशत्वाद्देशस्थितेरात्मनश्च वृत्तिप्रत्ययानुरूपं प्रवर्तेतेति वात्स्यायनः । *Kāma-Sūtra*, Ben. ed., p. 167.

3 शिष्टविप्रतिपत्तेरिति । शिष्टानां प्राच्याहिच्छत्रिकनागरकानां विप्रतिपत्तिर्दृश्यते । *Ibid.*, p. 167.

4 See V. A. Smith, *Early History of India*, third edn, p 377.

Mahābhārata which states that as the result of the defeat which Droṇācārya inflicted on Drupada, the Pañcāla king, the country was partitioned into two, and that the Brahmin teacher of the Kurus established his capital at Ahicchatra to the north of the Ganges,[1] and that up to this place the Kaurava battalions reached when the forces of the opposing armies assembled for the Great War.[2] It is a significant fact that we find a Brahmin family ruling at Ahicchatra in the second century B.C. and that it had marital relations with the great Brahmin imperial family of the Śuṅgas. The names of this family of Kings of *Adhichatra* which is apparently the same as Ahicchatra are given in two inscriptions in a cave at Pabhosā (the classical hill of Prabhāsa) 3 miles to the north-west of Kosam, the ancient Kauśāmbī. The inscription inside the cave records that it was "caused to be made by Âṣāḍhāsena, son of the Vaihidarî (i.e., Vaihidara-princess, and) son of King Bhāgavata, son of the Tevaṇî (i.e., Traivarṇa-princess), and son of King Vaṃgapāla, son of Śonakāyana (Śaunakāyana) of Adhichatra."[3] Another inscription on the rock outside

Brahmin Rulers at Ahicchatra

1 राजासि दक्षिणे कूले भागीरथ्याहमुत्तरे । ৭০
दक्षिणांश्चापि पाञ्चालान् यावच्चर्मण्वती नदी ।
द्रोणेन चैवं द्रुपदः परिभूयाथ पालितः ॥৭৪
अहिच्छत्रञ्च विषयं द्रोणः समभिपद्यत । ৭৬
एवं राजन्नहिच्छत्रा पुरी जनपदायुता ।
युधि निर्जित्य पार्थेन द्रोणाय प्रतिपादिता ॥৭৭

Mahābhārata, Adiparva, Ch. 138, Vaṅgavāsī edn.

2 अहिच्छत्रं कालकूटं गङ्गाकूलञ्च भारत ।

... ...

बभूव कौरवेयाणां बलेन सुसमाकुलः ।

Ibid, *Udyoga-parva*, Ch. 19. verses 30-31.

3 Trans. A. Fuehrer, *Epigraphia Indica*, II, p. 243.

the cave records the further fact that this Âṣāḍhasena was the maternal uncle of King Bahasatimitra, the son of Gopālī.[1] This King Bahasatimitra has been identified with the Śuṅga Emperor, Puṣyamitra by Mr. K. P. Jayaswal[2] who holds that "the Ahichatra family of Aṣāḍhasena was either gubernatorial or feudatory to the Magadha throne." He further points out that the "Ahichatra family were Brahmans like the Śuṅgas, an ancestor of Âṣāḍhasena being called Śaunakāyana." In the neighbourhood of Ahicchatra have been picked up the so-called Mitra coins and among them those of a King Agnimitra who is considered to be the same as the second emperor of the Śunga dynasty,[3] and a dedicatory inscription at Budh Gayā assigned to the earliar part of the first century B.C., records the gift of a queen of King Indramitra of Ahicchatra.[4] We know very little of the subsequent history of Ahicchatra but by the time that Vātsyāyana wrote his book, in the third century B.C., this city must have passed like the whole of the province to which it belongs through the hands of the Kushan monarchs. It is significant that while Vātsyāyana speaks of the people of Ahicchatra, he has nothing to record of the king or the king's harem as he does in other cases.

Saurasenas degraded since the Manu-saṁhitā by foreign contact

The *Saurasenas* occupied the country about the city of Mathurā, their capital. They are located by the commentary to the south of the river Kauśāmbī[5] which is apparently the stream flowing by the celebrated city of the same name. From the character that Vātsyāyana gives them they appear to have fallen off from the pure

1 *Ibid.*, p. 242.

2 *J. B. O. R. S.*, 1917, pp. 473—485.

3 Rapson, *Sources of Indian History, Coins*, p 13.

4 *Cambridge History of India* I. 526.

5 सौरसेनाः कौशाम्ब्या दक्षिणतः कूले ये निवसन्ति । *Kām. S.* (Benares), p.167.

and ideal conduct that characterised them in ancient times according to Manu who says, "The plain of the Kurus, the (country of the) Matsyas, Pāñcālas, and Śūrasenakas, these (form) indeed, the country of the Brahmarṣis (Brahmanical sages, which ranks) immediately after Brahmāvarta. From a Brāhmaṇa born in that country let all men on earth learn their several usages".[1] Evidently the Śaurasenas had fallen off from this high standard of purity under foreign domination. Mathurā had been occupied by the Greeks in the early years of the second century B.C. as pointed out by Kern on the authority of the *Gārgī-Saṃhitā* which says, "Then the viciously valiant Greeks, after reducing Sāketa, Pañcāla country and Mathurā will reach or take Kusumadhvaja (Palibothra)."[2] The Gārgī-Saṃhitā further adds that sometime after the Greeks, the country was occupied by the Śakas or Scythians.[3] This is fully corroborated by coins and inscriptions unearthed in Mathurā itself and the country in its neighbourhood showing that about the first century before Christ the Śaka satraps Hagāna, Hagāmasha, Rañjubula, Soḍāsa etc. were ruling at Mathurā.[4] Henceforth this city was under the domination of the Kushan monarchs for several centuries, so that in the third century after Christ when, according to our determination, Vātsyāyana wrote his work, the Śaurasenas had got much degraded by intercourse with foreigners of immensely inferior culture and had lost the ancient purity in their manners

1 Buchler, *Laws of Manu*, pp. 82-83.

2 ततः साकेतमाक्रम्य पञ्चालान् मथुरां तथा ।
यवना दुष्टविक्रान्ताः प्राप्स्यन्ति कुसुमध्वजम् ॥
Kern, *Bṛhat Saṁhitā*, Introduction, p. 37 et seq.

3 शकानां च ततो राजा ह्यर्थलुब्धो महाबलः ।
दुष्टभावश्च पापश्च विनाशे समुपस्थिते ॥ *Ibid.*, p 38.

4 See *The Cambridge History of India*, Vol. 1, pp. 526-7.

and customs that made Manu characterise them as an ideal people from whom all other peoples on earth were to imbibe good and decent behaviour.

The people of Sāketa who also passed through the same vicissitudes were almost as bad as those of Śūrasena, but the latter were worse in as much as they quoted scripture to support their vile a'uses. Sāketa (otherwise known as Ayodhyā) was the capital of the Kosala country, and this name which had been coming into prominence since the Buddhist times was in use in the second century B.C. as we see from its mention in the *Mahābhāṣya*[1] and later also we find it in the passage quoted above from the Gārgī Saṃhitā ; we find, therefore, in the Kāmasūtra this name in use in preference to Ayodhyā. I have shown elsewhere that Sāketa was on the boundary line between the Madhyadeśa and the Prācya division of India.[2]

Sāketa almost as bad as Sūrasena

It is notworthy that though Vātsyāyana refers to some of the practices of the Âhicchatrikas or the people of Ahicchatra, the ancient capital of northern Pañcāla, of the Pañcāla people as such he has got nothing to say. He speaks of the Pañcāla country no doubt but it will be observed from the way in which he does so that it was an ancient province to the achievements of which in the past he is referring, and he does nowhere in his work make any mention of any of the living practices of the Pañcāla people at the time that he lived. Thus he refers to the great Bābhravya Pāñcāla of old from whom he drew his materials but whose work was very little studied in his

Pañcāla people extinct in V.'s time

1 अरुणद् यवनः साकेतम्। *Mahābhāṣya* on Pāṇini III. 2, 111. See Goldstucker, *Pāṇini*, p. 230. अयं पन्थाः साकेतमुपतिष्ठते, *Mb.* on Pāṇini 1. 3, 2.

2 *Aryan Occupation of Eastern India*, pp. 12-14.

times;[1] he further points out the connection of the Pañcāla country with the division of the Ṛgveda into sixty-four chapters and draws an analogy between this fact and the invention of the sixty-four Pāñcāla *kalās* or arts[2] described by Bābhravya. But he notes no peculiarity in the conduct of the Pāñcālas of his day nor does he mention any contemporary practices in the relations between the sexes as he does of the other peoples of India. Evidently the Pañcāla people who occupied a prominent position among the Vedic Aryans in the period of the Brāhmaṇas and whose country made up one of the sixteen *Mahājanapadas* when the early works of the Theravāda school of the Buddhists were written, had lost their individuality as a separate people; at Ahicchatra, their ancient capital, the people must have been strongly influenced by foreign occupation—as at Mathurā.

The Udīcya Division of Northern India

Of the countries of the Udīcya or northern division, Vātsyāyana speaks still less than of the Madhyadeśa or the Midland proper. He nowhere mentions the Udīcya division by name but he refers to the customs and practices of some of the countries in the Udīcya division and even beyond the northern hills. Of the people on the Himalayas he speaks in general (*Haimavatānām*) without mentioning any particular country or state, saying that among the Haimavatas or people of the Himalayas, "adventurous citizens combining together bribe the sentinels and enter the harem."[3] The absence of specific mention of any

People on the Himalayas

1 बाभ्रवीयांश्च सूत्रार्थान् आगमय्य विमृश्य च ।
वात्स्यायनश्चकारेदं कामसूत्रं यथाविधि ॥ *Kāmasūtra*, Benares edition p. 381.
महदिति च बाभ्रव्यस्य दुरध्येयत्वात् संक्षिप्य सर्वमर्थमल्पेन ग्रन्थेन कामसूत्रमिदं प्रणीतम् । *Ibid.*, p. 7.

2 See *ante*, pp. 3–7.

3 अथन रक्षिणमुपगृह्य साहसिकाः संहताः प्रविशन्ति हैमवतानाम् । *Kāmas*, p. 294.

7

great people on the Himalayas indicates that the earlier hill states like those of the Śākyas, or their neighbours, the Koliyas, were extinct or at least, decadent, at the time that the *Kāmasūtra* was written.

Of the countries included in the Udîcya division by Indian writers, Vātsyāyana mentions Bāhlîka which the commentary explains as a country in Uttarāpatha,[1] that is, in the northern region. About the ladies of the Bāhlîka country (*Bāhlīkadeśyāḥ*), the *Kāmasūtra* informs us that they, like the women of the Madhydeśa, were of decent habits and averse to kissing and similar unclean practices.[2] Vātsyāyana also speaks of a very peculiar custom which the Bāhlîka country had in common with Strîrājya and the province of Grāmanārî : he avers that in these countries several young men were married to a single woman (*ekaikasyāḥ parigrahabhūtāḥ*) and they were in the same position there as ladies in the harem in other countries.[3] Vātsyāyana does not say exactly that these male spouses were confined in a harem by their lordly wives but that they had the same character as harem-ladies (*antaḥpurasadharmāṇaḥ*) that is, as the commentary explains, they had all to confine their services to the single lady who was their mistress and had to attend upon her either singly or in batches.[4] This rather unusual custom, no doubt refers to a system of polyandry carried to a refined excess. It was perhaps

Bāhlîka—Polyandry there in V.'s times

1 बाह्लीकदेश्याः उत्तरापथिकाः । *Ibid.* p. 125.

2 मध्यदेश्या आर्यप्रायाः शुच्युपचाराश्चुम्बननखदन्तपदद्वेषिण्यः । बाह्लीकदेश्याः...च ।
Kāmasūtra, p. 125.

3 ग्रामनारीविषये स्त्रीराज्ये च बाह्लीके बहवो युवानोऽन्तःपुरसधर्माण एकैकस्याः परिग्रहभूताः । *Ibid.* p. 140.

4 तेषामेकैकशो युगपच्च...रञ्जयेयुः । *Com.* एकैकेन क्रमशो यौगपद्येन चेत्यर्थः ।
Ibid., p. 140.

on account of the corrupt practices of the Bāhlīkas that they were characterised in the Great Epic as forming the very dregs of the earth.[1]

It is important to determine the geographical position of the country of Bāhlīka. The city of Balkh in Bactria which makes the closest approach to its name seems to indicate its ancient location though some scholars are inclined to doubt it and to suggest that it was somewhere near the Kuru land.[2] But that ancient India extended beyond the present north-western frontier seems indisputable from many considerations. The Chinese travellers, for example, found Balkh Indian to all intents and purposes. Yuan Chwang to reach the country which he calls Fo-ho-lo (I-tsing names it Fo-ko-lo),[3] travelled some hundreds of *li* from Tokhāra, crossed the Oxus and passed through some territories of small extent. He found Indian culture and civilisation predominating here, there being above hundred Buddhist monasteries with more than three thousand[4] brethren, all adherents of the "Small Vehicle" or the Hīnayāna system. He says that it reached on the north to the Oxus, the Wakhsch of Arab geographers and the Vakṣu or Vaṅkṣu of Kālidāsa. As we have shown before, Kālidāsa makes Raghu meet the Hūṇas on the banks of the Oxus.[5] Kālidādsa says that Raghu's horses relieved the fatigue of their long journey by rolling about on the banks of the Vaṅkṣu and shook their shoulders to which were attached filaments

Bāhlīka is the country about Balkh i.e., Bactria

Yuan-Chwang found Indian culture in Bactria

Kālidāsa's Vaṅkṣu is the Oxus in Bactria

1 मलं पृथिव्या बाह्लीकाः । *Mbt.* V. 39, 80.

2 *Camb. Hist.* I. p. 124 ; *Ved. Ind.* II. p. 62.

3 See Watters, *On Yuan Chwang*, I. p. 109.

4 *Ibid.*, p. 108.

5 See *ante.* p. 23, foot note 1.

of saffron[1]. Amara in his lexicon speaks of the yellow variety of the saffron grown in the Bāhlīka country,[2] and Kṣīrasvāmin, the earliest commentator of Amara, assures us that this Bāhlīka saffron was referred to by Kālidāsa.[3] Yuan Chwang also speaks of saffron (Curcuma=kuṅkuma, saffron) grown in the country about this region.[4] There can, therefore, be no doubt that the country about Balkh and reaching up to the Oxus was known as the Bāhlīka country at the time of Kālidāsa, that is, according to our calculations, about two centuries later than Vātsyāyana[5]

The *Atharva-Veda Pariśiṣṭa* leaves no doubt that the Vedic Bāhlīka was Bactria in as much as it speaks of the Bāhlīkas in a group *Śaka-yavana-Tukhāra-Bāhlīkāśca.*[6] These Tukhāras are no doubt the Tokharas (Tu-huo-lo) through whose country Yuan Chwang passed to the country of Balkh.

That Bāhlīka was regarded by Indians as belonging to the Udīcya division of the country is seen from Kālidāsa's verse immediately preceding the one we have referred to above where we are told that Raghu on his way to the Vaṅkṣu or the Oxus met the Udīcyas and inflicted a defeat upon them. This is also clear from a passage

Bāhlīka an Udīcya province

1. विनीताध्वश्रमास्तस्य वङ्क्षुतीरविचेष्टनैः ।
दुधुवुर्वाजिनःस्कन्धाँल्लग्नकुङ्कुमकेशरान् ॥ *Raghuvaṁśam*, IV, 67.

2 अथ कुङ्कुमम् । काश्मीरजन्माग्निशिखं वरं बाह्लीकपीतनम् ।
Amarakoṣa. Oka's edition, p. 110.

3 बह्लीकदेशजं (बाह्लीकं), यद्रघोरुत्तरदिग्विजये—दुधुवुर्वाजिनः स्कन्धाँल्लग्न-कुङ्कुमकेसरान् । *Ibid*. p. 110, Commentary.

4 See Watters, I, p. 124.

5 See *ante*. p. 23. foot note 1.

6 41. 3. 3. Ed. by Bolling and Negelein p. 351.

7 ततः प्रतस्थे कौबेरीं भास्वानिव रघुर्दिशम् ।
शरैरुस्रैरिवोदीच्यानुद्धरिष्यन् रसानिव ॥ *Raghuvaṁśam*, IV, 66.

in the *Nāṭyaśāstra* where Bharata tells us that of the seven local dialects (*Sapta bhāṣāḥ*) of India, the *Bāhlīka-bhāṣā* was spoken by the Udīcyas and the Khasas and was the language of their own country[1] (*swadeśajā*).

The earliest mention of Bāhlīka in Indian literature viz., in the *Atharva-Veda* shows that it was far away in the north even beyond the Mūjavants. "O fever," says a hymn of this Veda, "Go to the Mûjavants or to the Bāhlîkas, further off."[2] If Mûjavant is the name of a hill in or about Kāśmîr, the Bāhlîka country must have been farther in the north and evidently the same region where we find it in later Indian literature, though Zimmer[3] and the authors of the *Vedic Index*[4] are inclined to doubt it. The points raised by Zimmer have been answered by Weber[5] and we think, satisfactorily. We however, differ from Roth and Weber who thought that an Iranian tribe was here referred to. The Bāhlîkas are apparently an Indian tribe, or at least an Indo-Iranian tribe that had been under the Indian influence from very early times.

Bāhlīka in Atharva-Veda is far away in the North

Kauṭilya in his *Arthaśāstra* mentions three kinds of leather produced in the Bālhi country[6] and in this form it is mentioned by Kātyāyana in his Vārtika to Pāṇini IV. 2,99 where he says that like Kāpiśāyana which is

Bālhi in Kauṭilya and Pāṇini

1. मागध्यवन्तिजा प्राच्या शूरसेन्यर्धमागधी ।
बाह्लीका दाक्षिणात्या च सप्त भाषाः प्रकीर्त्तिताः ॥
Nāṭyaśāstra XVII 48.

बाह्लीकभाषोदीच्यानां खसानां च स्वदेशजा । *Ibid*. 52.

2. Whitney and Lanman *Atharva-Veda*. Harvard Oriental Series. VII, p. 260.
3. *Alt-Indisches Leben*, pp. 431-3.
4. II, 63.
5. *Berliner Sitzungsberichte* 1892, pp. 985-95.
6. सामूरं चीनसी सामुली च बाह्लवेयाः (or बाह्लेयाः). See Shama Sastri's first

formed by Pāṇini from Kāpiśî, Bālhāyana is formed from the word Bālhî.[1]

In this connection it may be noted that the word *Kāpiśī* in the main sūtra of Pāṇini which Kātyāyana supplements, refers no doubt to the country of Ka-pi-shih of Yuan chwang [2] in the neighbourhood of Bāhlîka;it was famous for its vine-yards now as in ancient times as is shown by the example by which the *Kāśikā-Vṛtti* explains the rule [3] and we observe that the soldiers of Raghu also relieved themselves from their fatigue with the liquor of that country in the rich vine-yards.[4] The Kāśikā-Vṛtti further compares the favourite drink of the Bāhlîkas with those of other well-known Indian tribes and peoples: "The Uśînaras drink milk (*Kṣîra*), while the favourite beverage of the Prācyas is *Surā*, that of the Bāhlîkas is *Sauvîra*, and that of the Gandhāras *Kaṣāya*"[5] In the *Śatapatha Brāhmaṇa* [6] we find mention of

The Kuru king Prātipîya succeeded to the Bāhlîka throne of his Maternal uncle

Bahlika-Prātipîya who is called a Kauravya King (Kauravyo rājā), and the same king apparently is the Mahārājā Bāhlika Prātipīya[7] of the Great Epic. We are told in the *Udyogaparva* that of the three sons of Pratîpa, the eldest

edition, p. 79. *Bāhleyāḥ* is the reading adopted by *Bhaṭṭasvāmin* in his *Ṭîkâ on Arthaśāstra*, p. 42 in *J. B. O. R. S.*, Vol. XI, pt. II ; he explains it as a part of the Himalayas: त्रिविधं बाह्लेयमाह, सामूरमित्यादि । बाह्लवा हिमवदेकदेशः ।

1. Cf. Weber, *Ind. Stud.* XIII, p. 369.

2. Watters, I, p. 122.

3. कापिशीशब्दात् ष्फक् प्रत्ययो भवति शैषिकः । फकारो ङीषर्थः । कापिशायनं मधु । कापिशायनी द्राक्षा । *Kāśikā-vṛtti* on Pāṇini, iv. 2, 99.

4. विनयन्तेस्म तद्योधा मधुभिर्विजयश्रमम् ।
आस्तीर्णाजिनरत्नासु द्राक्षावलयभूमिषु ॥ *Raghuvaṁśam*. iv. 65.

5. क्षीरपाणा उशीनराः । सुरापाणाः प्राच्याः । सौवीरपाणा वाह्लीकाः । कषायपाणा गन्धाराः । *Kāśikāvṛtti* on Pāṇini, viii. 4, 9.

6. तदु ह बह्लिकः प्रातिपीयः...कौरव्यो राजा । *Śatapatha Brāhmaṇa* XII. 9.3.3.

7. महाराजो वाह्लिकः प्रातिपेयः कच्चिद्विद्वान् कुशली सूतपुत्र ।
Mbt, *Udyoaparva*, 23. 9.

Devāpi being rejected by the representatives of the people—the Paurajānapada—went to the forest and became an ascetic and the second Bālhîka, obtaind the very rich kingdom of his maternal uncle and abdicated the paternal throne in fayour of the youngest Śāntanu.[1] He fought with his Bāhlîkas on the side of Duryodhana. This explains how a Kaurava prince came to rule over the Bāhlîka people in the distant north and shows that in ancient times the Kurus were connected by matrimonial bonds with ruling families in the North-west, even beyond the mountain-barriers; Pāṇḍu's marriage with Mādrî and that of Dhṛtarāṣṭra with Gāndhārî shows the intimacy of the relations between the Kurus and the Kṣatriya tribes in the North-west. In fact the Great Epic shows that the kingdoms on the North-west frontier and beyond—Madra, Gāndhāra, Kāmboja, Bāhlîka—were looked upon as Indian provinces and Vātsyāyana shows that this feeling continued so late as the third century A.C when the Kāmasūtra was written.

Greek occupation of the country as well as intermixture with other foreign peoples had considerably modified the customs and practices of the Bālhîkas from the moral standard of the Indians thus making them hateful to the latter, so that their rulers are placed among the barbarous and sinful kings who will rule on earth on the advent of the Kaliyuga,[2] and the people

1. बाह्लीको मातुलकुलं त्यक्त्वा राज्यं समाश्रितः ।
पितॄन् भ्रातॄन् परित्यज्य प्राप्तवान् परमर्द्धिमत् ॥
बाह्लीकेन त्वनुज्ञातः शान्तनुर्लोकविश्रुतः ।
पितर्युपरते राजन् राजा राज्यमकारयत् ॥
Mbt. V. 149. 27-8. See *JRAS.* 1910. p. 52.

2. बहवो म्लेच्छराजानः पृथिव्यां मनुजाधिप ।
मृषानुशासिनः पापा मृषावादपरायणाः ॥
आन्ध्राः शकाः पुलिन्दाश्च यवनाश्च नराधिपाः ।
काम्बोजा बाह्लिकाः शरास्तथाभीरा नरोत्तम ॥ *Mbt.* III. 188, 34-36

are considered, as we have seen before, as the very dregs of the earth.

In the Great Epic itself there is evidence that some of the Bāhlīkas at least were Asuras, that is, Asura-worshippers or Iranians: we are told of a very powerful king of the Bāhlīkas Darada by name who was a *Mahāsura* or a great Asura and this Darada, the Bāhlīka, is praised highly by Śiśupāla, an Indian sovereign with Asura tendencies.[1]

Iranians in Bāhlīka

The Uttarakāṇḍa of the Rāmāyaṇa records a very interesting and important tradition which goes to show that one of the most powerful ruling families of India was originally derived from the Bāhlīka country.[2] It is a variant of the well-known myth of *Ila* which is found in all the Purāṇas and both the Epics. We are told here that *Ila*, a son of the Prajāpati Kardama, was the king of the Bāhlīka country.[3] Then the story goes on to relate how he was turned into a woman and passed by the name of *Ilā*, and when in this condition, had a son Purūravas Aila, by Budha, the son

Rāmāyaṇa says Aila family was derived from Bāhlīka

1. असुराणान्तु यः सूर्य्यः श्रीमांश्चैव महासुरः ।
दरदो नाम बाह्लीको वरः सर्वमहीक्षिताम् ॥ *Mbt.* I. 67. 58.
दरदं स्तुहि बाह्लीकं इमं पार्थिवसत्तमम् ।
जायमानेन येनेयम् अभवद् दारिता मही ॥ *Ibid.* II. 44, 8.

In the Great Epic, Bāhlīka is sometimes confounded with Bāhīka or the region where the sindhu flows with its five branches, including the Madra country. over which Śalya ruled, and Mādrī is once called Bāhlīkā (I. 125, 21) and Nīlakaṇṭha in his gloss on *Mbt.* V. 39, 80, makes the same mistake :

बाह्लीकाः "पञ्चानां सिन्धुषष्ठानां नदीनां यत्र सङ्गमः । बाह्लीका नाम ते देशाः ।"

2 *Uttarakāṇḍa*, Ch 87.

3 श्रूयते हि पुरा सौम्य कर्दमस्य प्रजापतेः ।
पुत्रो बाह्लीश्वरः श्रीमानिलो नाम सुधार्मिकः ॥

Rāmāyaṇa VII. 87, 3.

of Sōma, the moon-god. He ultimately recovered his male form by virtue of an Aśvamedha sacrifice performed under the auspices of his father, Kardama. Then the story tells us that Ila gave up Bāhlîka, placing his first son, Śaśavindu on the throne of that country and himself founded a new city, *Pratiṣṭhāna-pura* by name in the Madhyadeśa and set up a kingdom there. After his death Purūravas Aila ascended the throne left vacant by Ila.[1] This Pratiṣṭhānapura was, as we know from the Purāṇas and Kālidāsa's *Vikramorvaśîyam*,[2] situated at the junction of the Ganges with the Yamunā, that is, was identical with Prayāga or Allahabad. The story as related here is virtually the same as in the other Purāṇas, but the importance of this version lies in its statement that Ila was originally a ruler of the Bāhlîka country and at last set up a kingdom in the Midland which was the centre of Vedic Aryan culture. The mythical character of the tradition tracing back the descent of some of the most important ruling families of India up to Soma, shows that it relates to the very earliest times of the Aryan settlement in India and its connection with Bāhlîka or Bactria may suggest that it is a reminiscence of the times when the Aryan race was dwelling in its cradle-land in Central Asia.

A Reminiscence of the Aryan Cradle in Central Asia

1 राजा तु बाह्लिमुत्सृज्य मध्यदेशे ह्यनुत्तमम् ।
निवेशयामास पुरं प्रतिष्ठानं यशस्करम् ॥
शशविन्दुश्च राजर्षिर्बाह्लिं परपुरंजयः ।
प्रतिष्ठाने इलो राजा प्रजापतिसुतो वली ॥ *Ibid.* VII 90, 21—23.

2 भअवदीए भाईरहीए जउँणा-संगमविसेस-पावणेसु सलिलेसु ओलोअन्तस्स विअ अत्ताणअं पइट्ठाणस्स सिहाभरणभूदं राएसिणो भवणं उवट्ठिदम्ह । *The Vikramorvaśîyam.* Edited by S. P. Pandit, 3rd edition, revised by B. R. Arte, Bombay, 1901, Act II.

8

Strīrājya—the Woman-governed State—a polyandrous country near Bāhlīka

Another country where, as we have seen above, men were kept in the same position as ladies in the harem, was *Strīrājya.* As its name indicates, here the women perhaps exercised power in state affairs and apparently polyandry was the rule here giving the women a greater preponderance than in Bāhlīka or any other country; that it was not entirely mythical is proved by the details about the character of the ladies that Vātsyāyana gives in two passages besides the one quoted above. One of them states that in Strīrājya artificial means of sexual enjoyment were resorted to by the women, and the other tells us of the character of women in the king's harem.[1] Vātsyāyana's mention of the Strīrājya along with Bāhlīka and the existence of the same sort of relations between the sexes in the two countries would seem to indicate that they were situated in the same region. The other two passages where Vātsyāyana mentions Strīrājya in his work[2] do not offer any clear indication of its geographical position. Nor does the Commentary help us here. The comment on one of the passages only gives a synonym for Strīrājya viz., Strīpurī, and the other tells us that the Strīrājya was to the West of the Vajravantadeśa or Vaṅgarakta[3] about whose position we know nothing. The *Bṛhat Saṃhitā* of Varāhamihira, however, supports us in the conjecture that it is about the north-western frontier of India that we have to look for this country of women,

1 दृढप्रहरणयोगिन्यः खरवेगा एव अपद्रव्यप्रधानाः स्त्रीराज्ये कोशलायां च । *Kāmasūtra*, p. 126.

तथा प्रवेशिभिरेव ज्ञातिसम्बन्धिभिर्नान्यैरुपयुज्यन्ते स्त्रैराजकानाम् । *Ibid.* p. 294.

2 *Ibid* p. 126 and p. 294.

3 स्त्रीराज्यः स्त्रीपुरी तत्र भवानाम् । *Ibid.* p. 295. वज्ररक्तदेशात् पश्चिमेन स्त्रीराज्यं । *Ibid.* p. 126. Durgaprasad in the Jaipur edition p. 130. reads—वज्रवन्तदेशात् पश्चिमेन ।

In as much as he definitely asserts that the Strîrājya belonged to the north-western quarter of India along with the Tuṣāras (Tokhāra of Yuan Chwang), the Aśmakas, the Madras and similar other tribes in that region.[1] *Parāśara* who belonged to a much earlier period and from whose *Siddhānta* Varāhamihira borrowed his statements, says expressly that in the north-west lived the Tuṣāras and other tribes, and beyond them was the Strîrājya[2] leaving no doubt that the Strîrājya was situated in the farthest quarter of the northwestern district. In the corresponding passage in the *Mārkaṇḍeya-Purāṇa*[3] we have a mention, in the north-western quarter, of the country of Strī vāhya which is evidently a misreading of the name Strîrājya. In the *Mahābhārata* we are told that at the *svayaṃvara* of a daughter of Citrāṅgada, the King of Kaliṅga, came Mahārāja Sugāla, the ruler of the Strīrājya,[4] but nothing can be ascertained about the position of the country from this mention, we can only be so far certain that the Strīrājya was looked upon as an integral part of India.

Yuan Chwang describes a country in the Himalayas far away to the north of the region about Gangādvāra

1 दिशि पश्चिमोत्तरस्यां माण्डव्यतुखारतालहलमद्राः ।
अश्मककुलूतलहडस्त्रीराज्यनृसिंहवनखस्थाः ॥
Bṛhat-Saṁhitā, XIV, 22. Edited by Kern, 1865.

2 तथा च पराशरः । अथ पश्चिमोत्तरस्यां दिशि गिरिमतिवेणुमतिरलमति-फल्गुलुकमाण्डव्यैकनेत्रमरुकुचतुषारतालमल्लहलडहलातवर्दिलीनविलीनदीर्घकेशग्रीवान्याङ्गश-रगविषवेषशूलिकगुलुहाः । परमतः स्त्रीराज्यमिति । *Bṛhat-Saṁhitā* Vol. I. p. 292; edited by Mahāmahopādhyāya Sudhākara Dvivedi with the commentary of Bhaṭṭotpala in two volumes. The Vizianagram Sanskrit Series, No. 12.

3 कुन्यता लड़हाश्चैव स्त्रीवाह्या वालिकास्तथा । *Mārkaṇḍeya-Purāṇam*, 58, 38.

4 सुगालश्च महाराजः स्त्रीराज्याधिपतिश्च यः । *Śāntiparva* iv, 7.

or Hardwar. Thus he goes on, "To the north of this country (Brahmapura), and in the Great Snow Mountains, was the Suvarṇa-gotra country. The superior gold which it produced gave the country its name. This was called the 'Eastern woman's country' (that is, of the Chinese) so called because it was ruled by a succession of women. The husband of the queen was king, but he did not administer the government. The men attended only to the suppression of revolts and the cultivation of the fields. This country reached on the east to T'u-fan (Tibet), on the north to Khoten, and on the west to San-p'o-ha (Malasa)."[1]

Polyandry—a living Custom in the Himalayas at present

The boundaries of this country as given by the Chinese pilgrim show that it lay near to the Tibetan frontier and it is seen from his account that there was a so called king of the country who was rather the Prince consort, and probably Mahārāja Sugāla, the *Strīrājyādhipati* of the *Mahābhārata* was one such *king* by courtesy. We have no reason to think that this Strīrājya was entirely mythical because we find that Strīrāj or polyandry is still prevalent about these regions, specially in the higher Himalayas. Thus we read in the Census Report,[2] "Polyandry or the custom of a woman having more husbands than one at one time, is peculiar to the Himalayas. It exists in the Kulu sub-division, the Bashahr state (Simla Hill States) and to a smaller extent in the Nahan, Mandi and Suket states." Again we have here, "Polyandry is confined to the upper Himalayas—i.e. Spiti, Lahul and Siraj in Kulu; Chamba Lahul in Chāmba, Siraj in Mandi, Rampur, Chini (including Kavawar) and the upper minor states in Bashahar (State) and the Transgiri part of the Nahan State."[3] Similar cus-

1 Watters, I. p. 330.
2 1911, Vol. XIV, by Paṇḍit Harakishan Kaul. R. B., C. I. E., p. 287.
3 *Ibid*. p. 289.

toms are also prevalent among the Brahmans and Rajputs in Kumaon.[1]

The *Rājataraṅgiṇī* mentions Strîrājya as one of the countries conquered by King Lalitāditya (first half of the 8th century A.C.) who we are told after vanquishing the Tukhāras who lived, as we have seen from Yuan-Chwang's account, in the immediate vicinity of Balkh or the Bāhlîka country, conquered the country of the Amazons and proceeded to the land of the Uttarakurus[2] which according to the *Aitareya Brāhmaṇa*[3] and the usual tradition was on the other side of the Himalayas, so that here it is seen that Strîrājya is considered to have been in the extreme north-west so as to agree with the location assigned to it by the *Bṛhat Saṃhitā*. If Strîrājya here is purely mythical like the Uttarakurus,[4] yet it is significant as a record of the tradition that the country is considered to have been in the far north. But the *Rājataraṅgiṇī* furnishes further details which would lead one to suppose that this Strîrājya of the *Rājataraṅgiṇī* might not have been entirely a mythical land, a product of the poet's imagination merely. Lalitāditya is said to have placed an image of Nṛhari (Viṣṇu) in the Strîrājya.[5] Again, Lalitāditya's grandson, Jayāpîḍa, who reigned towards the end of the eighth century, is also credited with the conquest of Strîrājya by Kalhana who says "wonderful it is that after he had conquered a territory in the 'land of the Amazons' (Strîrājya) the [other] kings esteemed [still

In Rājataraṅginî Strîrājya is near Bāhlîka

1 Bhagavanlal Indraji, *Ind. Ant.* VIII, p. 88.

2 Stein's *Rājataraṅginî*, (Trans.), Vol. I. pp. 136—138; Taraṅga IV. verses. 165-175.

3 परेण हिमवन्तम्। *AitareyaBrāhmaṇa*, VIII. 14.

4 See Stein, *Rājataraṅginî*, Vol. I. p. 137, foot note.

5 *Rājataraṅginî*, IV. 185.

[m]ore] highly his victory over the group of his-senses (indriyagrāma)."[1] Again he tells us of Jayāpîḍa's son, the debauchee Lalitāpîḍa, that "this king who was not satisfied with a few women, and who was full of violent desires, thought Jayāpîḍa an imbecile for having left the 'land of the Amazons' (Strîrājya) after he had conquered it."[2]

Bhaṭṭasvāmin, the celebrated commentator of the *Arthaśāstra*, quotes a verse in which Strîrājya forms one of the countries which contained mines of precious stones.[3] This verse has not been located as yet but it shows at least that in India Strîrājya was looked upon as an actual country and not as a mere mythical land.

Precious Minerals come from Strîrājya

The Strîrājya of Vātsyāyana, therefore, does not appear to have been a mythical land, but it must have been a state where polyandry was prevalent and where there was a *king*, apparently of the type described by Yuan-Chwang and it might have been located in the Himalayas to the north of the Panjab, but more probably in the region of the north-west beyond the Himalayas where the *Bṛhat Saṃhitā* and the *Rājataraṅgiṇī* place it.

Vātsyāyana himself speaks of another country where also similar customs prevailed ; He calls it the *Grāma-nārî-viṣaya*, the 'District of village women' which appears rather to be a descriptive epithet than a proper name. The Commentary explains that this district was situated near the Strî-rājya farther away.[4] It is

Grāma-nārî-Viṣaya—another polyandrous district

1 *Ibid*. IV. 587.
2 *Ibid*. IV. 666.

3 विन्ध्यो विदूरशैलो मलयो विन्ध्योपलक्षयोद्देशः।
स्त्रीराज्यञ्चेति पुनस्तस्याकरभूमयोऽभिहिता॥

Bhaṭṭasvāmin on Arthaśāstra, p. 31 *J. B. O. R. S.*, Vol. XI. Pt. II.

4 स्त्रीराज्यसमीप एव परतो ग्रामनारीविषयः। *Kāmasūtra* p. 140.

nowhere else mentioned by Vātsyāyana. Most probably it formed a group of villages where polyandrous people lived and apparently they did not form an independent state like the Strīrājya.

The Land of the Six Rivers

Another country in the north-west of India which Vātsyāyana refers to, is that through which flow the six rivers including the Sindhu or the Indus.[1] The people living in this region, says Vātsyāyana, were fond of the filthy practice of Aupariṣṭaka ; that they were sexually very corrupt is borne out by the character given them by Karṇa in the *Mahābhārata*[2] which also describes the country almost in the very same words as Vātsyāyana[3] and designates the people as *Bāhīkas.* This Bāhīka country is condemned in the strongest terms in the Mahābhārata and is declared as unfit for habitation by Âryas[4] showing apparently that at the time of the Great Epic itself, the people of the Punjab were at a far lower stage of culture than that of the Vedic Indo-Aryans.

This land of the five rivers with the Indus as the sixth does not exactly belong to the Udīcya division, but to the Pratīcya or Western Division ; yet we mention it here on account of its affinity with the Udīcya countries and in fact, in the *Mahābhārata*, its ancient name Bāhīka is sometimes confused with Bāhlīka, but that they were not the same country is quite apparent both from the descriptions of the two countries in the Epic itself, as well as the separate mention by Vātsyāyana

1 सिन्धुषष्ठानां च नदीनामन्तरालीया औपरिष्टकसात्म्याः । *Ibid.*, p. 128.

2 *Karṇaparva*, ch. 44 ff.

3 पञ्चानां सिन्धुषष्ठानां नदीनां येऽन्तराश्रिताः ।
तान् धर्मबाह्यानशुचीन् वाहीकान् परिवर्ज्जयेत् ॥ *Mbt.* viii, 44, 7.

4 पञ्च नद्यो वहन्त्येता यत्र निःसृत्य पर्व्वतात् ।
आरट्टा नाम वाहीका न तेष्वार्य्यो द्व्यहं वसेत ॥ *Ibid.*, viii, 44, 40.

of the two countries in sûtras[1] closely following each other in the same connection.

The Prācya or Eastern Division

Of the Eastern or the Prācya division of India Vātsyāyana mentions several countries and usages as well the general name *Prācya* itself as a designation for the whole of the district. We have already referred to his eulogium of the Prācya people who, as we have seen, unlike the Śaurasenas and the Sāketas were free from some of the grossest forms of sexual abuse.[2] The Commentary here explains that the Prācyas are people to the east of the *Aṅga* country, but here it is inconsistent with its own statement elsewhere ; we have seen that according to the Commentary the limits of Vātsyāyana's Madhyadeśa are the same as those of Vasiṣṭha in his *Dharmasūtra* and hence the Prācya district must lie to the east of Prayāga, or Allahabad, where that Madhyadeśa ends. As we shall show below, the Commentator's knowledge of Eastern India was far from satisfactory or reliable, and there is no reason to question that Vātsyāyana has used the word Prācya in its usual sense since the Vedic times, viz., the region from Allahabad to the farthest eastern limits of India.

Prācya Customs referred to by V.

In describing the abuses in the king's harem Vātsyāyana says that among the Prācyas, a number of ladies—nine or ten in number—would combine and hide a common lover against discovery ;[3] besides, he refers to some general customs prevalent in Prācya countries

1 Sūtras 22 and 25, pp. 125 and 126.

2 तस्माद्यास्त्वौपरिष्टकमाचरन्ति न ताभिः सह संसृज्यन्ते प्राच्याः ।

Kāmasūtra, p. 166.

3 संहत्य नव दशेत्येकैकं युवानं प्रच्छादयन्ति प्राच्यानामित्येवं परस्त्रियः प्रकुर्वीत ।

Ibid. p. 295.

(*Prācyopcārāḥ*) with respect to the conduct of the king towards his many wives[1] and also to the temporary so-called marriage of the daughter of a courtesan by a Nāgaraka.[2]

Of the countries included in the Prācya division, Vātsyāyana mentions *Kośalā*, but as he speaks of it only once, in describing a practice which it had in common with the Strīrājya,[3] we cannot be sure whether it is the northern Kośala which was a part of the Prācya region, or the Kośala in the south. But Vātsyāyana mentions, as we have already seen, Sāketa, the capital of the northern Kośala country in his time.

Kośalā

The country of *Kāśī* is also referred to by Vātsyāyana when speaking of the Kāsi-rāja Jayatsena who was murdered by his master of the horse when out on an affair of love.[4]

Kāśī

Vātsyāyana mentions three countries of the Prācya Division, Vaṅga, Aṅga and Kaliṅga in one passage where he refers to the love-episodes of the royal harem. He says that Brahmins of the city under the pretext of giving flowers to the ladies enter the harem with the knowledge of the king, and speak with them from behind a curtain, and from such conversations union afterwards takes place.[5] It is in his notes on this passage that the

Vaṅga, Aṅga and Kaliṅga

1 राजानश्च कृपाशीला विनाऽपि भावयोगादायोजितापद्रव्या यावदर्थमेकया रात्र्या बह्वीभिरपि गच्छन्ति यस्यां तु प्रीतिर्वासकऋतुर्वा तत्राभिप्रायतः प्रवर्तन्त इति प्राच्योपचाराः। *Ibid.*, pp. 289—290.

2 पाणिग्रहणाश्च संवत्सरमव्यभिचार्यस्ततो यथाकामिनी स्यात्। *Ibid.*, p 365.

3 दृढ़प्रहणानयोगिन्यः खरवेगा एव अपद्रव्यप्रधानाः स्त्रीराज्ये कोशलायां च। *Ibid.*, p 126.

4 काशिराजं जयत्सेनमश्वाध्यक्ष इति। *Ibid.*, p. 287.

5 See Burton's Translation, Reprint 1883, p. 285.

9

commentator, Yaśodhara, manifests his absolute ignorance of the geography of eastern India to which we have already referred. Thus he says that the Vaṅgas lived to the east of the Lauhitya or the Brahmaputra, the Aṅgas to the east of the Mahānadī and the Kaliṅgas to the south of the Gauḍa-viṣaya, and that the Gauḍas themselves were a Prācya people living in Kāmarūpa.[1] Except with regard to the situation of Kaliṅga which may be said to be practically correct, all his other locations are absurd showing that he had no personal acquaintance with this part of India.

Gauḍa of V. is a part of Modern Bengal

G a u ḍ a is mentioned several times by Vātsyāyana and appears to have been a separate kingdom from Vaṅga at the time that he wrote; thus he makes a separate mention of the love-intrigues in the king's harem in the two countries, though they are virtually of the same character, in as much as he says that among the Gauḍas these intrigues were carried on with Brahmins, relatives and servants etc.,[2] that is, with men who had ordinarily access to the harem as in Vaṅga. In two other passages Vātsyāyana refers to the sense of beauty of the men and the softness and delicacy of the women of Gauḍa: thus while comparing the various fashions of dressing the nails by men in different parts of India, he says, "Large nails, which give grace to the hands, and attract the heart of women from their appearance, are possessed by the Bengalees."[3] Burton here translates '*Gauḍānām*" by Bengalees. In another passage where Vātsyāyana compares the characteristics of the women

1 गौडाः कामरूपकाः प्राच्यविशेषाः । वङ्गा लौहित्यात् पूर्वेण । अङ्गा महानद्याः पूर्वेण । कलिङ्गा गौड़विषयाद्दक्षिणेन । *Kāmasūtra*, p. 225.

2 ब्राह्मणैर्मित्रैर्भृत्यैर्दासचेटैश्च गौडानाम् । *Ibid.*, p. 294.

3 Burton's Translation, Reprint 1883, pp. 52-3.

of various parts of India, he speaks of the ladies of Gauḍa as soft and sweet in their speech, full of love and tender in their bodies.[1] Here the Commentary explains *Gauḍyaḥ* as ***Pūrvadeśabhavāḥ***, and evidently Gauḍa of Vātsyāyana is northern Bengal. Vātsyāyana has separately mentioned Vaṅga showing that it formed a separate kingdom comprising the eastern districts of modern Bengal.

Gauḍa is Bengal Everywhere in Indian Literature

Gauḍa as the name of a city, a country, or a people, is found from very early times in Indian literture including the works of Pāṇini and Kauṭilya, and almost everywhere it appears to refer to Bengal. But as some scholars have expressed a doubt about it, the question deserves to be very carefully examined. Cunningham expressed the opinion that the ancient Gauḍa was "only a sub-division of Uttara-Kośala" [2] as against the mediæval city of Gauḍa in Bengal.[3] Again, the late Mr. A. M. T. Jackson also, in connection with an inscription wherein the Rāṣṭrakūṭa king, Kṛṣṇa II, is declared to have been *Gauḍānām vinaya-vratārppaṇa-guruḥ*,[4] observes "It is too often assumed that in the tenth century and earlier the name *Gauḍa* means Bengal. I think, however, that this is a mistake which is responsible for much misreading of Indian History. It was, I think, Professor R. G. Bhandarkar who first expressed doubts on the point, and suggested that Gauḍa meant Gonda in Oudh. The key to the riddle is to be found in Alberuni's notes on the 'Voelkertafel' of Varāhamihira (Sachau's Alberuni's

Doubts expressed by Cunningham and Jackson—entirely baseless

1 मृदुभाषिण्योऽनुरागवत्यो मृद्वङ्ग्यश्च गौड्यः। *Kāmasūtra*, p. 127

2 *Reports of the Archaeological Survey of India*, Vol. 1. p. 327.

3 *Ibid.*, p. 328.

4 *Epigraphia Indica*. IV, p. 283.

India, I, 300) which informs us that Guḍa = Tāneshar. This explains why the Sārasvat Brahmans of the holy Sarasvatī are the Gauḍas *par excellence*, and why Gauḍa and Vaṅga are mentioned separately in the Baroda Grant of 812 A.D. The Gauḍas whom Kṛṣṇa II 'humbled' or 'schooled' were therefore the rulers of 'Hindustan' in the narrow sense, or in other words the Gurjaras themselves."[1] Most of these opinions expressed here by Mr. Jackson can be clearly shown to be absolutely wrong. In the first place, as regards the tenth century, no serious historian now doubts that the Gauḍa emperor Devapāla who was the son of Raṇṇādevī, a sister of Kṛṣṇa II,[2] belonged to Bengal and not to the Gonda district of Cunningham or Thanesar of Mr. Jackson, so that this point need not be expatiated upon.

Gauḍeśvara Devapāla is Ruler of Bengal in the 10th Century

Devapāla is called *Gauḍeśvara* in Gurava Miśra's inscription on the Garuḍa-pillar at Bādal in the Dinajpur district in nothern Bengal,[3] and the Gauḍas whom Kṛṣṇa II could have taught a lesson were the people under this relative of his. In the Baroda Grant of 812 A.D.—no doubt he refers to the Baroda copper-plates, dated 734 Śaka-saṃvat of Rāṣṭrakūṭa Karka II—*Gauḍendra* and *Vaṅgapati* are separately mentioned,[4] because north western and eastern Bengal formed different kingdoms at the time, while the very fact that they are mentioned together shows that these kings were close neighbours. Their defeat by the Pratihāra-Gurjara king Vatsarāja had evidently been obtained before Gopāla, the founder of the Pāla dynasty of Bengal,

1 *JRAS*. 1905, pp. 163-4.

2 See *Gauḍalekhamālā*, pp. 36-37.

3 *Ibid*., p. 74.

4 गौडेन्द्र-वङ्गपति-निर्जय-दुर्व्विदग्ध सद्-गुज्जरेश्वर-दिगर्गलतां च यस्य । *Ind*, *Ant*. XII. p. 160, line, 9.

consolidated Gauḍa, Vaṅga and Magadha into one great empire.

Rājataraṅginī refers to Gauḍa in Bengal

The *Rājataraṅgiṇī* offers clear proof that so far west as in Kashmir also in the eighth and ninth centuries of the Christian era, Gauḍa was considered to be in Bengal and we must remember, as Stein observes,[1] that Kalhana is very reliable and precise as a guide to the scenes of his narrative. Thus we read of King Lalitāditya who reigned in the early years of the eighth century, that on his expedition of conquest, after vanquishing Yaśovarman of Kānyakubja, "his army proceeded with ease to the Eastern Ocean. His elephants, which there saw the land of their birth, were only with difficulty induced by the abuse of their impatient drivers to march on from the *Kaliṅga* country. Numberless elephants joined him from the Gauḍa lands as if attracted by friendship for the elephant [carrying] the couch of Lakṣmī, who was attached [to the king]. When his advanced troops reached the Eastern Ocean, it seemed as if the trunks of the hosts of his war-elephants grasped in the waves the hair of the Ocean." [2] Here we find that Gauḍa was near the Eastern Ocean in the neighbourhood of the Kaliṅga country, so that it was no doubt Bengal. In the same chapter, Kalhana also speaks of the assassination of the Gauḍa King who had sought refuge in Kashmir and of the wonderful bravery shown by that King's followers.[3] Again we are told that Lalitāditya's grandson, Jayāpīḍa who reigned in the last half of the eighth century, while travelling incognito "entered the city of Pauṇḍravardhana, subject to the

1 *Introduction to Rājataraṅginī*, p. 35.

2 *Rājataraṅginī*, IV. 148-149.

3 *Ibid.* IV. 323-338.

Kings of Gauḍa and [at that time] protected by a prince called Jayanta,"[1] and further that Jayāpīḍa married the daughter of Jayanta and "showed there his valour by defeating even without preparation, the five Gauḍa chiefs, and by making his father-in-law their sovereign."[2] Here the fact that the Gauḍas were ruling at Pauṇḍravardhana shows that the Gauḍa country was there in Bengal. Whether these events are to be regarded as based upon actual historical facts, or as creations of the poet's fancy, there can be no doubt that there was some historical tradition behind it and it is clear that there were some relations between Kashmir and Gauḍa in the eighth and ninth centuries and that this Gauḍa was in Bengal.

In the 7th Century Harṣacarita shows Gauḍa is Bengal

Coming to the seventh century we have the evidence of *Harṣacarita* wherein we find that Rājyavardhana of Thaneswar which Mr. Jackson considers to be identical with the Gauḍa country, was killed by the Gauḍa-king (*Gauḍâdhipa*)[3] Śaśāṅka, who, Yuan Chwang tells us, was the ruler of Karṇasuvarṇa in Bengal.[4] There can therefore be no room for doubting that in the seventh century A. C. Gauḍa was a part of Bengal.

In the 6th Century Haraha Inscription says Gauḍa is on the Sea

That Gauḍa meant Bengal in the sixth century also is proved to a certainty by the Haraha inscription of the reign of the Maukhari King Iśānavarman of 554 A. C. (Vikramasaṃvat 611) stating that this sovereign made "the Gauḍas living on the seashore, in future to remain within

1 *Ibid.*, IV. 421.

2 *Ibid.*, IV. 46, 8.

3 गौडाधिपेन...भ्रातरं व्यापादितमश्रौषीत् । *Harṣacarita*. *Ucchvāsa* VI.; I. C. Vidyāsāgara's Edition. p. 161.

4 Watters, I. p. 343; Beal, *Buddhist Records*. p. 210.

their proper realm."[1] The Gauḍas on the sea-coast could certainly not have lived near the hills in the Gonda district.

Varāhamihira (6th Century) places Gauḍa near Pauṇḍra and Utkala

Varāhamihira who lived about the same time as King Iśānavarman,—that is, the first half of the sixth century after Christ[2]—in his *Bṛhat Saṃhitā*, also places Gauḍa in the immediate neighbourhood of Pauṇḍra in the eastern region,[3] and Vaṅga and Kaliṅga in the south-east[4]. He thus gives a correct position for Gauḍa and Vaṅga, and the Taneshar of Mr. Jackson is not Gauḍa but Guḍa, which again, is only the second half of the name of a country the full designation of which according to Varāhamihira[5] was *P ā ṇ ḍ u g u ḍ a*, as may be seen from the way in which Bhaṭṭotpala reads the passage in his celebrated commentary on the *Bṛhatsaṃhitā*;[6] the error of dividing the single name into two is most probably not of Albiruni who

1 कृत्वा चायतिमौचितस्थलभुवो गौडान् समुद्राश्रयान् अध्यासिष्ट नतक्षितीश्वरचरणः सिंहासनं यो जिती । *Ep. Ind.* XIV. Translated by Hiranandа Sāstri. M. A. *Ep. Ind.* XIV. p. 120.

2 Thibaut *Pañcasiddhāntikā Introduction*, p. LV.

3 अथ पूर्वस्यामञ्जनवृषभध्वजपद्ममाल्यवद्गिरयः ।
व्याघ्रमुखसुह्मकर्वटचान्द्रपुराः शूर्पकर्णाश्च ॥
खसमगधशिबिरगिरिमिथिलसमतटोड्राश्ववदनदन्तुरकाः ।
प्राग्ज्योतिषलौहित्यक्षीरोदसमुद्रपुरुषादाः ॥
उदयगिरिभद्रगौडकपौण्ड्रोत्कलकाशिमेकलाम्बष्ठाः ।
एकपदताम्रलिप्तककोशलका वर्धमानश्च ॥

Bṛhatsaṁhitā XIV. 5-7 Edited by Kern.

4 आग्नेय्यां दिशि कोशलकलिङ्गवङ्गोपवङ्गजठराङ्गाः । *Ibid.* XIV. 8.

5 गौरग्रीवोद्देहिकपाण्डुगुडाश्वत्थपाञ्चालाः । *Ibid* XIV. 3.

6 गौरग्रीवाः । उद्देहिकाः । पाण्डुगुडाः । अश्वत्थाः । पाञ्चालाः । *Bṛhatsaṁhitā with the Commentary of Bhaṭṭotpala.* Vol. I. p. 286. Edited by Mahāmahopādhyāya Sudhākara Dvivedī.

was well acquainted with the commentary,[1] but of the Translator.

The same location of Gauḍa is also assigned in the work of Parāśara (one of the very early Indian astronomers) who enumerates the countries in the east in the order Utkala, Puṇḍra, Karvaṭa, Samataṭa, Uḍra, and Gauḍaka.[2] Certainly this indicates clearly, without any doubt, that with the guidance of Parāśara we have to look for Gauḍaka in the same region as Puṇḍra, Samataṭa, and Uḍra, that is, in Bengal and not in the Gonda district. We must also here note carefully what Kern points out with regard to Parāśara's work : "Interesting for the geography of India is an entire chapter which Varāhamihira only changing the form, but leaving the matter almost intact, has given in the 14th chapter of Bṛihat Saṃhitā ; therefore we have to consider that chapter as really representing the geography of Parāśara tantra or perhaps yet more ancient works."[3] Paráśara's exact date cannot be ascertained but as he places the Yavanas,—Greeks—in south-western India, he probably belongs to the period about the beginning of the Christian era to which period Kern assigns Garga, another ancient astronomer of the same type as Parāśara.[4]

Parāśara (beginning Christian era) places Gauḍa near Samataṭa and Uḍra

In the fourth century before Christ we meet with a mention of Gauḍa in the *Arthaśāstra* of Kauṭilya who describes a variety of silver called "Gauḍika which is the

1 *Albiruni's India.* I, p. 298. Translated by Sachau.

2 उत्कलपुण्ड्रकर्वटसमतटोड्रगौडक ... । . MM. Dvivedi's edition of *Bṛhatsaṁhitā* vol I. p. 287.

3 *Introduction to Bṛhat Saṁhitā.* p. 32.

4 *Ibid.* p. 40.

product of a country known as Gauḍa."[1] The ancient commentary of Bhaṭṭasvāmin here explains that Gauḍikam or Gaulikam was the silver from Kāmarūpa (*Kāmarūpajam*).[2] Here his geography is a little faulty like that of Yaśodhara who calls the Gauḍas, as we have seen before, a Prācya people living in Kāmarūpa. Evidently to commentators living in the far south or west, the distance between Bengal and Kāmarūpa which are contiguous countries, was immaterial, especially as the boundaries varied quite often with the advent of every ambitious monarch. The commentators prove at least the fact that according to Indian tradition, Gauḍa was in the East and not in the region near Thaneswar or Gonda. We may also observe that Kauṭilya's name for Kāmarūpa is *Pāra-Lauhitya*,[3] or 'the Trans-Lauhitya country'—the country on the other side of the Brahmaputra. Evidently therefore Kauṭilya's Gauḍa was not Kāmarūpa, but must have been the same as the Gauḍa of Parāśara who was not much removed from him in date.

Kauṭilya speaks of the silver of Gauḍa which must have been Bengal

It must now be amply clear that the country that was known as Gauḍa in ancient times, was a part of Bengal and it seems more than probable that it is in Bengal also that we have to locate the *Gauḍapura* of Pāṇini[4] who says that when the words *Ariṣṭa* and *Gauḍa* stand before the word *pura* so as to form the words Ariṣṭapura, and Gauḍapura, the acute accent is placed

Gauḍapura of Pāṇini must have been the City of Gauḍa in Bengal

1 तुत्थोद्गतं गौडिकं काममलं कन्रूकं चाक्रवालिकं च रूप्यम् ।
Arthaśāstra, p. 86. Translation. Shama Sastri. p. 103.

2 गौल्िकं कामरूपजं तगरपुष्पाभम् ।
Bhaṭṭasvāmin on Arthśāstra. See *JBORS*. Vol XI. Pt. II p. 62

3 *Arthaśāstra*, p. 78.

4 पुरे प्राचाम् । अरिष्टगौड़पूर्व्वे च । *Pāṇini*. VI. 99-100.

10

on the final syllable of the first member. The only *pura* or city bearing the name of Gauḍa at any time was situated in Bengal. No city of the same name occurs in the Gonda district or anywhere else in India.

A Gáuḍa-deśa near S'rāvastī is mentioned only in some Purāṇas

The only passage that shows the existence of a Gauḍa country in the Gonda district is found in a verse that occurs in the list of kings of the Ikṣvāku family in the *Matsya*[1], *Kūrma* and *Liṅga* Purāṇas, as pointed out by Cunningham[2], where Śrāvastī is said to have been founded by Śrāvasta of that dynasty in the Gauḍa-deśa. The corresponding passage in the other Purāṇas, for example, *Vāyu*, *Viṣṇu*, *Bhāgavata* etc., speaks of the foundation of Śrāvastī by king Śrāvasta but does not mention the Gauḍa-deśa. This *Gauḍa* therefore must have been merely a Sanscritization by some writers of the local name *Gonḍa* and hence it is no wonder that it was very rarely used in literature. It is nowhere found in any record of historical importance whether literary or epigraphical, it is only an unimportant local name Sanscritized in imitation of the Gauḍa *par excellence* in Bengal. It is remarkable that in Buddhist literature where Śrāvastī and the country around is frequently referred to, *Gauḍa* is nowhere mentioned. The Gauḍa of Kauṭilya and early geographical works and of inscriptions was no doubt, in Bengal ; it acquired a great political importance since the later Gupta times, and even before that, formed a well-known province of Eastern India. There is every reason to believe that the G a u ḍ a p u r a of Pāṇini was the capital of this Gauḍa country.

It occurs nowhere else in Literature or Inscription

1 श्रावस्तश्च महातेजा वस्तकस्तत्सुतोऽभवत् ।
निर्म्मिता येन श्रावस्ती गौडदेशे द्विजोत्तमाः ॥

Matsyapurāṇa, 12. 30. Vaṅgavāsī edition. This passage has been quoted by Mr. B.C. Mazumdar, *JRAS*, 1905, p. 412.

2 *Arch. Surv. Rep.* 1. p. 327.

In culture the Gauḍas had won a distinct position for themselves in early times and created an independent style of poetic composition—the *Gauḍī-rīti*, and it is positively certain that Gauḍa here refers to Bengal and not the Gonda district. We have already seen Bāṇabhaṭṭa speak of Śaśāṅka, the king of Bengal (Karṇasuvarṇa of Yuan Chwang) as *Gauḍādhipa.* When the same author in one of the introductory verses [1] to his *Harṣacarita* speaks of the fondness for a display of sonorous words (*akṣara-ḍambara*) as the characteristic of the people of Gauḍa, he cannot mean by the word any other country than Bengal. Daṇḍin, the author of the *Kāvyādarśa*, who also is generally supposed to have flourished about the same time as Bāṇa, i.e., the seventh century after Christ, expatiates at some length on the differences of the two styles of Vidarbha and Gauḍa and besides, speaks of them as the Southern (Dākṣiṇātya) and the Eastern (Paurastya) styles.[2] This characterisation of the *Gauḍī* as the *Paurastyā* or the Eastern style shows that the Gauḍa of Daṇḍin must have been in Eastern India and without doubt, Bengal, in as much as we find his contemporary, Bāṇa, placing Gauḍa in Bengal.

Gauḍī-Rīti of Rhetoricians is the Style of Bengal

A comparison with the *Nāṭyaśāstra* of Bharata and the *Kāvyamīmāṃsā* of Rājaśekhara leaves, moreover, no room for doubt that *Gauḍī-rīti* was the style

1 श्लेषप्रायमुदीच्येषु प्रतीच्येष्वर्थमात्रकम् ।
उत्प्रेक्षा दाक्षिणात्येषु गौडेष्वक्षरडम्बरः ॥
Harṣacarita Introductory verse, No. 7.

2 Winternitz: *Geschichte der Indischen Litteratur*, iii. p. 11 ff.
अतो नैवमनुप्रासं दाक्षिणात्याः प्रयुञ्जते ।
इत्यनालोच्य वैषम्यमर्थालङ्कारडम्बरौ ॥ 1. 60
अपेक्षमाणा ववृधे पौरस्त्या काव्यपद्धतिः ॥ 1 .50.
Kāvyādarśa edited by Jivananda Vidyasagara.

of Bengal. Thus the *Nāṭyaśāstra* which is much earlier than *Kávyádarśa*, mentions four styles (*pravṛttis*),—Âvantî, Pañcāla-madhyamā, Dākṣiṇātyā and Oḍra-Māgadhî,[1] of which the last two correspond to the Vaidarbhî and Gauḍî styles of Daṇḍin[2] and it is apparent that what Bharata calls Oḍra-Māgadhî or the style of Orissa-Magadha is called Gauḍî or Paurastyā by Daṇḍin, and Bharata expressly tells us that his Oḍra-Mâgadhî flourished in Bengal, Orissa, Magadha, Prāgjyotiṣa, Tāmralipta and the adjoining countries[3]. That this Oḍra-Māgadhî is identical with Gauḍî is made clear by Râjeśekhara who shows the connection between the earlier and the later ways of enumeration; he says that in the countries Aṅga, Vaṅga, Suhma, Brahma, Puṇḍra, etc. the *Oḍra-Mágadhî Pravṛtti* and the *Gauḍīyā Rīti* were prevalent and he cites in this connection a verse describing the Gauḍa ladies (*Gáuḍāṅganāsu*).[4] There can, therefore be no doubt that the Gauḍî-rîti of the rhetoricians refers to Bengal.

1 आवन्ती दाक्षिणात्या च तथा चैवोड्रमागधी ।
पाञ्चालमध्यमा चेति विज्ञेयास्तु प्रवृत्तयः ॥

Bhāratîya-Nāṭya-Śāstram, VI. 26, Edited by Grosset.

2 वैदर्भगौडीयौ वर्ण्यते प्रस्फुटान्तरौ

Kāvyādarśa, I. 40.

3 अङ्गा वङ्गाः कलिङ्गाश्च वत्साश्चैवोड्रमागधाः ।
पौण्ड्रा नैपालिकाश्चैव अन्तर्गिरिबहिर्गिराः ॥
तथा प्रवङ्गमा ज्ञेया मलदा मल्लवर्त्तकाः ।
ब्रह्मोत्तरप्रभृतयो भार्गवा मार्गवास्तथा ॥
प्राग्ज्योतिषाः पुलिन्दाश्च वैदेहास्ताम्रलिप्तकाः ।
प्राच्यप्रभृतयश्चैव युञ्जन्ति ह्योड्रमागधीम् ॥

Nś., Grosset, XIV. 45-47.

4 अथ सर्वं प्रथमं प्राचीं दिशं शिश्रियुर्यत्राङ्गवङ्गसुह्मब्रह्मपुण्ड्राद्या जनपदाः तत्राभियुञ्जाना तमौमेयीयं वेषं यथेष्टमसेविष्ट । स तत्रत्याभिः स्त्रीभिरन्वक्रियत । सा प्रवृत्तिरोड्रमागधी । तथाविधाकल्पयापि तया यदवशम्वदीकृतः समासवदनुप्रासवद्योगवृत्तिपरम्परागभजगाद सा सागौडीया रीतिः । *Kāvyamīmāṁsa*, Gaekwad's Oriental Series No. 1; edited by C. D. Dalal and R. Anantakrishna Shastry, p. 8; for *Oḍramāgadhî* the text wrongly gives *audramāgadhî*, but the learned editors give the correct reading in their note (p. 3 of notes).

Paundra

The country of Paundra is not mentioned by Vātsyāyana, but is once referred to by the Commentary to illustrate the sport of *Kadamba-yuddha* in which, it is said that instead of the soft balls of Kadamba-flower, the Paundras used sticks and stones[1]. Mithilā is similarly mentioned by the commentator in connection with a local sport[2].

Pāṭaliputra

The only other place that Vātsyāyana mentions in Eastern India is Pāṭaliputra at the request of the courtesans of which city, Dattaka composed his monograph on the section of the Kāmaśāstra dealing with them [3]. Beside this, Yaśodhara, the Commentator, considers Pāṭaliputra to be implied by the term *Nagara* in two passages of Vātsyāyana, it being perhaps, in his opinion, the 'n a g a r a' *par excellence*: thus he explains the word *Nāgarikyaḥ* in a passage by *Pāṭaliputrikyaḥ*[4], and *Nāgarakāḥ* in another, by *Pāṭaliputrakāḥ*[5]. Yaśodhara has not stated on what authority, or from what considerations,

Nagara is not Pāṭaliputra

he was led to offer this explanation, but bearing in mind his poor knowledge of the geography of Eastern India, as we have seen before, this identification is not worthy of any serious consideration. We can, therefore, have no hesitation in rejecting his identification as a mere haphazard guess. Besides, the very fact that Vātsyāyana mentions Pāṭaliputra expressly when speaking of Dattaka, precludes the supposition that

1 कदम्बयुद्धानि...यथा--पौण्ड्रानाम् युद्धं कचित्क्कचिद्दृश्यते । *Kāmasūtra*, p. 55.

2 पाञ्चालानुयानम् । भिन्नालापचेष्टितैः पाञ्चालक्रोडा, यथा मिथिलायाम् । *Ibid.*, p. 54.

3 तस्य षष्ठं वैशिकमधिकरणं पाटलिपुत्रिकाणां गणिकानां नियोगाद्दत्तकः पृथक्चकार । *Ibid.* p. 6.

4 नागरिक्य इति । पाटलिपुत्रिक्यः । *Ibid.* p. 127.

5 नागरकाः पाटलिपुत्रकाः । *Ibid*; 166.

he should use another word when speaking of the same place in a different part of the same book. We shall presently discuss the question of the location of Vātsyāyana's *Nagara*.

Gonarda in Eastern India

Another country which was apparently in the Prācya division is G o n a r d a, implied in the name Gonardīya of one of the predecessors of Vātsyāyana[1]. It is doubtful, as we have already pointed out[2], whether this Gonardīya is the same as the grammarian Gonardīya and Kielhorn is most probably right in holding that the latter cannot be the same person as Patañjali, the author of the Mahâbhāṣya[3]. The country of Gonarda is located by some Indian scholars in Kashmir, and by others in Oudh[4]. The first view has its origin probably in a fancied connection with the Kashmir kings called *Gonanda*[5], or rather *Gonarda*, as they are more correctly styled by Kalhana[6]. There is no reason to think that Gonarda was the Punjab as Mr. N. L. Dey does, because it was conquered by Gonarda of Kashmir[7]. All that we can say with certainty about the location of Gonarda is that it is a country in the Eastern Division of India. The Kâśikā-vṛtti gives the example *Gonardīya* in illustration of the rule of Pâṇini according to which the suffix *'cha'* is aded to names of Prācya countries whose first vowel is *'e'* or *'o'*[8]. Again, the *Matsya-Purāṇa*

1 See *ante*, p. 3ff.

2 *Ibid.*, pp. 11-12.

3 *Indian Antiquary*, vol. xv, pp. 87ff. and Vol. xvi. pp. 101ff.

4 अयं च गोनर्ददेशः कश्मीरेषु इति प्राञ्चः अयोध्याप्रान्ते इति पौरस्त्याः ।
MM. Pandit S'ivadatta D. Kudala in his edition of the *Mahābhāṣya*. Int. p. 16 f n. 3

5 Cunningham, *Rep. Arch. Survey*, Vol. II. p. 10.

6 Stein, *Rājatarṅginî*, Int. p. 59.

7 *Dictionary of Ancient Indian Geography* Gonardda

8 एङ् प्राचां देशे । Pāṇini. I. 1, 75.
एङ् यस्याचामादिस्तत् प्राग्देशाभिधाने वृद्धसंज्ञं भवति । गोनर्दीयः
Kāśikā-vṛtti on the above.

mentions Gonarda as a country in the Prâcya or Eastern division along with Prāgjyotiṣa, Puṇḍra, Videha, Tāmralipta, Magadha etc[1]. . The same statement is also found in the *Brahmāṇḍapurāṇa* [2]. Varâhamihira, however, places Gonarda in the south[3] but the location in Eastern India seems to be the correct one,as it is supported by the *Kāśikāvṛtti*, and its situation near Ayodhyā would tally with this view.

Dakṣiṇāpatha or Dākṣiṇātya —the Southern Division

Southern India is designated by Vâtsyāyana both as *Dakṣiṇāpatha* as well as *Dākṣiṇātya*, and in some cases, he speaks in general of the Dâkṣiṇâtyas or the people of the South, while in other passages he mentions some of the individual provinces making up the southern region. With regard to the area comprised in the Southern Division, the Commentator explains that the country to the south of the river Narmadā or Nerbudda was called *Dakṣiṇāpatha*[4] ; this agrees well with the limit fixed by Râjasêkhara in his *Kāvyamīmāṃsā* where we are told that Dakṣiṇâpatha lies to the south of the city of Mâhiṣmatî[5], that is, Mândhātā on the Nerbudda[6] ; Bharata in his *Nāṭyaśâstra* which belongs to about the same period as *Kāmasūtra*[7] also gives a definition of Dakṣiṇâpatha which virtually agrees with the above : he says that Dakṣiṇâpatha is the area containing the mountains Mahendra, Malaya, Sahya etc, and besides, that the *Dākṣiṇātya* or the southern style (*pravṛtti*) is found

1 प्राग्ज्योतिषाश्च पुण्ड्राश्च विदेहास्ताम्रलिप्तकाः ।
शाल्व-मागध-गोनर्दाः प्राच्या जनपदाः स्मृताः ॥
Matsya-Purāṇa, ch 114. V. 45.

2 *Brahmāṇḍa-purāṇa*, Bhā. 16.

3 *Bṛhat-Saṁhitā*, ch. XIV. 12.

4 नर्मदाया दक्षिणेन देशो दक्षिणापथः । *Ibid.* p. 126.

5 माहिष्मत्याः परतो दक्षिणापथः । *Kāvyamīmāṁsā*, p. 93.

6 Fleet, *JRAS.*, 19.0, p. 444.

7 Winternitz. *Geschichte der Indischen Litteratur*. III p. 3. f.n. 3.

in vogue in all the countries between the Vindhyas and the Southern Sea[1].

Peculiarities of the Dākṣiṇātyas noted by V.

Dakṣiṇāpatha is mentioned by Vātsyāyana in connection with the custom of marriage with the daughter of the maternal uncle in that region[2] and the Dākṣiṇâtyas are referred to four times. One peculiar custom of the South is referred to by him as consisting of something like circumcision[3]. Vātsyāyana refers to the peculiar way in which the Dākṣiṇâtyas dress their finger-nails as distinguished from the Gauḍas, while the Mahârāṣṭrakas, he assures us, follow a middle course[4]. The Dākṣiṇātyas, says Vātsyāyana, are also characterised by a fondness for delivering artistic strokes at ladies in their amorous sports as an expression of strong passion[5]. This was a local custom with them and Vātsyāyana gives several examples from the court life of the South. The women of the South, says he, bear on their bodies marks of these strokes[6] which sometimes were so

1 महेन्द्रो मलयः सह्यो मेकलः पलपिन्जरः ।
एतेषु ये श्रिता देशाः स ज्ञेयो दक्षिणापथः ।
कोशलास्तोशलाश्चैव कलिङ्गा यवनोऽश्वाला: ।
द्रविडान्ध्रा महाराष्ट्रा वैष्णा वै वानवासजाः ॥
दक्षिणस्य समुद्रस्य तथा विन्ध्यस्य चान्तरे ।
ये देशास्तेषु युन्जीत दाक्षिणात्यां तु भित्यशः ॥
Bhāratīya Naṭyaśāstra, Edited by Grosset XIV. 39—61.

2 मातुलकुलानुवर्त्ती दक्षिणापथे । *Kāmasūtra*, p. 200.

3 दाक्षिणात्यानां लिङ्गस्य कर्णयोरिव व्यधनं बालस्य । *Ibid*. p. 374.

4 ह्रस्वानि कर्म्मसहिष्णूनि विकल्पयोजनासु च स्वेच्छावपातीनि दाक्षिणात्यानाम् । *Ibid*. p. 115. मध्यमान्युभयभाञ्जि महाराष्ट्रकाणामिति ।

5 कीलामुरसि कर्तरीं शिरशि विद्धां कपोलयोः संदंशिकां स्तनयोः पार्श्वयोश्चेति पूर्व्वैः सह प्रहणनमष्टविधमिति दाक्षिणात्यानाम् । *Ibid*. pp. 147—8.

6 तद्युवतीनामुरसि कीलानि च तत्कृतानि दृश्यन्ते, देशसात्म्यमेतत् । *Ibid*. p. 148.

violent as to deprive them of their lives. It was by just such a stroke—the K a r t a r ī imparted on the head —that Kuntala Śātakarṇi Śātavāhana killed his chief queen, Malayavatî,[1] the Chola king killed the courtesan, Citrasenā, by a similar stroke on the chest, called K î l ā in the technical language of the *Kāmasutra*[2], and a stroke, the V i d d h ā, aimed at the forehead of a dancing girl by Naradeva, who, as the Commentary informs us, was Chief of the Pāṇḍya king's forces, made her lose an eye.[3] Besides, he refers to an evil practice of the Dākṣiṇātyas[4].

D r a v i ḍ a and V a n a v ā s i

Besides the general mention of the people of the Deccan, Vātsyāyana delineates some peculiarities in the character of the women of D r a v i ḍ a (*Drāvidyaḥ*)[5] and V a n a v ā s i (*Vānavāsikyaḥ*)[6]. Yaśodhara, whose ignorance of the geography of the East, as we have seen, was quite lamentable, shows an accurate knowledge of the location of the countries of the South. Thus he says, the *Draviḍa Viṣaya* was to the south of the Karṇāṭa country[7] (Kanara of modern days) and the *Vanavāsa-viṣaya*, he says, was to the east of the province of Koṅkaṇa[8]. In connection with this mention of *Vanavāsī* by Vātsyāyana, Mahāmahopādhyāya Haraprasad Sastri in his lectures on *Magadhan Literature* has expressed the opinion that the ancient name, Vaijayantî, "became Vanavāsî about the begin-

1 कर्तर्य्या कुन्तलः शातकर्णिः शातवाहनो महादेवीं मलयवतीम् (जघान) । Ibid., p. 149.

2 रतियोगे हि कीलया गणिकां चित्रसेनां चोलराजो जघान । Ibid., p. 149.

3 नरदेवः कुपाणिर्विद्धया दुष्प्रयुक्तया नटीं काणां चकार । The Commentary explains, नरदेवः पाण्ड्यराजस्य सेनापतिः । Ibid., p. 149.

4 अघोरतं पायावपि दाक्षिणात्यानाम् । Ibid., p. 141.

5 मृद्यमानाश्चाभियोगान्मन्दं मन्दं प्रसिञ्चन्ते द्राविड्यः । Ibid., p. 127.

6 मध्यमवेगाः सर्वंसहाः स्वाङ्गप्रच्छादिन्यः पराङ्गहासिन्यः कुत्सिताश्लीलपरुष-परिहारिण्यो वानवासिक्यः । Ibid., p. 127.

7 कर्णाटविषयाद्दक्षिणेन द्रविडविषयः । Ibid., p. 127.

8 कोङ्कणविषयात् पूर्वेण वनवासविषयः । Ibid. p.127.

11

ning of the Christian era"[1], and thence he derives an argument in favour of his theory that Vātsyāyana is to be placed in the first century A. C. But we find from inscriptions that the name Vaijayantī continued for several centuries of the Christian era. Thus we find Viṇhukaḍa-Cuṭukulānanda Sātakaṇṇi calls himself V a i j a y a n t i—p u r a-r ā j ā in an inscription on a pillar in front of the Kalleśvara temple at Malavalli in the Shikarpur Taluka of Mysore.[2] As Fleet observes, "This king of Vaijayantī, that is Banawāsi in the North Kanara district, Bombay, may be referred to any time in or about the first or second century A. D.[3]" In a later inscription on the same pillar the Kadamba king, Śivakhada-Vamma or Śivaskanda-varman calls himself the 'lord of Vaijayantī' and Rice has "marked its date as about 250 A. D.[4]"

Vidarbha and Vatsagulmaka

Vātsyāyana also mentions V i d a r b h a or Berar twice in his work in connection with the abuses in the king's harem[5], and the Commentary explains that the country to the south of Kālāñjara was called Vidarbha[6]. Another people, the V a t s a g u l m a s are also mentioned in the same connection as the Vaidarbhas and are to some extent characterised by similar abuses; among both these peoples, we are informed by Vātsyāyana, beautiful women were sent to the king's harem[7]. This agreement is not to be wondered at, in as much

1 *Magadhan Literature*, p. 87.

2 *Epigraphia Carnatica*, Vol. vii, p. 251.

3 *JRAS.* 1905, pp. 304-5.

4 *Ep. Car.* vii. Introduction, p. 6.

5 रूपवतीर्जनपदयोषितः प्रीत्यपदेशेन मासं मासार्धं वा वासयन्त्यान्तःपुरिका वैदर्भाणाम्। ** स्वैरेव पुत्रैरन्तःपुराणि कामचारैर्जननीवर्जमुपयुज्यन्ते वैदर्भकाणाम्। *Ks.* pp. 257 and 294.

6 कालाञ्जराद्दक्षिणेन विदर्भो नाम देशः। Ibid., p. 288.

7 महामात्रेश्वराणामन्तःपुराणि निशि सेवार्थं राजानमुपगच्छन्ति वात्सगुल्मकानाम्। ** प्रेष्याभिः सह तद्वेषान्नागरकपुत्रान् प्रवेशयन्ति वात्सगुल्मकानाम्। Ibid., p. 287 and p. 294. Cf. Note 5.

as we learn, from Rājaśekhara's *Kāvyamīmāṃsā* that Vatsagulma was a city in the Vidarbhas and that it was a favourite haunt of the god of love[1]. The Commentator, Yaśodhara, says that in the Dakṣiṇāpatha there were two brothers called Vatsa and Gulma, and the country where they lived was designated Vatsagulma[2]. Evidently he had no personal knowledge of the place and his information was gathered from some such work as Kṣemendra's *Bṛhatkathāmañjarī* where we are told that Somaśarmā, a Dākṣiṇātya Brahmin had two sons named Vatsa and Gulma[3] whose nephew (sister's son) was Guṇāḍhya, the author of the *Bṛhatkathā*, the great storehouse of stories in Paiśācī Prakrit. The same story is told also in the *Kathāsaritsāgara*[4], and the two brothers Vatsa and Gulma are also mentioned there ; but in neither of these stories is there any record of the foundation of the city, which, as we learn from Rājaśekhara, was situated in Berar. By the time that Yaśodhara wrote his Commentary, the name Vatsagulma must have gone out of use.

Andhra

The people of the Andhra country, which the Commentator tells us, was in the Dakṣiṇāpatha, to the east of the Karṇāṭa-Viṣaya[5], is referred to several times. The Andhra ladies are referred to in two passages[6] and Vātsyāyana speaks

1 तत्रास्ति मनोजन्मनो देवस्य क्रीड़ावासो विदर्भेषु वत्सगुल्मं नाम नगरम् ।
Kāvyamīmāṃsā, p. 10.

2 दक्षिणापथे सोदर्य्यौ राजपुत्रौ वत्सगुल्मौ ताभ्यामध्यासितो देशो वत्सगुल्मक इति प्रतीतः । *Kāmasūtra*, p. 288

3 अभूतां दाक्षिणात्यस्य द्विजातेः सोमशर्म्मनः ।
वत्सगुल्माभिधौ पुत्रौ श्रुतार्था कन्यका तथा ॥
Bṛhatkathāmañjarī. Kāvyamālā edition. I, 3, 4.

4 *Kathāsaritsāgara*. Lambaka 1, Taranga 6. Nirṇayasāgara edn., p. 15ff.

5 कर्णाटविषयात् पूर्व्वेणान्ध्रविषयः । *Kāmasūtra*, p. 126.

6 प्रकृत्या मृद्वङ्गो रतिप्रिया अशुचिरुचयो निराचाराश्चान्ध्र्यः । तदान्ध्रीषु प्रायेणेति संवेशनप्रकारा वाभ्रवीयाः । *Ibid*. p. 126 and p. 135

of a custom by which a newly married damsel among the Andhras was sent to the king's harem on the tenth day with some presents[1].

Mahārāṣṭra

The Mahārāṣṭrakas whose country is located by Yaśodhara between the Narmadā and the Karṇāṭa district[2], are mentioned in two passages, one of which refers to the method of dressing the finger-nails of the men[3] and the other gives some characteristics of the ladies[4] who are said to have been fond of all the sixty-four Pāñcāla arts.

Daṇḍaka

Another indirect mention of a southern country is that implied in the name of Dāṇḍakya, the Bhoja king who met with extermination along with his whole family and kingdom for ravishing a Brahmin girl[5]. This is one of those passages which have apparently been quoted by Vātsyāyana from the Arthaśāstra of Kauṭilya.[6] The story is related in the Uttarakāṇḍa of *Rāmāyaṇa*[7] how the flourishing dominions of Dāṇḍakya were changed into the forest of Daṇḍaka. The Bhoja kings ruled in the south not only at the time of Kauṭilya but also much earlier; they go back without any doubt to the age of the *Brāhmaṇas*, and most probably, even so far back as the Ṛgvedic period. Thus we are told by a passage in the *Aitareya Brāhmaṇa*[8] that in the south, the kings of the Satvats were called Bhojas and

1 प्रत्ता जनपदकन्या दशमेऽहनि किंचिदौपायनिकमुपगृह्य प्रविशन्त्यन्तःपुरमुपभुक्ता एव विसृज्यन्त इत्यान्ध्रानाम् । Ibid., p. 287.

2 नर्मदाकर्णाटविषययोर्मध्ये महाराष्ट्रविषयः । Idid. p. 127.

3 मध्यमान्युभयभाञ्जि महाराष्ट्रकानामिति । Ibid., p. 115.

4 सकलचतुःषष्टिप्रयोगरागिन्योऽश्लीलपरुषवाक्यप्रियाः शयने च सरभसोपक्रमा महाराष्ट्रिक्यः । Ibid., pp. 126 127.

5 यथा दाण्डक्यो नाम भोजः कामाद् ब्राह्मणकन्यामभिमन्यमानः सबन्धुराष्ट्रो विननाश । Ibid., p. 24.

6 Eng. trans. of Kauṭiya's *Arthaśāstra* by S. Shamasastry, Introduction. p. xi.

7 Bombay edition, Chapters 92-94.

8 *Ait. Br.* viii. 14.

a passage in the *Ṛgveda*[1] mentions Pākasthāman, the Bhoja; besides, other passages in the Ṛgveda and the comments in the Bṛhaddevatā on them, show clearly that B h o j a as the designation of a line of kings was well known in the Ṛgvedic era[2].

The Western Division

A western division with general characteristics is not mentioned by Vātsyāyana and it appears that there was no uniformity of character and habits in Western India as in the Prācya country and the Dākṣiṇātya. We have already referred to the land of the five rivers with the Indus as the sixth, i.e., the Punjab in the north-west in connection with the U d ī c y a division and only the countries in the South-West now remain to be dealt with. Vātsyāyana

Mālava and Avantī

mentions the ladies of Mālava and A v a n t ī[3], the former being properly the Eastern or P ū r v a-M ā l a v a with its capital at Vidiśā, and the latter, Western or A p a r a-M ā l a v a with its capital at Ujjayinī as the Commentary correctly points out[4]. Avantī and Mālava are also separately mentioned in Bharata's *Nāṭyaśāstra* where we are told that the people of Avantī, Sorāṣṭra, Mālava etc. have the same style as Avantī[5]. Another name for eastern Malava was Ā k a r a as we find from *Bṛhat-Saṃhitā* which mentions Ākara among the countries in the South West[6] as also from several inscriptions of the Śātavāhanas where we find Ākara and Avantī

1 *Ṛ.V.* viii. 3, 24.

2 The matter has been exhaustively dealt with by me in *Aryan Occupation of Eastern India*, p. 46 and pp 59-62.

3 *Kāmasūtra*, p. 125.

4 आवन्तिका उज्जयिनीदेशभवाः । ता एवापरमालव्यः । Ibid. p. 125.

5 अवन्तिका वैदिशिकाः सौराष्ट्रा मालवास्तथा । *Nāṭyaśāstra* xiii. 29 (Kāvyamālā edn.). Grosset reads—आवर्तका etc. (xiv. 4).

6 फणगिरियवनमाकरकर्णप्रात्रेयपारशवशूद्राः । बर्बरकिरातखण्डकव्यास्थाभीरचञ्चकाः ॥ *Bṛhat-Saṃhitā*, XIV. 18.

mentioned side by side[1]. These inscriptions and also coins go to show that the two Mālavas were by the first century A.D. included in the empire of the Śātavāhanas[2], but with the disruption of that empire, they must have again become independent, as their separate treatment by Vātsyāyana shows.

The Âbhîras

The Â b h î r a s are mentioned prominently. The Âbhîra ladies are said to be the same in their likes and dislikes with the ladies of Mālava[3], and the love intrigues of the ladies in the harems of Âbhîra kings are also referred to. In this connection we are told that the Âbhîra harem was defended by guards who bore the designation of ***Kṣatriyas***[4], showing that the Âbhîras themselves had not yet acquired the status of Kṣatriyas and it seems that these latter were employed as guardians of the royal seraglio, in consideration of the lesser chance of their communication with the ladies than of warders taken from their own clan. An Âbhîra Koṭṭarāja or king of Koṭṭa, which, the Commentator informs us, was a place in Gurjarāta (modern Gujrat) is mentioned as an illustration of the dangers to kings in entering the houses of others on love intrigues. The Commentary gives the detail that this Âbhîra king had entered the house of Śreṣṭhî Vasumitra to meet his wife, and there he was assassinated by a washerman employed by the king's brother who had a claim to the throne[5].

1 *Ep. Ind.* VIII, p. 44 and p. 60.

2 *Camb. Hist.* I, p. 533.

3 परिष्वङ्गचुम्बननखदन्तचूषणप्रधानाः क्षतवर्जिताः प्रहणनसाध्या मालव्य आभीर्यश्च । *Kāmasūtra*, p. 125.

4 क्षत्रियसंज्ञकैरन्तःपुररक्षिभिरेवार्थं साधयन्त्याभीरकानाम् । Ibid. p. 294.

5 गूर्जराते कोट्टं नाम स्थानं, तस्य राजानमाभीरनामानं, परभवनगतमिति श्रेष्ठिवसुमित्रस्य भार्यामधिगन्तुं तद्भवनगतं, रजको राज्यार्हेण तद्भ्रात्रा प्रयुक्तो जघान । Ibid., p. 287.

Saurāṣṭrakas, or the people of Surāṣṭra, that is, the peninsula of Kathiawar, are mentioned in connection with the pratice of the city as well as the

Saurāṣṭra or Kathiawar

country women among them, of living in the royal harem either individually or in a body for sporting with the king[1]. Lāṭa or Northern Kathiawar is referred to twice,—some

Lāṭa or Northern Kathiawar

characteristics of the ladies of Lāṭa being given in one passage[2] and those of the men in another[3].

The people of Aparānta are referred to several times; in one passage the Aparānta ladies are said to resemble those of Lāta[4], and another refers

Aparānta—the Western Coastline

to an immoral custom prevalent among the Aparānta people that they sent their own handsome wives to kings and high officers in order to win their favour[5]. A third passage states that in Aparānta, the king's harem was not so strictly guarded as in other parts of India[6]. As regards the location of the province, the Commentary says that the Aparānta country was situated near the Western Sea[7]. It is now generally considered to be "Northern Konkan with a capital at Śūrpāraka (now Sopārā)"[8] but very often the name appears to have been applied to designate a much wider region from Malabar to Sindh. Kālidāsa, for

1 राजक्रीडार्थं नगरस्त्रियो जनपदस्त्रियश्च संघश एकशश्च राजकुलं प्रविशन्ति सौराष्ट्रकाणामिति । Ibid., p. 287–8.

2 चण्डवेगा मन्दसीत्कृता आपरान्तिका लाट्यश्च । Ibid. p. 126.

3 ऊरुसंधिबाहुनाभिमूलेषु लाटानाम् । Ibid., p. 103.

4 See note 2.

5 दर्शनीयाः स्वभार्याः प्रीतिदायमेव महामात्रराजभ्यो ददत्यपरान्तकानाम् । Ibid., p. 287.

6 नातिसुरक्षितत्वादापरान्तिकानाम् । Ibid., p. 294.

7 पश्चिमसमुद्रसमीपेऽपरान्तदेशः । Ibid. p. 126.

8. *Cam. Hist.* I. p. 603.

example, appears to have used the word in its literal sense of ' the land on the western boundary line" or the " western marches " including the entire-coast line from Malabar to Sindh. He makes Raghu cross the Sahya range or the Western Ghats between the two peaks Malaya and Dardura[1] which are no doubt Dodabetta in the Nilgiri District and the Anaimalai hills of which the highest is the Anaimudi peak ; here is in fact the well-known Palghat gap which forms the only wide opening through the Western Ghats in these regions and through which the Railway line crosses the Ghats. Next, we are told that Raghu's immense army, bent upon conquering the Aparānta country, filled up, as it were, the narrow strip of land between the Ghats and the Sea, and the very next verse takes us to Kerala characterised by its noble palms[2] and extending, in its widest signification, as far north as Kangarote river near Goa in North Kanara[3]. Immediately after this, the poet speaks of the date palms[4] which flourish most in the north, especially in the dry, arid regions of Sindh and in the verse following, he again speaks of the sea paying tribute to Raghu through the kings of Aparānta[5]. Apparently therefore the whole western coast from Kerala up to

Kālidāsa's Aparānta includes the entire coast from Malabar to Sindh

1 स निर्विश्य यथाकामं तटेष्वालीनचन्दनौ । स्तनाविव दिशस्तस्याः शैलौ मलयदर्दुरौ । *Raghuvaṁśam*. IV. 51.

2 भयोत्सृष्टविभूषाणां तेन केरलयोषिताम् ।
अलकेषु चमूरेणुश्चूर्णप्रतिनिधीकृतः ॥
मुरलामारुतोद्धूतमगमत्कैतकं रजः ।
तद्योधवारबाणानामयत्नपटवासताम् ॥
अभ्यभूयत वाहानां चरतां गात्रशिञ्जितैः ।
वर्मभिः पवनोद्धूतराजतालीवनध्वनिः ॥ Ibid. IV. 54-56.

3 See *JRAS*. 1897. p. 867.

4 खर्जूरीस्कन्धनद्धानां मदोद्गारसुगन्धिषु ।
कटेषु करिणां पेतुः पुंनागेभ्यः शिलीमुखाः ॥

5 अवकाशं किलोदन्वान् रामायाभ्यर्थितो ददौ ।
अपरान्तमहीपालव्याजेन रघवे करम् ॥ Ibid. IV. 57.

Sindh was included in Kālidāsa's Aparānta. Sir R. G. Bhandarkar was the first to identify Aparānta with the western coast : he says, "Aparānta must be the western coast below the Sahyādri ; for, Kālidāsa represents Raghu, in the fourth canto of the Raghuvaṃśa to have crossed the Sahya to conquer that country, and to have by means of his immense army made the sea appear 'as if it touched the Sahya mountain."[1] Dr. Bhagavanlal Indraji following him, says, "It corresponds with modern Konkaṇa, the district extending from Gokarṇa, in the Karwar collectorate to the Damān Gaṅgā, the frontier river of Gujrāt, or perhaps even further north to the Tāpī."[2] He quotes in support of his statement a passage from the Commentary to the Kāmasūtra and a passage in the Mahābhārata, where it is asserted that Arjuna visited all the holy places in Aparānta up to Prabhāsa in Kāthiāwār. Dr. G. Bühler in a note also accorded his agreement with this view.[4] Pundit Indraji also observes[5] on the authority of the *Viśvakoṣa* quoted by Mallinātha that Śūrpāraka or Sopārā was the capital of Aparānta. Dr. Burgess also agrees with this view.[6]

Coins show that Aparānta extended to Sindh

On the evidence offered by the Aparānta coins, however, General Cunningham shows Aparānta to extend farther north and also to include territories considerably inland. Thus Cunningham observes, "Aparāntika is placed by Varāhamihira in the western division of India

I *Trans. Second Int. Congress of Orient.* (1874), p. 313.

2 *Ind. Ant.* vii, p. 259

3 सोऽपरान्तेषु सीर्थानि पुण्यान्यायतनानि च ।
सर्वानिवानुपूर्व्येन जगामामितविक्रमः ॥
समुद्रे पश्चिमे यानि तीर्थान्यायतनानि च ।
तानि सर्वानि गत्वा स प्रभासमुपजग्मिवान् ॥

4 *Ind. Ant.* vii. p. 263.

5 Ibid., p. 259.

6 *JBBRAS.* XV, p. 274. See *Ind. Ant.* 1901, p. 387 .

12

along with Sindhu-Sauvîra and Pañcanada, or Sindh and the Punjab."[1] He further argues, "The coins of the Aparāntikas, bearing the inscription *Aparatasa Maharājasa*, were found chiefly in Rajputana about Nimach and Ajmer, by Colonel Stacy, while my own specimens have been obtained in north Rajputana and Mathurā. For these reasons I conclude that the country known as Aparāntika or "West Land," was actually in the west of India, and that it did not extend geographically to the south of the Narbadā. Politically Sopārā and other places to the south of that river may have been included." But this is not the view of Kālidāsa as we have shown above. Yet, at the same time, it has to be admitted that Cunningham's argument has much force. Fleet also points out that "One of the Aśoka edicts classes the Yavanas, Kāmbojas and Gandhāras as Âparānta," and thinks that Aparānta includes "the Konkan, with also Northern Gujrat, Kathiawad, Cutch and Sindh."[2] But as we have shown above, Kālidāsa takes it further south and includes the whole of the Malabar coast in it. It is difficult to say what region exactly is meant by Vātsyāyana but we can form a guess from the context in which it occurs. In the group of *sūtras* where Aparānta occurs, Vātsyāyana is illustrating a local custom (*Deśapravṛtti*), and all the people that he mentions belong to south-western India : thus they occur in the order—*Andhras* (whose dominions had before the days of Vātsyāyana extended to the western coast and Mālava), the *Vatsagulmas* and the *Vidarbhas*, (both of whom belong to Berar), the *Aparāntas* and lastly the *Saurāṣṭrakas*. Aparānta of Vātsyāyana appears therefore to be the western coast including the Konkan and extending to the south

1 *Coins of Ancient India*, pp. 102—3.
2 *Ind. Ant.* xxii, p. 178 and *JRAS.*, 1910, p. 427.

of Kathiawar. It did not include Saurāṣtra, nor Sindh in as much as the *Saindhavas* are mentioned separately.

Saindhavas

These latter are only once mentioned in connection with the love affairs of the ladies in the king's harem.[1] The Commentary informs us that the Saindhava people dwelt in the land to the west of the Indus.[2]

Nagara—a City in present Jaipur State

The question now remains for us to determine the position of Nagara referred to in Vātsyāyana's *Nāgarikyaḥ* and *Nāgarakāḥ*. The Commentary is certainly right in holding that they are proper names referring to a particular place and are not used in the literal sense of 'the women or men of a city' in general, and this will be evident from the context in which they occur. In neither of the cases is there any contrast between the town and the village. Both the words are used in connection with other proper names, the former in the order—*Āndhryaḥ*, *Māhārāṣṭrikyaḥ*, *Nāgarikyaḥ*, *Drāviḍyaḥ*, *Vānavāsikyaḥ* etc., and the latter in the order *Āhicchatrikāḥ*, *Sāketāḥ*, *Nāgarakāḥ*[3]. In the second case it is found that the names are those of well-known towns, Ahicchatra, the capital of the North Pañcāla and Sāketa or Ayodhyā, and the conclusion becomes irresistible that *Nagara* is also the name of a particular town, and as we have seen that Vātsyāyana is more familiar with Western India than with the other parts of the country, we are led to expect Nagara in this region. We find here 'the great ancient city of Nagara'[4] the ruins of which now lie scattered over an area of nearly four square miles in extent in the territory of the Mahārājā of Jeypore, 25 miles to the south-south-east of

1 परिस्कन्दाः कर्मकराश्चान्तःपुरेष्वनिषिद्धा अन्येऽपि तद्रूपाश्च सैन्धवानाम् ।
Yāmasūtra, p. 294.

2 सिन्धुनामा नदस्तस्य पश्चिमेन सिन्धुदेशस्तत्र भवानाम् । Ibid, p. 295.

3 See *Ks*. pp. 126–7. and p. 166.

4 Cunningham's *Report of the Archæological Survey of India*, vol. vi, pp. 161-162.

Tonk and 45 miles to the north-north-east of Bundi"[1] Mr. Carlleyle who made an archæological survey of the place, picked up here several thousands of very ancient types of coins, many of the punch-marked variety and many bearing the legend *Jaya Mâlavâna* in Brāhmî characters.[2] The city is not very far from Malwa and we think the democratic coin-legend speaking of the "Triumph of the Mālava people" refers to the celebrated Mālava-gaṇa who are known to have instituted the era now called the Saṃvat[3]. There is another ancient city *Nāgarī* or *Tambabatī Nagari* (about eleven miles north of Chitore) which has been identified with the Madhyamikā of Patañjali[4]; this city might also claim identity with Vātsyāyana's *Nagara*, but I think the former is the more probable one, as the latter was evidently called *Majhamikā* or *Madhyamikâ*[5] about the beginning of the Christian era, and probably also a few centuries later. Pāṇini appears to have known *Nagara* as the name of a particular city as it appears in the *Gaṇa* or group *kattryâdi* referred to in one of his Sūtras[6]. The *Kāśikâ* commentary enumerates fifteen names as belonging to this class. That the word *Nagara* in this list is older than the Kāśikā and is a proper

Pāṇini knew a City called Nagara

1 *Ibid.*, p. 162.

2 These coins are described by Mr. Carlleyle and also by Sir A. Cunningham, Ibid, pp. 180–3, also Cunningham, vol. XIV, p. 150.

3 Fleet, *Gupta Inscriptions*, pp. 87, 158; *JRAS.*, 1913, pp. 995–8, and 1914, p. 747, Prof. D.R. Bhandarkar, *Ind Ant*,. 1913, p. 161; Thomas, *JRAS.*,1914,pp. 1012–3. etc.

4 Carlleyle, op. cit., pp. 200 ff.; Cunningham, Vol XIV p. 146. See also Prof. D.R. Bhandarkar, The *Archæological Remains and Excavations at Nāgarî*, Mem. Arch. S. of India, No. 4.

5 The coins found here bear the legend *Majḥamikāya Sibijanapadasa*, Carlleyle, *op. cit.*, p. 202.

5 कत्र्यादिभ्यो ढकञ् । Pāṇini, iv. 2, 95. Prof. D.R. Bhandarkar who first drew attention to this *sūtra*, says in the *Indian Antiquary*, 1911, p. 34. footnote 45, " Nagara as the name of a town, was known to the author of Kāśikā." He considers *Nagarkot* or *Kāṇgḍā* as the Nagara from which the Nāgar Brāhmaṇas derived their name.

name, appears from what the Kāśikā says in connection with another *sūtra* of Pāṇini (IV. 2, 128); it states that Nagara is read in the *Kattryādi* group as the designation of a particular city as it occurs in company with other such names there.[1] From a city called Nagara also the Nāgari alphabet might have derived its name. The existence of a city called Nagara therefore cannot be questioned. There is, however, no justification for holding that the *Nagara* we have referred to was the city where Vātsyāyana composed his work, it being only one of the many places that he has mentioned in illustrating his *sūtras*; the utmost that we can say is that from the uncompromising and straightforward manner in which he has exposed the evils practised by the king's officials and queens, he must have belonged to a *Gaṇa-rājya* or a democratic government like the city of the Mālavas described above. This is also apparent from the importance he attaches to the assembly of citizens (*nāgarikasamavāya*) alluded to before.

Vātsyāyana did not belong to Magadha or Pāṭaliputra

It is hopeless to attempt to decide definitely which part of India Vātsyāyana belonged to. Some scholars (including Mahāmahopādhyāya Haraprasād Śāstrī) hold that Vātsyāyana wrote his Kāmasūtra at the city of Pāṭaliputra, but there is hardly any justification for this belief in the book itself. It depends mainly upon the Commentator's identification of Vātsyāyana's Nagara with Pāṭaliputra which, as we have seen, is absolutely without any founda-

1 कत्र्यादिषु तु संज्ञाशब्देन साहचर्यात्संज्ञानगरं पठ्यते तस्मिन् नागरेयकमिति प्रत्युदाहार्यम्। *Kāśikā* on Pāṇini, IV. 1, 178. The last part of the quotation would have *Nāgareyaka* as the correct form of derivative to designate a citizen of this particular *Nagara*, but Vātsyāyana has apparently not followed Pāṇini here, perhaps in deference to popular practice. The *Kāśikā* in accordance with the *sūtra* of Pāṇini, here lays down that the form *Nāgaraka* is derived from *Nagara* to signify abuse or expert knowledge (कुत्सन-प्रावीण्ययोः), otherwise, it will be *Nāgara*, and the example given to illustate this point is नागरा ब्राह्मणाः. Does it show that Nāgara Brāhmaṇas were known to Kaśika ?

tion. It is remarkable that Vātsyāyana has got nothing to say of the people of Magadha. In his days, Magadha was still a great country and not extinct like Pañcāla, and its capital was still the greatest city in India. There is, therefore, no reason why Vātsyāyana should not mention the characteristics of the people of Magadha, as he has done with regard to those of other parts of India. It is argued by some (who favour the theory of Vātsyāyana being a man of Pāṭaliputra himself), that he did not like to calumniate his own people by expatiating on their sexual abuses. But this argument cannot hold, inasmuch as our author has not everywhere enumerated mere defects or abuses, but has not unoften delineated simple and faultless customs and habits without the least suggestion of any evil in them. It was open to him to bring out the good points in their character, as he has done in the case of the men and women of Gauḍa. We cannt think of any other reason than personal ignorance of the country of Magadha and its people for this omission on the part of Vātsyāyana. MM. Haraprasād Śāstrī has pointed out that in the introduction to the *Harṣacarita*, Bāṇa who belonged to the *Vātsyāyana-gotra* says that his ancestors dwelt at some place in Magadha and hence he has argued that all the Vātsyāyanas in literature must have belonged to the same country[1]. This is a large generalisation which it is hard to accede to. There are Brahmins of the *Śāṇḍilya-gotra* now in Bengal; it would hardly be a sane conclusion to derive from this fact that all the Śāṇḍilyas that lived at any time in India were Bengalees, that the author of the *Śāṇḍilya-sūtras*, for example, hailed from Bengal. Our Vātsyāyana was separated from Bāṇabhaṭṭa by about four centuries, and according

1 *Magadhan Literature*, p. 73 ff.

to the findings of the Mahāmahopādhyāya himself, by not less than six. Is it not rather rash to imagine that they belonged to the same family located in the same spot for these many hundreds of years ?

V. knows S. W. India more thoroughly than any other Part

Now, we observe that though Vātsyāyana possesses more or less knowledge of all parts of India, yet he appears to have been acquainted more thoroughly with South-Western India than with the other portions. Of the country from Rajputana to the south up to the Konkan coast, he speaks of almost all the various provinces and peoples. For example, he speaks of A v a n t î and M ā l a v a (i.e. Eastern and Western Mālava), A p a r ā n t a, L ā ṭ a, S a u r ā ṣ ṭ r a, V i d a r b h a, M a h ā r ā ṣ ṭ r a, etc., he mentions twice the V a t s a g u l m a k a s of Berar and the A n d h r a s and the Â b h î r a s are mentioned again and again, and he treats them with a wealth of detail which is not observed in his delineation of the peoples in other parts of India. Of the countries to the North-West he speaks of the people of Sindh and the Punjab and of some customs of the B ā h l î k a country or Bactria. The people in the South he knows only as the D ā k ṣ i ṇ ā t y a s and their country as D a k ṣ i ṇ ā-p a t h a and he once mentions the D r ā v i ḍ a s and only incidentally a *Colarāja*. The people in the East he speaks of as the P r ā c y a s, "the Eastern people," though he seems to know the G a u ḍ a s and makes a collective mention of *Vaṅgāṅgakaliṅga* in one passage. He does not, as we have seen, even once speak of Magadha, nor does he notice any characteristics of the people of its capital, and of the entire country from Magadha to Rajputana he has very little to say. Once only he speaks of the M a d h y a d e ś a and once each of the Ś a u r a s e n a s, S ā k e t a and A h i c c h a t r a,

Vātsyāyana probably belonged to South Western India

This meagre mention of the countries of the central and eastern portions of Northern India and the detailed description of the customs of Western India makes it abundantly clear that Vātsyāyana had personal knowledge of the western portion alone, and that his information about the eastern regions was derived probably from the works of his predecessors like the treatise on the *Vaiśika* section of the science of Erotics by Dattaka of Pāṭaliputra. That Vātsyāyana belonged to Western India may also be guessed from the fact that he makes a large number of quotations from Âpastamba's *Gṛhyasūtra*[1] as we have shown before, and it is known that the Vedic school of the Âpastambins flourished in Western India, specially in the land of the Andhras.[2]

1 See *ante*, pp. 12-14.

2 Buehler, *Âpastamba Dharmasūtra*, Introduction, p. xxxiii.

CHAPTER III

SOCIAL LIFE IN ANCIENT INDIA : AS DEPICTED IN VÂTSYÂYANA'S KÂMASŪTRA

I CASTES AND OCCUPATIONS

Vātsyāyana in the *Kāmasūtra*, presents a beautifully vivid and realistic picture of various aspects of social life in India about seventeen hundred years ago. Though mainly concerned with erotics, yet he throws light on many an obscure side of Indian society, furnishing facts and circumstances hardly available from any other source. From his work we get a picture of ancient Indian society under the operation of the *Varṇāśrama Dharma* of the religious law-books and while discussing the ideals and forms of marriage, Vātsyāyana gives us an insight into the actual life of the young people, their loves and jealousies, their courtship and coquetry. He depicts the gay life of the N ā g a r a k a, the city-bred man of fashion of his days—his house and gardens, his daily round of pleasures, his sports and festivities, his many-sided culture and refinement. He furnishes a picture of the Indian home, of the sweet, pure and devoted Indian wife, the mistress of the household and controller of the family purse. From Vātsyāyana also we can glean an account of the arts and crafts that flourished in this age of fine aesthetic tastes and artistic pursuits, and we see how the artiste, the g a ṇ i k ā, by virtue of her intellectual accomplishments and skill in the fine arts, occupied a position of no mean importance in society. At the same time, we realise that the merry life depicted in Vātsyāyana's work, representing, as it does, but one side of the entire Indian social structure, supplements the picture as obtained from the *Dharmaśāstras*, and the ideal life, according to Vātsyāyana, is one in which the three elements of *dharma*, *artha* and *kāma* are harmoniously blended together.

Indian Society founded upon Varṇāśrama according to V.

As in the *Dharmaśāstras* and the other sacred literature of India, we find, in Vātsyāyana's work, Indian society founded upon the fourfold classification of the entire people into v a r ṇ a s or castes, and the fourfold division of the life of each individual into ā ś r a m a s or stages. Vātsyāyana himself declares that the very existence of the social structure is effected by the observance of the rules rendered obligatory for the maintenance of the institutions of *varṇa* and *āśrama*;[1] and though the subject Vātsyāyana has to deal with, does not offer many occasions for expatiating upon these matters, yet it is amply clear from casual references in the work that it was a society controlled by the *varṇāśrama* system that Vātsyāyana was depicting. Thus when referring to the various ways in which Vātsyāyana's *beau ideal*, the Nāgaraka, was to acquire the wealth necessary for leading his life in ease and comfort, Vātsyāyana enumerates four methods of earning money, viz., acceptance of gifts (p r a t i g r a h a), conquest (j a y a), trade (k r a y a) and wages (n i r v e ś a).[2] Of these, as the Commentary points out, *pratigraha* or acceptance of gifts is the standard means of subsistence for a Brahmin[3]; of the six kinds of work which according to Manu a

The Four Varṇas divided according to Occupations

1 वर्णाश्रमाचारस्थितिलक्षणत्वाच्च लोकयात्रायाः । *Kāmasūtra* p. 20.

2 गृहीतविद्यः प्रतिग्रहजयक्रयनिर्वेशाधिगतैरर्थैरन्वयागतैरुभयैर्वा गार्हस्थ्यमधिगम्य नागरकवृत्तं वर्तेत । Ibid., p. 42.

3 तत्र ब्राह्मणः प्रतिग्रहेण, तद्वृत्तित्वात् । Ibid. p. 42.

Brahmin may partake in, three enable him to earn a living, as Manu points out himself, viz., sacrificing for others (*yājana*), teaching (*adhyāpana*) and the acceptance of gifts from pure men (*pratigraha*)[1] and of these three again, if looked at closely, the last *viz.*, *pratigraha*, is evidently the actual means of earning money in the case of sacrificing and teaching also, as the remuneration offered in most cases was voluntary. Vātsyāyana who was trying to condense these matters into as few words as possible in his pithy paradigms, has spoken of pratigraha only as the means of acquiring a fortune in the case of Brahmins, that being essentially the only method for the purpose.

In the case of the Kṣatriya, similarly, Manu declares that the bearing of arms is the means of subsistence[2], so that Vātsyāyana's conquest (jaya) is practically equivalent to it. In the same way, of the three approved means of subsistence prescribed for the Vaiśya, viz., trade, rearing of cattle and agriculture[3], trade is the essential element, as the produce from cattle and agriculture have to be bartered to bring money. Lastly, in the case of the Śūdra, we find Manu ordaining for him the earning of a living as an artisan or craftsman[4] which

1 अध्यापनमध्ययनं यजनं याजनं तथा ।
दानं प्रतिग्रहश्चैव षट् कर्माण्यग्रजन्मनः ॥
षण्णां तु कर्मणामस्य त्रीणि कर्माणि जीविका ।
याजनाध्यापने चैव विशुद्धाच्च प्रतिग्रहः ॥
Mânava Dharmaśâstra, X. 75-76.

2 शस्त्रास्त्रभृत्त्वं क्षत्रस्य । Ibid., x. 79.

3 वणिक् पशुकृषी विशः । Ibid., x. 79.

4 अशक्नुवंस्तु शुश्रूषां शूद्रः कर्तुं द्विजन्मनाम् ।
पुत्रदारात्ययं प्राप्तो जीवेत्कारुककर्मभिः ॥
यैः कर्मभिः प्रचरितैः शुश्रूष्यन्ते द्विजातयः ।
तानि कारुककर्माणि शिल्पानि विविधानि च ॥ Ibid., X. 99-100.

is the same as the n i r v e ś a or working for wages of Vātsyāyana. This fourfold division of the means of earning money according to birth, shows that in Vātsyāyana's time, occupation was controlled by the caste in which one was born. In connection with another important matter of life also, *viz.*, marriage, Vātsyāyana speaks of the four castes, of higher and lower castes, and also on the advisability of the union between men and women of the same caste (s a v a r ṇ a) as we shall show in the next chapter.

Brāhmaṇa

The B r ā h m a ṇ a s he mentions several times and as receiving special respect. Blessings vouchsafed by good Brāhmaṇas are to be coveted by everyone, says Vātsyāyana, as a source of long life and renown[1]. The gift of a thousand cows to Brāhmaṇas is considered to be one of the highest aims in life of a lady, even in the case of a courtesan when she is rich, although in her case the gift had to be made through a third person, as a direct gift by a fallen woman would not be acceptable to them . Even into the royal harem where the ladies were guarded against intrusion by any male person, the Brāhmaṇa had right of entry and could converse with them separated by a screen[3]. With regard to medical preparations for recovering health or restoring vigour, Vātsyāyana advises the use of those only that are approved of by friends and Brāhmaṇas[4], the underlying

1 ब्राह्मणानां प्रशस्तानामाशिषः (यशस्यमायुष्यम् । *Kāmasūtra*, p. 380.

2 गोसहस्राणां पात्रान्तरितं ब्राह्मणेभ्यो दानं.. ...गणिकानां लाभातिशयः । Ibid., p. 340.

3 नान्तःपुराणां रक्षणयोगात् पुरुषसन्दर्शनं विद्यते । पुष्पदाननियोगान्नगरब्राह्मणा राजविदितमन्तःपुराणि गच्छन्ति –पटान्तरितश्चैषामालापः । Ibid., pp. 286 and 294.

4 तपोयुक्तः प्रयुञ्जीत शिष्टैरनुगतान् विधीन् ।
ब्राह्मणैश्च सुहृद्भिश्च मङ्गलैरभिनन्दितान् ॥ Ibid., p. 371.

idea in such recommendations being that the Brāhmaṇa was believed to be unselfish and honest.

The Brāhmaṇas as performing various religious functions and as forming various orders of monks or ascetics, are mentioned by Vātsyāyana : for example, the Ś r o t r i y a and the fire maintained constantly in his house for offering daily sacrifices, are referred to several times in the chapter on marriage[1], and besides, in other places. Moreover, we find a mention of the *Brahmacārin*, the *Dīkṣita* or the man initiated to perform a sacrifice, the *Vratin* or the man who has taken a special vow, and the *Liṅgin* or person who like the *Sannyāsin* of later times, has adopted certain special dress and marks[2]. The Commentary explains the *Liṅgin* as the *Parivrājaka*—the wandering ascetic who has renounced the world[3].

Brahmanical Sacrifices

Vātsyāyana's work amply demonstrates the fact that sacrificial performances still formed an important element in the Brahmanical faith, in as much as the setting up of large and costly fire-places or A g n i - c a i t y a s is considered a popular form of public service along with the erection of temples, excavation of tanks, laying of parks and building of bridges etc.[4] The sacrificial performances on a large scale (y a j ñ a) afforded one of the common occasions on which it was permissible for ladies to go out of their inner apartments (*antaḥpura*)[5] to take part in

1 प्रतिपत्तामभिप्रेतावकाशवर्त्तिनीं नायकः श्रोत्रियागारादग्निमानाय्य कुशानास्तीर्य यथास्मृति हुत्वा च त्रिः परिक्रमेत् । Ibid., pp. 219-220.

2 श्रोत्रियस्य ब्रह्मचारिणो दीक्षितस्य व्रतिनो लिङ्गिनो वा । Ibid., p. 351.

3 लिङ्गी प्रव्रजितः । Ibid., p. 301.

4 देवकुलतडागारामाणां करणं, स्थलीनामग्निचैत्यानां निबन्धनं, गोसहस्राणां... ब्राह्मणेभ्यो दानम् । Ibid., p. 310.

5 आवाहे विवाहे यज्ञे गमनं सखीभिः सह गोष्ठीं देवताभिगमनमित्यनुज्ञाता कुर्यात् । Ibid., p. 26 ,

the public or private festivities. Again, the utility of religious or scientific treatises (*Śāstra*) for the performance of concrete practical works like sacrifices (*yajñas*)[1], is referred to by Vātsyāyana, and moreover, he adds that priests officiating at sacrifices (*yājñikāḥ*), even though ignorant of grammar, were able to apply at the sacrificial rites (*Kratus*) the principle of *ū h a* or drawing of inference which depends upon a knowledge of grammar[2]. These sacrificial festivities which the maidens went out of tneir homes to join, also afforded opportunities, according to Vātsyâyana, to a youngman for choosing his partner for life and winning the love of the girl of his selection[3]. At the sacrificial festivities again, the amorous lover sought for an opportunity of arranging a rendezvous with his mistress with the help of a female go-between[4]. Thus we observe that *Gṛhya* or household sacrifices like those performed at the household fire of the Śrotriyas, as well as the more elaborate *Śrauta* rites on a large scale, formed common occurrences in the society that Vātsyāyana depicts.

Of the second caste in the social order, we find the Rājā playing a prominent part in society in Vātsyāyana's days, but it is evident that the Rājā or king,
Kṣatriya though generally a Kṣatriya, was not unoften derived from other classes like the Âbhîras, and sometimes

1 अलौकिकत्वाददृष्टार्थत्वादप्रवृत्तानां यज्ञादीनां शास्त्रात् प्रवर्तनम्, लौकिकत्वाद् दृष्टार्थत्वाच्च प्रवृत्तेभ्यश्च मांसभक्षणादिभ्यः शास्त्रादेव निवारणं धर्मः । Ibid., p 12.

2 अस्ति व्याकरणमित्यवैयाकरणा अपि याज्ञिका ऊहं क्रतुषु प्रयुञ्जते । Ibid., p. 26.

3 यज्ञे विवाहे यात्रायामुत्सवे व्यसने प्रेक्षणकव्यापृते जने तत्र तत्र च दृष्टेङ्गिताकारां परीक्षितभावामेकाकिनीमुपक्रमेत । Ibid., p. 213.

4 स तु देवताभिगमने यात्रायामुद्यानक्रीडायां जलावतरणे विवाहे यज्ञव्यसनोत्सवेष्वग्न्युत्पाते चौरविभ्रमे जनपदस्य चक्रारोहणे प्रेक्षाव्यापारेषु तेषु तेषु च कार्येष्विति ।
Ibid., p. 274.

perhaps he was a Brahmin. The word *Kṣatriya* is used by Vātsyāyna only once, and even there, as the special designation of a class of guards employed by the Âbhîra monarchs. This passage tells us that the seraglios of the Âbhîra kings were guarded by sentries who bore the designation of *Kṣatriyas*[1]. This shows apparently that the Âbhîras themselves were not Kṣatriyas, but were outside the fourfold classification of Indian society, and that they emyloyed these Kṣatriyas considering them to be more trustworthy in guarding the harem than their own tribesmen.

Vaiśya and S'ūdra

The Vaiśyas and the Śûdras are not expressly mentioned by Vātsyāyana, but we have seen that their caste occupations are referred to by him, and besides, he mentions a number of artisans and craftsmen whose occupations are in some way connected with the life of luxury and ease that the Nāgaraka led. These are the Mālākāra—'the maker of garlands', the Gāndhika—'the perfumer', the Rajaka and the Nîlîkusumbharañjaka—'the dyer and the cleaner of clothes, the Nāpita—'the barber', the Śauṇḍika—'the vendor of spirituous liquors', the Tāmbūlika—'the seller of betel leaves', the Suvarṇika or Suvarṇakāra—'the goldsmith', the Maṇikāra—'the jeweller', the Vaikaṭika—'the diamond-cutter', the Kuśîlâva—'the actor', the Gāyana—'the singer' and so on[2]. We may compare with these last the artiste spies of Kauṭilya having opportunities of espying the private character of citizens, *viz.* the actor (*naṭa*), the dancer (*Narttaka*), the singer (*Gāyana*), the

1 क्षत्रियसंज्ञकैरन्तःपुररक्षिभिरेवार्थं साधयन्त्याभीरकाणाम् । Ibid., p. 294.

2 मालाकारगान्धिकशौण्डिकरजकनापित... (*KS.*, p. 300)...सुवर्णकारमणिकारवैकटिकनीलीकुसुम्भरञ्जकादिषु...(p. 259), ···ताम्बूलिकसौवर्णिक...(p. 69), कुशीलवाश्चागन्तवः...(p. 50), परिचारकमुख्यान् संवाहकगायनवैहासिकान् । (p. 306)-

musician *(Vādaka)*, the man who lives on his tongue (*Vāgjīvana*) and the bard (*Kuśīlava*)[1]. Many of the craftsmen no doubt formed separate castes that varied according to their occupations but were commonly included under the general name of *Śūdra*. We have a mention of some females that were skilled in the arts, the Śilpakārikā—'a woman practising the arts', the Naṭī or Nāṭakīyā—'the actress', and the Kalāvidagdhā—'the female artiste'[2]. Here also we are reminded of Kauṭilya's *Śilpavatyaḥ striyaḥ*,—'the women proficient in the arts', who had access to the inner apartments of the people[3]. He speaks of the *Śilpakārikā* also[4].

Of the higher professions, we have a reference to the astrologer (Daivajña)[5] and the physician (Vaidya)[6]. There is no indication in Vātsyāyana's work to show whether they formed separate castes. The *Vaidya* probably occupied a respectable position, in as much as in two passages in the *Kāmasūtra*, he is mentioned with the Mahāmātra as an influential person and in another passage, the Vaidya is considered to be a person whose favour is worth acquiring by a courtesan[7]. The literature used by the Vaidya, that is the science of

1 नटनर्तकगायनवादकवाग्जीवनकुशीलवाः स्त्रियश्चाभ्यन्तरं चारं विद्युः। *Arthaśāstra* p. 21.

2 ततो वेश्या आभ्यन्तरिका नाटकीयाश्च। *KS.* p 24. तभिक्षुक्यः कलाविदग्धाः ...व्याख्याताः। Ibid. p. 57.

3 अन्तर्गृहचरास्तेषां कुब्जवामनषण्डकाः।
शिल्पवत्यः स्त्रियो मूकाश्चित्राश्च म्लेच्छजातयः॥ *AŚ.* p. 21.

4 शिल्पकारिकाः कुशीलवा दास्यो वा। *AŚ.* p. 21.

5 दैवज्ञा। *KS.* p. 300.

6 शूरो वैद्यश्चेति। Ibid p. 301.

7 वैद्यमहामात्रभवनसंनिकर्षे। *KS.* p. 257. वैद्यमहामात्रयोरुपकारक्रिया कार्यहेतोः। p. 319.

mdeicine is called Vaidyaka by Vātsyāyana and the *Āyurveda*, or the 'science of life' is also mentioned along with the *Veda* and the *Vidyātantras*, i.e. works on various branches of science[1].

Vātsyāyana mentions a number of government officials, but there is nothing to indicate their caste. Their position in society, however, appears to suggest that they must have belonged to the higher castes, but they need not necessarily have belonged to the Brahmin or the Kṣatriya castes. We find that the Rāṣṭriya or governor appointed by the emperor Candragupta Maurya, in Western India, was the Vaiśya Puṣyagupta and the man holding the same position in Aśoka's time was the Yavana Tuṣāspa, while Rudradāman's governor was the Pahlava Suviśākha[2], of foreign extraction no doubt, but thoroughly Indianised.

In the first place, the Mahāmātra is mentioned many times in the book, side by side with the king, as of a very high position in society. Vātsyāyana, when writing his work, had in mind as his prospective readers the daughters of kings and Mahāmātras who were likely to profit by his book, because in the first place, as he observes, among females it was specially they who received a liberal education—had their intellect sharpened by a study of the literature on a subject (*śāstra*)[3]. On festive occasions near the house of the Māhamātra, a lover would try to meet and win over the lady he

1 रसवीर्यविपाका हि श्वमांसस्यापि वैद्यके ।
कीर्त्तिता इति तत् किं स्याद्भक्षणीयं विचक्षणैः ॥ *KS.* p. 170.
आयुर्वेदाच्च वेदाच्च विद्यातन्त्रेभ्य एव च ।
आप्तेभ्यश्चावबोद्धव्या योगा ये प्रीतिकारकाः ॥ p. 371.

2 Junagadh Inscription of Rudradāman, *Ep. Ind.* viii. p. 43.

3 सन्त्यपि खलु शास्त्रप्रहतबुद्धयो गणिका राजपुत्र्यो महामात्रदुहितरश्च । *KS.* p. 30.

14

loved[1]. A person who was in the good books of the Mahāmātra was considered a desirable lover by the hetaræ[2]. The favour of the Mahāmātras was sought to be won by men in some parts of India in ways that were far from honorable, and certainly not sanctioned by codes of morality[3]. Vātsyāyana advises the Mahāmātras never to enter another's house on any amorous expedition, because other people would imitate the conduct of great men like themselves, and he adds that just as the sun, high up in the sky, is watched by all people in his journey across the heavens, similarly the movements of the Mahāmātras are keenly watched by men; therefore they should not do anything that was unworthy or dishonourable[4]. Vātsyāyana also speaks of persons that were harassed by the Mahāmātras[5] and he speaks in similar terms of the R ā j a v a l l a b h a or the favourite of the king[6] who was marked generally by violent and sinister conduct. The Mahāmātra of Vātsyāyana appears to be, as in the Arthaśāstra of Kauṭilya[7], a designation for high government officials in general, including provincial governors, as in Aśoka's edicts. Besides the Mahāmātra, Vātsyāyana also mentions the

1 मित्रज्ञातिमहामात्रवैद्यभवनसंनिकर्षे विवाहयज्ञोत्सवव्यसनोद्यानगमनादिषु । Ibid., pp. 257–8.

2 राजनि महामात्रे च सिद्धः । *KS.* p. 800.

3 महामात्रेश्वराणामन्तःपुराणि निशि सेवार्थं राजानमुपगच्छन्ति... दर्शनीयाः स्वभार्याः प्रीतिदायमेव महामात्रराजभ्यो ददति । *KS.* p. 187. एतै रेव कारणैर्महामात्रसंबद्धा राजसंबद्धा वा तत्रैकदेशचारिणी काचिदन्या वा कार्यसंपादिनी विधवा पञ्चमीति चारायणः । p. 65.

4 न राज्ञां महामात्राणां वा परभवनप्रवेशो विद्यते, महाजनेन हि चरितमेषां दृश्यतेऽनुविधीयते च । सवितारमुद्यन्तं त्रयो लोकाः पश्यन्त्यनूर्यान्ति च गच्छन्तमपि पश्यन्त्यनुप्रतिष्ठन्ते च । तस्मादशक्यत्वाद् गर्हणीयत्वाच्च न ते वृथा किञ्चिदाचरेयुः । *KS.* p. 281.

5 महामात्राभितप्तानाम् । *KS.* p. 285.

6 तस्यैव राजवल्लभस्य क्रौर्यप्रभावाधिकस्य... । *KS.* p.. 349.

7 *AŚ*. pp. 16 and 20.

Mantrin on whose shoulders rested the heavy burden of state,[1] as a person who should never have anything to do with filthy practices. This Mantrin, the pillar of the state, seems to be the Prime-minister and superior to the Mahāmātras, or he may be a member of the *Mantri-pariṣad* of Kauṭilya.[3] Of the superior officers, Vātsyāyana also speaks of the Dharmasthas or Dharmādhikaraṇasthas, the dispensers of law and justice[4] and four of the Adhyakṣas or superintendents in charge of the departments of state, beside the Uttarādhyakṣa or a superior officer in general.[5] These *adhyakṣas* or departmental superintendents mentioned by Vātsyāyana, are only such as come in contact with women in the ordinary course of their duties and have thus opportunities, as Vātsyāyana avers, of winning their love without much risk to themselves. Such an officer is the Gavādhyakṣa who had access to cowherdesses.[6] The Sūtrādhyakṣa, the Superintendent of spinning and weaving, had dealings with widows, helpless women and female mendicants[7] who spun yarn for the Government and brought it to him for his approval and also for their wages ; Kauṭilya gives a fuller list of such women—"Widows, cripple women, mendicant or ascetic women (*pravrajitā*), women compelled to work in default of paying fines (*daṇḍa-pratikāriṇī*), mothers of prostitutes, old women-servants

1 मन्त्री वा राजधर्धरः। *KS.* p. 170.

2 न कारयेदौपरिष्टकम्। *KS.* p. 170

3 *AŚ.* I. 15.

4 धर्मस्थेषु व्यवहारयेदिति। *KS.* p. 343. धर्माधिकरणस्थाः, p. 300.

5 अङ्कुशभूत उत्तराध्यक्षोऽस्यागमिष्यति स्वामी पिता वा। *KS.* p. 343.

6 यथा व्रजयोषिद्भिः सह गवाध्यक्षस्य। *KS.* p. 282. गोध्यक्ष of Kauṭilya. *AŚ.* II. 29.

7 विधवाऽनाथाप्रव्रजिताभिः सह सूत्राध्यक्षस्य। Ibid., p 282,

of the king, and prostitutes (*devadāsī*) who have ceased to attend temples on service, shall be employed to cut wool, fibre, cotton, panicle (*tūla*), hemp and flax,"[1] The Paṇyâdhyakṣa – the Superintendent of merchandise—the same as the *Paṇyādhyakṣa* of Kauṭilya, has dealings with women in the course of purchase and sale of various articles[2]. But he says that honest women also often earn a living for themselves by spinning: "Those women who do not stir out of their houses (*aniṣkāśinyaḥ*), those whose husbands are gone abroad, and those who are cripple or girls, may when obliged to work for subsistence, be provided with work (spinning out threads) in due courtesy through the medium of maid-servants (of the weaving establishment)." He therefore prescribes strict rules so that they may work with honour: "Those women whe can present themselves at the weaving house shall at dawn be enabled to exchange their spinning for wages (*bhāṇḍavetanavinimayam*). Only so much light as is enough to examine the threads shall be kept." Besides, he provides punishment if the Superintendent is tempted to look at the faces of such women or presumes to talk with them on any other topic except that of the business immediately in hand.[3]

A similar person is the Nāgara, the officer in charge of a city, that is, the Superintendent of the city police who in his rounds in the town at night meets wandering women going to meet their lovers and has power over them, in as much as he comes to be in possession of the secrets of their movements.[4] In the

1 Shama Sastri's Translation of the *AŚ*. p. 140.

2 क्रयविक्रये पण्याध्यक्षस्य । *KS*. p. 283.

3 *AŚ*., Shama Sastri's Translation, p. 141.

4 मर्मज्ञत्वाद्रात्रावटने चाटन्तीभिर्नागरस्य । *KS*. p. 283.

villages also the government officer, Âyuktaka, in charge of a village, when he is a young man and the son of a leading husbandman himself, has easy access to the village-women who can be won over simply for the asking and who are called *Carṣaṇīs.*[1] With them he gets into contact on various accounts such as in works which they have to render without wages (*viṣṭi*), in storing and taking out things from the store-house, in cleaning the house, in work on the fields, in receiving cotton and wool and the fibrous skin of flax and hemp, in accepting yarn spun by them, and in sale, purchase and exchange of various articles.[2]

The Aśvādhyakṣa or the Master of the horse is also referred to in another connection.[3] Two female officers, the Kañcukīyâ, the female overseer of the women's apartments and the Mahattarikā are mentioned by Vâtsyâyana as employed in the harems of kings.[4] They are employed by the queens in sending messages accompanied by various presents to the king.[5] In the dramas we generally find male officers of advanced years employed as the *Kañcukin* or Chamberlain, but here a woman is found to be so appointed.

We may add here a few words with regard to the institution of *Āśrama* which, as we have already seen,

1 ग्रामाधिपतेरायुक्तकस्य हलोत्थवृत्तिपुत्रस्य यूनो ग्रामीणयोषितो वचनमात्रसाध्या ताश्चर्षण्य इत्याचक्षते विटाः । *KS.*, p. 282.

2 ताभिः सह विष्टिकर्मसु कोष्ठागारप्रवेशे द्रव्याणां निष्क्रमणप्रवेशयोर्भवनप्रतिसंस्कारे क्षेत्रकर्मणि कर्पासोर्णातसीशणवल्कलादाने सूत्रप्रतिग्रहे द्रव्याणां क्रयविक्रयविनिमयेषु तेषु तेषु च कर्मसु संप्रयोगः । *KS.* p. 282.

3 काशिराजं जयत्सेनमश्वाध्यक्षः । *KS.* p. 287.

4 कञ्चुकीया महत्तरिका वा । *KS.* p. 243.

5 तदादाय राजा निर्माल्यमासां प्रतिप्राभृतकं दद्यात् । *KS.* p. 243.

Āśramas

Vātsyāyana speaks of as forming beside Varṇa, the other great foundation of Indian society[1]. He makes it clearer in his introductory chapter on the realisation of the threefold goal of human life (*Trivarga*). Thus he says, "Man, whose term of life, is a hundred years, should divide the whole of this period and practise the *trivarga*, that is *Dharma*, *Artha* and *Kāma*, in such a manner that they may harmonize together and not clash in any way."[2] He explicitly lays down also directions for making this division. Thus he advises that in the first part of life (*Bālya*) which appears to include both boyhood and adolescence, one should devote oneself to such objects as the acquisition of learning, and in youth—*Yauvana*—to enjoyment (*Kāma*). In old age one should practise *Dharma* and further, seek the realisation of the ultimate goal of man's life viz. *Mokṣa* or the final emancipation from the bonds of life and death ; but, he goes on, as life is uncertain, these objects should be pursued just as they come to hand. However, he enjoins strictly that until a man finishes his education, he should practise b r a h m a c a r y a, or lead a life of perfect chastity,[3] that is,as both Manu and Yājñavalkya affirm, so long as he is a student, he must not swerve from the vow of chastity (*avipluta-brahmacarya*).[4] This is the B r a h m a c a r y ā ś r a m a or the first stage of life of the *Dharmaśāstras*. The Brahmacārin is also referred to in the Vaiśika section of the *Kāmasūtra*.[5]

Of the second stage of life, Vātsyāyana says that

1 See *ante*, p. 98.

2 शतायुर्वै पुरुषो विभज्य कालमन्योन्यानुबद्धं परस्परस्यानुपघातकं त्रिवर्गं सेवेत । *KS.* p. 11.

3 बाल्ये विद्याग्रहणादीनर्थान् । कामं च यौवने । स्थाविरे धर्मं मोक्षं च । अनित्यत्वादायुषो यथोपपादं वा सेवेत । ब्रह्मचर्यमेव त्वाविद्याग्रहणात् । Ibid., pp. 11—12.

4 *Manu*, iii. 2. *Yājñavalkya*, i. 52.

5 Ibid., p. 351.

after getting one's education one should enter into the life of the householder (G ā r h a s t h y a), that is, one should marry and settle down as a Nāgaraka[1]. As the *Kāmasūtra* occupies itself entirely with this period when one enjoys life, Vātsyāyana has very little occasion to speak of the third and fourth *āśramas* of the *Vānaprastha* and the *Yati* respectively But he speaks of the *Lingins*—that is, ascetics who wore the special marks and garments of their respective sects.[2] Female asectics find more prominent mention as *Pravrajitā*, *Śramaṇā*, *Kṣapaṇikā*, *Tāpasī*, *Bhikṣukī*, *Muṇḍā* etc.[3] Of these, as we shall show hereafter, the Ś r a m a ṇ ā appears to be the Buddhist nun and the K ṣ a p a ṇ i k ā, the Jain S ā d h v î, while the T ā p a s î seems to belong to the Brahmanical faith. The name *Pravrajitā* appears to be applied to female ascetics in general. The *Pravrajitā* sometimes earned a living, as we have seen, by spinning.[4] In the case of the *Bhikṣuka*[5] and the *Bhikṣukî* it is difficult to decide whether these are Sanscritized forms of the Buddhist *Bhikṣu* and *Bhikṣuṇī*, or mean religious mendicants in general. In the inscriptions of the Śātavāhanas who were not very much anterior to Vātsyāyana, as well as of the contemporary epigraphic records of the Kṣaharātas, we find permanent endowments being made sometimes in favour of Buddhist *Bhikṣus* and sometimes again, in favour of *Bhikṣus* of all denominations. For example, Vāsiṣṭhiputra Śrî-Pulumāvi records a grant[6] to

Ascetics—Male and Female

1 गृहीतविद्यः......गार्हस्थ्यमधिगम्य नागरकवृत्तं वर्तेत। Ibid., p. 42.

2 Ibid., pp. 301 and 351.

3 Ibid., pp. 65–67. 225, 275 etc. We shall speak of them more fully hereafter.

4 See *ante*. p. 107. f.n. 7.

5 *KS*.. p. 300.

6 *Ep. Ind.* viii. p. 60.

Buddhist B h i k ṣ u s of the Bhadāyaniya sect, while Usavadāta, the son-in-law of the Kṣaharāta ruler, Nahapāṇa, records in a rock-cave at Nāsik that he had made a gift of some land for the *Bhikṣus* coming from all quarters, that is, as Senart translates, "From it food will be procured for all monks, without distinction, dwelling in my cave.[1]"

All these ascetics, male and female, belong to the fourth stage of life, inasmuch as they had avowedly renounced the world, though some, as we see from what Vātsyāyana says of them, might have been persons of questionable morals. But we must remember that Vātsyāyana has occasion to speak of them only as persons who were likely to be of help (s a h ā y a) to Nāgarakas and their mistresses and besides, to courtesans, in carrying their messages of love, as they had easy access to houses of citizens, and even to the *antaḥpura* or the inner apartments of the ladies.[2] It is, besides, a dilemma for a courtesan to solve whether it would be right conduct (*dharma*) for her, or the reverse, to reciprocate the feelings of an avowed ascetic like a *Brahmacārin* or a *Liṅgin*, when it becomes apparent that love unrequited would bring about his death :[3] one way she would be guilty of abetting a breach of the vow of chastity, and the other way, she would make herself responsible for the death of a holy man, as the Commentary explains.

To the Vānaprastha we have absolutely no reference at all, as the recluse in the forest was beyond the scope of the *Kāmaśāstra* even as a helper in the course of love. Moreover, it seems that this Brahmanical institution of the third *Aśrama*

Vānaprastha Stage going out of vogue when V. wrote

1 Ibid., p. 79.

2 *KS.* p. 274, 225, 285, etc.

3 श्रोत्रियस्य ब्रह्मचारिणो दीक्षितस्य व्रतिनो लिङ्गिनो वा मां दृष्ट्वा जातरागस्य मुमूर्षोर्मित्रवाक्यादानृशंस्याच्च गमनं धर्मोऽधर्म इति संशयः । *KS.* p. 351.

was going out of vogue. The *Vaikhānasa Dharmapraśna* tells us, that it was Brāhmaṇas alone who passed through all the four stages, the Kṣatriyas went through only three, and the Vaiśyas two—the stages of the student and the householder[1]. The Śūdra, apparently, was a householder throughout. The Great Epic shows the Kuru elders as passing to the forest life, but none of them emerged out of it into the life of the *Yati* or the *Parivrājaka* which was reserved for the Brahmins alone. Due to the influence of Buddhism and Jainism and the innate religious tendency of the Indian mind, there were many ascetics in the country—the L i ṅ g i n s of Vātsyāyana, but very few of them appear to have come through the regular course of four stages as prescribed in the *Dharma-śāstras*. It seems that the third *āśrama*, that of the V ā n a p r a s t h a, was going out of vogue in Indian society by the time that Vātsyāyana wrote his book, though of ascetics of various denominations there was no dearth at any time.

---

1 ब्राह्मणस्याश्रमाश्चत्वारः । क्षत्रियस्याद्यास्त्रयः । वैश्यस्याद्यौ । तदाश्रमिणश्चत्वारो ब्रह्मचारी गृहस्थो वानप्रस्थो भिक्षुरिति । i. 1, 10—13.

CHAPTER IV

SOCIAL LIFE IN ANCIENT INDIA AS DEPICTED IN VÂTSYÂYANA'S KÂMASŪTRA

II. MARRIAGE AND COURTSHIP

V. agrees with Sacred Literature in Marriage Rules and Ideals

With regard to marriage, Vâtsyâyana is in general agreement with the *Dharmaśâstras*, both with reference to the ideals as well as the procedure to be followed in the preliminary pourparlers leading to a settlement between the parties and also the ceremonies with which the hymeneal knot was finally tied. We have already seen how he quotes Âpastamba with regard to the selection of a bride[1]. The influence of Manu upon him must have been immense, in as much as we find that according to Vātsyāyana it was Manu that separated the Dharma portion from the all-embracing cyclopædia of Prajâpati.[2] Yājñavalkya, again, according to the generally accepted view of scholars, could not have been far removed from his time,[3] and an agreement between the two may naturally be expected. In addition to the *Dharmaśāstra* rules, however, Vātsyāyana often looks at matters from the common sense point of view and delineates the actual state of things in his time.

In the society depicted by Vātsyāyana, no marriage could take place, as we have already seen, until a young

1 See *ante*. pp. 12-15.

2 तस्यैकदेशं स्वायंभुवो मनुर्धर्माधिकारिकं पृथक् चकार । *KS*.. p. 4.

3 Winternitz, *Geschichte*, p. 4982 says that he cannot be earlier than the third or fourth century A.C.

man had completed his education[1], until he had passed through to the end of the Vedic lore, as Yājñavalkya asserts[2]. Again, in his chapter on marriage, Vātsyāyana emphasises the point that it was an educated man (ś r u t a v ā n) who was to look for a bride[3]. "It is only the educated man who is entitled to the householder's life," declares Medhātithi while expounding the corresponding passage of Manu and moreover, he affirms in the same connection, "Mere study of the Veda is not enough, its meaning also must have been mastered[4]." Even Siddhārtha, the Śākya prince was refused the hand of Gopā by her father, Daṇḍapāṇi the Śākya, who according to the L a l i t a v i s t a r a, thus made reply to the proposal for marriage offered by Śuddhodana : "His Highness the Prince has been nurtured amidst ease and comfort, while it is our family-custom that a girl is to be given away to one proficient in the arts and not to one ignorant of them. The Prince is neither skilled in the arts nor is he acquainted with the art of warfare with the sword and the bow. How then could I bestow my daughter upon one ignorant in the arts."[5] The Prince, the same book informs us, had to exhibit his learning and prowess, his proficiency in the arts and sciences, before he could get the hand of the girl of his choice. When

Marriage after Education is completed

1 See *ante*. pp. 110–11.

2 वेदं व्रतानि वा पारं नीत्वाप्युभयमेव वा । अविप्लुतब्रह्मचर्य्यो लक्षण्यां स्त्रियमुद्वहेत् ।
Yājñavalkya Saṁhitā, I. 51—52.

3 श्रुतवान् शीलयेत् । *KS.*, p. 184.

4 विद्वानेव हि गार्हस्थ्येऽधिक्रियते । ...अतः स्थितमेतत् नाधीत्यैव विवाहो यावद्दार्थो नाधिगतः । *Medhātithi* on *Manu*, III, 2.

5 दण्डपाणिराह । आर्यकुमारो गृहे सुखसंवृद्धः । अस्माकं चायं कुलधर्मः शिल्पज्ञस्य कन्या दातव्या नाशिल्पज्ञस्येति । कुमारश्च न शिल्पज्ञो नासिधनुष्कलापयुद्धसालम्भविधिज्ञः । तत् कथमशिल्पज्ञायाहं दुहितरं दास्यामि ।
Lalitavistara, ed. *Lefmann*, p.143.

we bear in mind that the *Lalitavistara* was written about the same time as the *Kāmasūtra*[1], the above episode in the life of Buddha gives us an insight into the mentality of the people of the period with regard to the necessity of a liberal and technical education before marriage.

V.'s Ideals of Marriage both Secular and Spiritual

The object of marriage, according to Indian ideals, was the obtainment of a son who would be competent to offer gifts and oblations after one is gathered to one's forefathers.[2] Vātsyāyana although mainly concerned with the physical side of marriage, relating to the pleasures and amenities of married life, yet is not unmindful of the other ideals of worldly gain, social position and the spiritual welfare of the couple. To him a good marriage secures the ends of *Dharma* and *Artha*,—that is, both spiritual as well as social and economic welfare and besides, progeny, increase of relatives and friends and also untarnished,genuine love. With this we may compare the five things that determine marriage according to the *Mānava Gṛhyasūtra, viz.* wealth,personal charms, learning, wisdom and friends[3] The objects of marriage, says Vātsyāyana,can best be secured by a man by his acquisition,according to the laws sanctioned by the holy writ (*śāstra*), of a virgin not given to any one before, and coming from the same caste as himself.[4] He further adds that with men of all the four *Varṇas* in society, when love is fixed upon a

Marriage only with a Girl of the same Caste

1 Winternitz. *Op. cit.*, ii, 200.

2 पुत्रार्थे क्रियते भार्या पुत्रः पिण्डप्रयोजनः।

3 पञ्च विवाहकारणानि भवन्ति—वित्तं रूपं विद्या प्रज्ञा बान्धवा इति। *Mānava-Gṛhyasūtra*, ed. Knauer, p. ·

4 सवर्णायामनन्यपूर्वायां शास्त्रतोऽधिगतायां धर्मोऽर्थः पुत्राः सम्बन्धः पक्षवृद्धिरनुपस्कृता रतिश्च। *KS.*, p. 134.

virgin who belongs to the same caste and who has been won in accordance with the prescriptions of the sacred laws, then it provides the means of getting lawful progeny, secures a good name in the world and besides, obtains the approval of the public. The contrary practice, he goes on, of *Kāma* or love directed towards women of the higher castes, or towards those that have been married to others, even though belonging to the same caste, is prohibited.[1] Love only, and not marriage, may be offerred to a woman of a higher caste, when she is a *svairiṇī*, that is, of unrestrained movements—a woman who has had many lovers before,[2] and in such a case, Vātsyāyana assures us, there will be no violation of *Dharma* or Law. Love with women of a caste lower than one's own, but even then not excommunicated from their own castes, with public women or with the *Punarbhūs*, that is, widows who, unable to lead a life of continence and restraint, sought for a lover, was neither approved of as decent conduct (*śiṣṭa*),nor was it prohibited, as the object in these cases was pleasure only.[3] In this last case, Vātsyāyana means to say that while such practice was not favoured by the better section of the community, it was not absolutely condemned by the public as the object of such union was simply pleasure and the woman was not expected to partake with him, like the lawful wife (*patnī*), in the ceremonial rites, nor was she expected to give birth to lawful progeny as the

Love not Marriage, permitted with other Castes

1 कामश्चतुर्षु वर्णेषु सवर्णतः शास्त्रतश्चानन्यपूर्वायां प्रयुज्यमानः पुत्रीयो यशस्यो लौकिकश्च भवति। तद्विपरीत उत्तमवर्णासु परपरिगृहीतासु च प्रतिषिद्धः। Ibid., p. 59.

2 स यदा मन्यते स्वैरिणीयमन्यतोऽपि बहुशो व्यवसितचारित्रा तस्यां वेश्यायामिव गमनमुत्तमवर्णिन्यामपि न धर्मपीडां करिष्यति। Ibid, p. 61.

3 अवरवर्णास्वनिरवसितासु वेश्यासु पुनर्भूषु च न शिष्टो न प्रतिषिद्धः सुखार्थत्वात्। Ibid., p. 59,

Commentary explains[1]. This is an important point to bear in mind as it serves to explain the mentality of the Indian law-givers. Offerings made by the progeny begot on such women would not be acceptable to the gods or the manes, therefore to take them to wife for having sons from them was unthinkable. Manu, though permitting *anuloma* marriage with a woman of a lower caste, including the Śūdra, proceeds, in the very same breath, most emphatically to condemn such marriage with a Śūdra woman and quotes a number of ancient authorities of whom even the most liberal would not permit a person of the twice born castes to have a son on a Śūdra woman. Thus says Manu, "According to A t r i and to (G a u t a m a) the son of Utathya, he who weds a Śūdra woman, becomes an outcast, according to Ś a u n a k a, on the birth of a son and according to B h ṛ g u, he who has (male) offspring from a (Śūdra female, alone). A Brāhmaṇa who takes a Śūdra wife to his bed, will (after death) sink into hell ; if he begets a child by her, he will lose the rank of a Brāhmaṇa. The manes and the gods will not eat the (offerings) of that man who performs the rites in honour of the gods, of the manes, and of guests chiefly with a (Śūdra wife's) assistance and such (a man) will not go to heaven."[2] Yājña-valkya condemns such marriage categorically :"What is said about the acquisition of a wife from the Śūdra caste, does not commend itself to me, for the reason that one's

1 तासु...प्रयुज्यमानो न शिष्टो न विहितः, ..परिगृह्यापि न प्रतिषिद्धः, सुखार्थत्वात्, तदानीं सुखार्थैव प्रवृत्तिः, न पुत्रार्था। । Ibid. p. 60.

2 शूद्रावेदी पतत्यत्रेरुतथ्यतनयस्य च । शौनकस्य सुतोत्पत्त्या तदपत्यतया भृगोः ॥
शूद्रां शयनमारोप्य ब्राह्मणो यात्यधोगतिम् । जनयित्वा सुतं तस्यां ब्राह्मण्यादेव हीयते ॥
दैवपित्र्यातिथेयानि तत्प्रधानानि यस्य तु । नाश्नन्ति पितृदेवास्तन्न च स्वर्गं स गच्छति ॥
Manu, III. 16—18. Trans. Buehler, *Manu*. pp. 78--9

own self is born in her."[1] At the present day, intermarriage between castes is not permitted by Hindu India under any circumstances, whether with superior or inferior castes, and we already notice a stiffness growing towards the question during the few centuries that intervened between Manu and Vātsyāyana. While Manu permits *anuloma* marriage, and that even with a Śūdra girl, though under protest, Yājñavalkya would exclude the Śūdra absolutely from its scope. Vātsyāyana who gives a nearer view of the actual condition of society, would not countenance anything but marriage inside one's own caste, all connection with a woman of an inferior caste (*avaravarṇā*) is placed by him in the same category as love with public women, and he would not consider it as serious marriage at all.

Growing unpopularity of Inter-caste Marriage in Hindu India

After laying down this first requisite about marriage connected with *Dharma*, Vātsyāyana next proceeds to speak of the purely secular circumstances about which a person thinking about marriage should be satisfied. He says that to obtain the full benefits of a marriage, one should seek for mate a girl satisfying the following conditions. She should have both her parents alive, she must be younger than himself by three years or more ; she should come of a family of decent and approved conduct, possessed of wealth and rich in adherents, a family, the members of which are numerous and attached to one another, her relatives both on the father's side as well as on the mother's, should be large in number ; and for herself, she must be a girl possessed of physical charms, of

Long List of Requirements of a Bride

1 यदुच्यते द्विजातीनां शूद्राद्दारोपसंग्रहः । न तन्मम मतं यस्मात्तत्रात्मा जायते स्वयम् ॥ तिस्रो वर्णानुपूर्व्येण द्वे तथैका यथाक्रमम् । ब्राह्मणक्षत्रियविशां भार्याः स्वा शूद्रजन्मनः ॥ *Yājñavalkya-Saṁhitā*. I. 56—57.

excellent conduct, with lucky marks on her body ; she should have neither more nor less than the proper number of teeth, nails, ears, hair, eyes and breasts, nor should any of these limbs have been lost by her ; she should be of a sound and healthy constitution ; the young man should, of course, be possessed of all these qualities himself and must have completed his studies.[1] Vātsyāyana, perhaps feeling that a girl possessed of all these qualities would be rare indeed, quotes in the very next *sūtra* the opinion of an earlier writer on the subject, G h o ṭ a k a m u k h a, who simplifies the whole thing by advising that a man should fix his affections on a girl when he would feel himself fortunate and happy in having her and at the same time would not incur the censure of his equals[2].

V. advises—"Marry the Girl that will make you happy"

It is not to be understood, however, that Vātsyāyana advises a young man to seek for a bride of a social rank higher than his own ; on the other hand, he specially sounds a distinct note of warning against all unequal unions, showing his intimate knowledge of the world. Here he quotes certain verses :—"Social games, such as, for example, filling up '*bouts rimes*,' marriages, and intercourse generally, should be with a man's equals, not with those either above or below him. A man marries above him when he marries a girl only to be treated by her and her friends as a servant ever afterwards ; no

Marriage to be happy, must be between Equals in Social Status

1 तस्मात्कन्यामभिजनोपेतां मातापितृमतीं त्रिवर्षात्प्रभृति न्यूनवयसं श्लाघ्याचारे धनवति पक्षवति कुले सम्बन्धिप्रिये सम्बन्धिभिराकुले प्रसूतां प्रभूतमातापितृपक्षां रूपशील-लक्षणसम्पन्नामन्यूनाधिकाविनष्टदन्तनखकर्णकेशाक्षिस्तनीमरोगिप्रकृतिशरीरां तथाविध एव श्रुतवान्शीलयेत् । *KS*, p. 184.

2 यां गृहीत्वा कृतिनमात्मानं मन्येत न च समानैर्निन्द्येत तस्यां प्रवृत्तिरिति घोटकमुखः । Ibid. p. 185.

man of spirit will do that. He marries below him when he and his people lord it over the girl, that is a bad marriage ; it too is censured by the good. When the love between husband and wife adds lustre to both, and is a source of joy to both families, that is the only marriage which is approved. Let a man, if he will, marry above him, and walk humbly among his wife's relations ever afterwards ; but on no account let him do, what all good men disapprove of, marry beneath him."[1]

Vātsyāyana's List of Defects and Disqualifications of a Bride

With regard to the qualities of a desirable bride, Vātsyāyana again specifies certain physical and other defects which would render a girl unfit for selection. Here, as we have shown before, Vātsyāyana quotes from the G ṛ h y a-s ū t r a of Â p a s t a m b a : thus he prescribes—"Let him give up a girl who, when the wooers come to woo, is found asleep, in tears, or out. Let him shun also these sixteen—1, a girl with an unlucky name ; 2, one who has been kept in concealment ; 3, one who is betrothed to another man ; 4, one with red hair ; 5, one with spots ; 6, a masculine woman ; 7, one with a big head ; 8, a bandy-legged woman ; 9, one with a broad forehead ; 10, one ceremonially impure ; 11, the fruit of an improper marriage ; 12, one who has menstruated ; 13, ono who is or has been pregnant ; 14, an old friend ; 15, one who has a younger sister much handsomer than herself ; and 16, one that hath a moist hand".[2]

Many of the terms in which these short-comings are worded are technical expressions the meanings of which are doubtful, we having to depend upon the explanation offered by the commentators. The above translation is based upon the commentary to the *Kāma-*

1 *Kāmasūtra*, pp. 190-1. Trans. Peterson, *JBBRAS.*, xviii, p. 117.

2 Ibid., pp. 113—114.

16

sūtra, whereas the commentators of Āpastamba such as Haradatta and Sudarśanārya, interpret some of the words in a different way. As the terms, however, are not of any great importance, we need not be detained by them.

Defects in Names—never considered a Serious Disability

Vātsyāyana also quotes another rule about the name of the girl—"A girl bearing the name of a constellation, a river, or of a tree is objectionable and besides a girl, the last letter but one of whose name is *l* or *r*, is to be avoided in wooing." [1] A woman who is too white or too dark in complexion, should be avoided even as a mistress and *pari passu* as a wife, and similar prohibition holds in the case of a woman afflicted with leprosy, insanity etc., [2] It may be observed here that inspite of the insistence of law-givers and Vātsyāyana's support of them, the defects about names have never been considered in India as a serious disability, and they appear to have been more obeyed in their breach than in their observance. Thus in ancient times as at the present day, some of the most popular names are names, of constellations like Rohiṇī and Citrā, of rivers like Gaṅgā and Yamunā, or names with penultimate '*l*' or '*r*' like Apālā and Viśvavārā—authoresses of Ṛgvedic hymns[3], and Kamalā and Tārā of later days.

V.'s final Advice—'Marry the Girl on whom the Heart and the Eyes are set'

Conscious that some of the many defects enumerated above are unavoidable and others are of a too technical character, Vātsyāyana, as in a previous case, when he quoted Ghoṭakamukha, quotes a simpler and more liberal rule from an ancient authority, in this case the Gṛhyasutra of Āpastamba.

1 नक्षत्राख्यां नदीनाम्नीं वृक्षनाम्नीं च गर्हिताम् । लकाररेफोपान्तां च वरणे परिवर्जयेत् ॥ *KS*., p. 188.

2 अगम्यास्त्वेवैताः, कुष्ठिन्युन्मत्ता पतिता भिन्नरहस्या प्रकाशप्रार्थिनी गतप्राययौवनाऽतिश्वेताऽतिकृष्णा दुर्गन्धा सम्बन्धिनी सखी प्रव्रजिता संबन्धिसखिश्रोत्रियराजदाराश्च । Ibid. p. 67.

3 *ṚV*. viii. 91, 7 and V. 28.

"He will be a happy husband who marries the woman on whom his heart and his eye are set. Let a man not think of any other. So some say." [1] Here Vātsyāyana approves of a selection made not according to minute and detailed technical rules, but on the general impression produced by the whole appearence. As in the everyday world, people were likely to be guided by this impression at first sight. Hence Vātsyāyana advises the parents and relatives of a girl when she has reached the marriageable age, to array her in a smart dress, and thus dressed she should sport every afternoon with her girl friends ; at festivities like sacrifices, marriage celebrations, and, in fact, wherever there is a concourse of people, care should be taken to show her to advantage in society, for the reason, Vātsyāyana asserts, that such a girl is of the nature of an article of trade. [2]

Compara-tive age of Bride and Bridegroom.

With regard to the comparative age of the couple to be married, Vātsyāyana prescribes that the bride should be younger by three years or more [3]. In another passage which Vātsyāyana quotes from the *Gṛhyasūtra* of Âpastamba, an expression (s v a n u j ā) is taken by the Commentator[4] to mean "considerably less in age" and in support of his statement, he quotes a text, most probably from a *Dharma*-

1 यस्यां मनश्चक्षुषोर्निबन्धस्तस्यामृद्धिर्नेतरामाद्रियेतेत्येके । Ibid. p. 188. Trans. Peterson, *op. cit.*, p. 114. *Âp. GṛS.* I. 3, 20.

2 नित्यं प्रसाधितायाः सखीभिः सह क्रीडा, यज्ञविवाहादिषु जनसन्द्रावेषु प्रायत्निकं दर्शनं तथोत्सवेषु च पण्यसधर्मत्वात् ॥ Ibid., p. 188.

3 त्रिवर्षात् प्रभृति न्यूनवयसम् । *KS.*, p. 184.

4 स्वनुजामिति,त्रिवर्षात् प्रभृति न्यूनवयसमित्यस्य शेषः सुष्ठु पश्चाज्जातामित्यर्थः । यथोक्तम्–'चतुर्थादष्टमं यावत्कनिष्ठां वत्सरे वरात्। कन्यां परिणयेच्छस्तां नैतरातिवयाश्च या'॥ *KS.*, pp. 187—188.

śāstra, which lays down that one should marry a girl who is in the fourth to the eighth year below him, that is, who is younger in age by three to seven years, neither more nor less. But the word *svanujā* is taken by others to mean a girl who has a fine younger sister [1]. The *Dharmaśāstras*, however, contemplate a far greater disparity in years, the correct ratio prescribed being generally one to three. Thus we have in the *Viṣṇu-Purāṇa*: "One should marry a wife whose age is a third of one's own", [2] and the same rule is also laid down by the *Mahābhārata*—that a man of thirty years should marry a girl of ten [3]. Manu also prescribes the same thing, the relative proportion being either thirty and twelve or twenty-four and eight [4]. This seems to have been the ideal of the religious lawgivers, but Vātsyāyana seems to represent the actual state of things more closely. And it should be noticed that both Medhātithi and Kullūka in their comments on the passage of Manu quoted above, states that the rule about age was not absolute [5] but only shows the approximate relation between the ages of the couple.

1 See Buehler, S B E. Vol. XXX. p. 257, and Peterson, *J B B R A S.* Vol XVIII. p. 114.

2 वर्षरेकगुणां भार्य्यामुद्वहेत् त्रिगुणः स्वयम् । *Viṣṇu Purāṇa*, III. 10. 16.

3 त्रिंशद्वर्षो दशवर्षां भार्य्यां विन्देत नग्निकाम् । एकविंशतिवर्षो वा सप्तवर्षामवाप्नुयात् ॥ *Mbt.* XIII 44. 14

4 त्रिंशद्वर्षो वहेत् कन्यां हृद्यां द्वादशवार्षिकीम् । त्र्यष्टवर्षोऽष्टवर्षां वा धर्मे सीदति सत्वरः ॥ *Manu*, IX. 94.

5 इयता कालेन यवीयसी कन्या वोढव्या न पुनरेतावद्वयस एव विवाह इत्युपदेशार्थः । अथापि न यथाश्रुतवर्षसङ्ख्यैव किं तर्हि बहुना कालेन यवीयसी वोढव्या । *Medhātithi.* एतच्च योग्यकालप्रदर्शनपरं न तु नियमार्थं प्रायेणैतावता कालेन गृहीतवेदो भवति । *Kullūka.*

Marriage after Puberty of Girls

Though Vātsyāyana in the rule quoted from Âpastamba prohibits the marriage of a *rākā* or a *phalinī* [1], that is, a girl who has reached the age of puberty, yet many other passages in his book seem to show that he is speaking of virgins who have passed that age and were considerably advanced in youth; for example, he speaks of a wife just after marriage as *Vigāḍha-yauvanā* or advanced in youth[2] and many passages in his chapter on courtship presuppose a virgin who is of sufficient age to respond to offers of love. The rule of Âpastamba quoted by Vātsyāyana also appears to suggest that the bride has passed the age of puberty[3]—and again the rule held in common by Baudhāyana and Vātsyāyana that the *gāndharva* was the best form of marriage[4], seems to indicate that both the parties had passed the age of puberty. It is impossible to conceive of Gāndharva marriage before the couple could feel mutual love.

Marriage before Puberty

Marriage of a girl before puberty, also appears to have been equally, if not more prevalent, as is evidenced by Vātsyāyana's section on *Bālopakrama*, that is, the courtship of a *bāla* or a girl of tender years. Similarly in a passage that we have already referred to above, he contrasts a wife who is of tender years, with one of advanced youth.[5] This is also supported by the *Gṛhyasūtras* which speak of the

1 *KS.* p. 187, *sūtra* 12; *Âp. Gṛ. Sū.* I. 3. 11.

2 विगाढयौवनायाः पूर्वसंस्तुतायाः। *KS.* p. 193.

3 संगतयोस्त्रिरात्रमधःशय्या ब्रह्मचर्यं क्षारलवणवर्जमाहारस्तथा सप्ताहं सतूर्यमङ्गलस्नानं प्रसाधनं सहभोजनं च प्रेक्षासम्बन्धिनाम् पूजनमिति सावर्णिकम्।
KS. p. 191 *sūtra* 1; *Âp. Gṛ. Sū.* III. 8. 8.

4 See *ante.*, p. 15, foot-notes 1 and 2.

5 दीपालोके विगाढयौवनायाः पूर्वसंस्तुतायाः, बालाया अपूर्वायाश्चान्धकारे।
KS. p. 193.

marriage of a *nagnikā*, technically, a girl of ten years of age, as the most approved.[1]

The truth seems to be that marriage took place of both tender girls before puberty as well as of those more advanced in years. In the earlier Vedic times, including the Ṛgvedic age, both these forms of marriage seem to have been in vogue. While on the one hand, there were virgins considerably advanced in years like G h o ṣ ā, there were others like R o m a ś ā for example, who were evidently married before puberty. In a hymn addressed to the Aśvins, the father of Ghoṣā, Kakṣīvat who is supposed to have been the author, says, "You bestowed, Aśvins, a husband upon Ghoṣā growing old, and tarrying in her father's dwelling".[2] Ghoṣā in a hymn of her own also says addressing the Aśvins, "You Nāsatyas, are the good fortune of a damsel growing old in (her father's) mansion[3]" and the *Bṛhaddevatā* adds that "in the days of old she remained in her father's house for sixty years, when she in two hymns[4] praised the Aśvins who gave her a husband."[5] Romaśā was jeered at by her husband, the king Bhāvayavya for her immaturity in years.[6] The

Marriage of both tender and aged Virgins in the Vedic age

1 समानवर्णामसमानप्रवरां यवीयसीं नग्निकां श्रेष्ठाम् । *Mānava Gṛ. Sū.*, 1. 7. 8. Edn. by Knauer, p. 9.

2 युवं नरा स्तुवते कृष्णियाय विष्णाप्वं ददथुर्विश्वकाय । घोषायै चित् पितृषदे दुरोणे पतिं जूर्यन्त्या अश्विनावदत्तम् ॥ *Ṛv.* i. 117. 7. Trans. Wilson, I. 315.

3 अमाजुरश्चिद्भवथो युवं भगोऽनाशोश्चिदवितारापमस्य चित् । अन्धस्य चिन्नासत्या कृशस्य चिद्युवामिदाहुर्भिषजा रुतस्य चित् ॥ *Ṛv.* X. 39, 3. Trans. Wilson, vi. 104.

4 *Ṛv.* X. 39 and 40.

5 आसीत् कक्षवती घोषा पापरोगेन दुर्भगा । उवास षष्टिं वर्षाणि पितुरेव गृहे पुरा ॥ चिन्तयन्तीति सूक्ते द्वे यो वां परि ददर्श सा । भर्तारं ददतुस्तस्यै सुहस्त्यं च सुतं मुनिम् ॥ *Bṛhaddevatā*, vii 41. 46 and 47. Mac Donell's Trans. pp. 262—263.

6 *Ṛv.* 1. 126, 7 and *Bṛhaddevatā.* III. 156.

story of Uṣasti Cākrāyaṇa who lived in a village with his child-wife when there was a great famine, is also well-known.[1] Girls that were given away at the *svayaṃvara* must have reached youth. Sāvitrî is spoken of as *Yauvanasthā* at the time of marriage and Damayantî as *Prâptayauvanā*.[2] Yaśodharā is said to have been born on the same day as Prince Siddhārtha.[3]

Vātsyâyana sums up the whole thing in a verse in his section on courtship where he says that a maiden of tender years should be won over with the help of childlike sports and playthings, a damsel come of age by skill in the arts, and a spinster of more advanced years—*vatsalā*—with the help of persons in whom she confides.[4]

V. says a marriageable Virgin may be Bālā, Yuvatî or Prauḍhā

We may now pass on to Vātsyāyana's description of Varaṇa or choice of the bride. The selection was generally made and the marriage settled by the parents and other relatives and friends, and not by the parties to the marriage themselves, unless under exceptional circumstances. In the Vedic age too, the Vara or the wooer was often a friend

Varaṇa—Choice of the Bride

1 मटचीहतेषु कुरुष्वाटिक्या सह भार्ययोषस्तिर्ह चाक्रायण इभ्यग्रामे प्रद्राणक उवास । *Chāndogya Up.* I. 10. 1.

2 सा विग्रहवतीव श्रीर्व्यवर्द्धत नृपात्मजा । कालेन चापि सा कन्या यौवनस्था बभूव ह ॥ यौवनस्थां तु तां दृष्ट्वा स्वां सुतां देवरूपिणीम् । अयाच्यमानां च वरैर्नृपतिर्दुःखितोऽभवत् ॥ क्वगताभूत् सुतेयं ते कुतश्चैवागता नृप । किमर्थं युवतीं भर्त्रे न चैनां सम्प्रयच्छसि ॥ *Mbt.* III. 2ɛ2, 25; 31; 293. 4. स समीक्ष्य महीपालः स्वां सुतां प्राप्तयौवनाम् । अपश्यदात्मना कार्यं दमयन्त्याः स्वयंवरम् । *Mbt.* III. 54. 8.

3 यस्मिं पन समये अम्हाकं बोधिसत्तो लुम्बिनिवने जातो तस्मिं येव समये राहुलमाता देवी...च जाता । *Introduction to the Pāli Jātakas* in *Fausbœll's Jātaka*, Vol. 1. p 54.

4 बालक्रीडनकैर्बाला कलाभिर्यौवने स्थिता । वत्सला चापि संग्राह्या विश्वास्यजनसंग्रहात् ॥ *KS.* p. 207.

of the bridegroom. We are told in a hymn of the *Ṛgveda* that when the god Soma was desirous of getting a bride, the two Aśvins became his *varas* or wooers, and presented the suit before *savitṛ*, the father of the bride,[1] and we are assured by another verse in the same hymn that when the Aśvins went in their three-wheeled car, soliciting the marriage of Sûryā, all the Gods signified their assent.[2] The *Gṛhya-Sūtras* also prescribe that *Varas* or woores are to be sent for selecting the girl [3]

Propitiation of Bride's Parents

Vātsyāyana says, that for the selection of the girl, the father, mother and relatives of the young man should stir themselves and besides, mutual friends of the two parties should carry on messages between them.[4] Vātsyāyana gives the advice that those charged with the *varaṇa* should exaggerate the defects present and prospective, of other suitors and should expatiate on the qualifications of their *Nāyaka*, both personal and hereditary, as well as such qualities as are likely to further their object ; besides, they should enlarge upon such advantages possessed by him at the time, or likely to accrue to him in subsequent years, as would commend themselves to the girl's mother.[5] The advantage of winning the favour of the girl's mother[6] is emphasised upon and clever tricks also are recommended by Vātsyāyana for assuring success in the endeavour. Some of the friends of the youngman should drive the mother wild

1 सोमो वधूयुरभवदश्विनास्तामुभा वरा । सूर्यां यत्पत्ये शंसन्तीं मनसा सविताददात् ॥ *Ṛv.* x. 85. 9.

2 यदश्विना पृच्छमानावयातं त्रिचक्रेण वहतुं सूर्यायाः । विश्वे देवा अनु तद्वामजानन्पुत्रः पितराववृणीत पूषा ॥ *Ṛv.* X. 85, 14.

3 वरान् प्रहिणुयात । *Âp. Gṛ.* 1. 4, 1, *Śānkh. Gṛ* 1. 6. 1 ff *Âs. Gṛ.* 1. 5.

4 तस्या वरणे मातापितरौ संबन्धिनश्च प्रयतेरन् मित्राणि च गृहीतवाक्यान्युभयसंबद्धानि । *KS.* p. 185..

5 तान्यन्येषां वरयितृणां दोषान् प्रत्यक्षानागमिकांश्च श्रावयेयुः । कौलान् पौरुषेयानभिप्रायसंवर्धकांश्च नायकगुणान् विशेषतश्च कन्यामातुरनुकूलांस्तदात्वायतियुक्तान्दर्शयेयुः । *KS.* pp. 185– 186.

6 विशेषतश्च कन्यामातुरनुकूलान्; *KS.* pp. 185—186.

by enumerating to her his chances of winning girls from other desirable parties.[1] One of the youngman's friends, again, may get himself up as an astrologer and give an account of the wealth and prosperity that would come to the *Nāyaka* in after years as promised by omens and portents, by the position of the planets and also by marks on his body.[2]

Influence of Astrology, Omens and Portents on Choice of Bride

Vātsyāyana, though he speaks above of sham astrologers yet gives it as his decided opinion that a girl should be sought for, and also given away, when signs and omens, and portents and voices (*upaśruti*), are favourable[3], and to support himself, he also quotes the earlier authority of Ghoṭakamukha, who says that marriages should not be contracted on human choice alone[4], that is, *daiva* or superhuman tests should be applied by both the parties, in order to be satisfied that happiness and prosperity would result from the match. We must remember that the age of Vātsyāyana was the age of the growth and development of Indian astronomy which was hardly ever dissociated from astrology, when as a result of this alliance between science and pseudo-science grew up that large body of Siddhānta works culminating in the great books of Varāhamihira—the *Pañcasiddhāntikā*, the *Bṛhatsaṃhita*, and the *Bṛhajjātaka*.[5] Though faith

1 अपरे तु पुनरस्यान्यतो विशिष्टेन कन्यालाभेन कन्यामातरमुन्मादयेयुः । *KS*. p. 186.

2 दैवचिन्तकरूपश्च, शकुननिमित्तग्रहलग्नबललक्षणदर्शनेन नायकस्य भविष्यन्तमर्थसंयोगं कल्याणमनुवर्णयेत् ॥ *KS*. p. 185.

3 दैवनिमित्तशकुनोपश्रुतीनामानुलोम्येन कन्यां वरयेद्दद्याच्च । *KS*. p. 185.

4 न यदृच्छया केवलमानुषयेति घोटकमुखः । *KS*. p. 187.

5 See Thibaut, *Astronomie. Astrologie und Mathematik*, pp. 4 and 20.

in extra-human tests in marriage had been in favour since the time of the *Gṛhyasūtras* as the *Mānava Gṛhyasūtra*, the *Kauśikasūtra* and the others testify,[1] yet they seem to have been more popular than ever before in the age of Vātsyāyana who presses into service even *upaśrutis*—supernatural oracular voices heard as a result of mystic invocations of Gods or sometimes miraculous utterances heard specially at night, as the Commentary explains[2].

Signs and Omens at the time of Varaṇa

The signs observed at the time of *varaṇa*, that is, when the bridegroom's party went to the parents of the girl to formally present their suit, were considered as very important factors in the final choice and hence Vātsyāyana quotes from Âpastamba the rule that at the time of *varaṇa*, a girl who is found sleeping or weeping or has gone out of the house should be given up, [3] these being considered as inauspicious portents; then follow rules about the name borne by the girl and similar other things that we have already referred to before[4]. However, many of these defects are insignificant, artificial or accidental and Vātsyāyana was too astute an observer of the world to be led merely by such meaningless portents, and he at last quotes a simple rule, as we have seen before, [5] from the same legal authority, that happiness and prosperity attend the choice of a girl in whom the heart and the eyes are pleased and none other should be favoured. To capture the heart and the eyes of the wooers therefore, Vātsyāyana

1 *Mânava Gṛ. Sū.* Edn. by *Knauer*, p. 9,

2 निशीथे चोपश्रुतिर्ग्राह्या । *KS.* p. 187.

3 सुप्तां रुदतीं निष्क्रान्तां वरणे परिवर्जयेत् । *KS.* p. 187. Sūtra 11 = *Ap. Gṛ. Sū.* 1. 3, 10.

4 See *ante.* pp. 121-22

5 See *ante.* p. 123

prescribes that the parents and relatives of a marriageable girl would be best advised to show her off in beautiful dress and ornaments and that thus got up, she should sport with her playmates every afternoon, and attend all festive gatherings[1].

He next proceeds to give an account of the way in which the girl's parents and relatives are to receive the

Reception of the Suitors

suitors. He thus goes on : "When men fair to look on, courteous in speech, and accompanied by their connexions, come to propose marriage, the parent of the girl should receive them hospitably, and on same pretext or other show the girl in all her ornaments. They should come to no decision as to giving the girl before they have consulted the oracles. The wooer's party will be asked to bathe and take their meal and so forth. They should say, 'All that will come later.' They should not that day accept such attentions".[2] The *varaṇa* is to fructify, says Vātsyāyana, in one of the four approved forms of marriage, *viz*, *Brāhma*, *Prājāpatya*, *Ārṣa* or *Daiva*, or according to the forms in vogue in one's own country.[3]

It would be seen that this ceremony of *varaṇa* is not exactly courtship as Peterson takes it to be, because, here

Varaṇa is not Courtship

the actual parties to the marriage have very little to do. They have no choice to exercise, the whole matter is settled by the parents and relatives, including the selection of the bride. Personal courtship by the young people themselves has a secondary importance only with Vātsyāyana ; it was to be resorted to when other means failed. Hence he does not describe courtship first and marriage afterwards, but he

1 See *ante*. p. 123.

2 Trans. by Peterson, *J B B R A S*, XVIII, pp 115 and 117. *KS*. p. 189.

3 देशप्रवृत्तिसात्म्याद्वा ब्राह्मप्राजापत्यार्षदैवानामन्यतमेन विवाहेन शास्त्रतः परिणयेदिति । *KS*. p. 189.

first of all deals with the acquisition of a wife in the method approved of by society and by ancient tradition as contained in the sacred literature, and when this fails, a man may try to win over a girl by honest courtship, and even that failing, he may use tricks and even violence to secure his end. A girl also, under certain circumstances, though rather rare, may according to Vātsyāyana, take up the task of getting her husband in her own hands as we shall presently see.

Circumstances necessitating Courtship

A young man is to give up the idea of preferring his suit (*varaṇa*) in the approved method and think of winning the affections of a girl by his own personal exertions when he finds himself placed under certain unfavourable circumstances: thus, he may be poor though otherwise fully qualified as a suitor; or when possessed of mediocre qualifications (*madhyastha-guṇa*), he may be of rather mean birth; or though rich, he may be a neighbour and therefore would not be liked on account of his high pretensions, or he may be disliked because of the possibility of quarrels springing up over boundaries etc., as the Commentary observes;[1] or though possessing parents and brothers, he may be dependent on others; or he may be considered a mere boy;—in all such cases when he cannot hope for a favourable response to his suit, he should try to gain the love and esteem of the girl on whom his heart is set from her childhood.[2]

Vātsyāyana gives an example here from the people

1 स्वगृहसमीपवासी सीमासम्बन्धेन कलहादिजनकत्वात्। *KS.* p. 200.

2 धनहीनस्तु गुणयुक्तोऽपि, मध्यस्थगुणो हीनापदेशो वा, सधनो वा प्रातिवेश्यां, मातापिताभ्रातृषु च परतन्त्रा, बालवृत्तिरुचितप्रवेशो वा कन्यामलभ्यत्वान्न वरयेत्। बाल्यात् प्रभृति चैनां स्वयमेवानुरञ्जयेत्। *KS.* p. 200.

Marriage between Cousins in Dakṣiṇāpatha

of the south: thus, for example, says he, in the Dakṣiṇāpatha, one separated from one's mother when a child, and living in a subordinate position in the family of his maternal uncle, should try to gain over the daughter of the uncle when beyond his reach on account of her wealth, even if she may have been provisionally betrothed to another.[1] He may attempt to win over other girls also from childhood, for Ghoṭakamukha, who is Vātsyāyana's great authority for all matters appertaining to nuptials, declares that this courtship from childhood is unexceptionable as union is brought about by honest and honourable means (*dharma*).[2] Here Vātsyāyana confirms what Baudhāyana says about the irregular practice of the people of the south, that they marry the daughter of a maternal uncle.[3] Kumārila Bhaṭṭa also casts a fling at the Dākṣiṇātya who, he says, is overjoyed to get the daughter of his maternal uncle.[4] "The marriages between cousins," as Bühler points out, "occur among the Karhāḍa Brāhmaṇas of the Dekhan."[5] The existence of this custom in high circles in the South,

Historical Confirmation of Cousin-marriage in Dākṣiṇātya

receives historical confirmation from the inscriptions of the powerful royal house of the Rāṣṭrakūṭa sovereigns of Malkheḍ. Thus the Rāṣṭrakûṭa monarch Kṛṣṇa II, who reigned during the last part of the ninth

1 तथायुक्तश्च मातुलकुलानुवर्ती दक्षिणापथे बाल एव मात्रा च वियुक्तः परिभूतकल्पो धनोत्कर्षादलभ्यां मातुलदुहितरमन्यस्मै वा पूर्वदत्तां साधयेत् । *KS.*, p. 200.

2 अन्यामपि बाह्यां स्पृहयेद् बालायामेवं सति धर्माधिगमे संवननं श्लाघ्यमिति घोटकमुखः ।*KS* p. 200.

3 पञ्चधा विप्रतिपत्तिर्दक्षिणतस्तथोत्तरतः । यानि दक्षिणतस्तानि व्याख्यास्यामः ...मातुलपितृष्वसृदुहितृगमनमिति । *Baud. Dh. Śāst.* 1, 1, 2, 1–3. Edn. by Hultzsch. p.2.

4 स्वमातुलसुतां प्राप्य दाक्षिणात्यस्तु तुष्यति । Kumārila Bhaṭṭa, quoted by Govindasvāmin in his Commentary on the *Baud. Dh. Śāst.* Mysore edn. p. 8,

5 *SBE.* vol XIV, p. 146,

and the beginning of the tenth century, had as his *mahādevī* or chief queen, a daughter of the Haihaya Cedi king Kokkalla, and from them was born Jagattuṅga II who married Lakṣmī, the daughter of his maternal uncle. Raṇavigraha, a son of Kokkalla. From this union sprang up Indra III, who again married Vijāmbā, the daughter of Ammaṇadeva, who himself was the son of Arjuna, another son of Kokkalla.[1]

Courtship of a Girl of tender years

Vātsyāyana gives detailed instructions about the methods of courtship, varying according to age. A mere girl (*bālā*) is to be wooed by sharing in her child-like sports and occupations, a damsel who is come of age (*yauvanasthitā*), by an exhibition of skill in the arts or *kalās*, and a woman more advanced in years is to be courted through the help of those in whom she places her confidence.[2] Thus the young swain is advised to collect flowers and make garlands in company with the maiden whose heart he wishes to win and to carry on with her games befitting their age or the degree of familiarity between them, or only such as are agreeable to her disposition.[3] He should form the acquaintance of and propitiate her female friends, specially the daughter of her nurse, by little acts of kindness and service—as she would be very helpful in his quest.[4] The man should get for the girl things that she takes a fancy to.[5] Vātsyāyana then gives a fairly

1 Cambay Plates of Govindarāja IV, verses 14–20, *Ep. Ind.* vii, p. 38.

2 See *ante*. p. 127.

3 तथा सह पुष्पावचयं ग्रथनं गृहकं दुहितृकाक्रीडायोजनं भक्तपाककरणमिति कुर्वीत परिचयस्य वयसश्चानुरूप्यात् । *KS*. p. 201.

4 धात्रेयिकां चास्याः प्रियहिताभ्यामधिकमुपगृह्णीयात्, सा हि प्रीयमाणा विदिताकाराऽप्यप्रत्यादिशन्ती तं तां च योजयितुं शक्नुयादनभिहिताऽपि प्रत्याचार्यकम्। *KS*. p. 202.

5 क्रीडनकद्रव्याणि यान्यपूर्वाणि यान्यन्यासां विरलशो विद्युस्तान्यस्या अप्रयत्नेन संपादयेत् । *KS*. p. 202.

long list of presents that would be prized by her especially such as would show her off on days of public and private festivities.[1] When he has won the confidence to some extent then he may amuse her by relating agreeable stories or entertain her with music[2]. He himself must always be faultlessly dressed and never be offensive to sight, because, Vātsyāyana argues, when maidens reach youth they get to love men whom they frequently see[3]. He should now carefully take note of her movements and see if he can detect any signs of growing partiality for him.[4]

Signs that betray a growing love in the Girl

Vātsyāyana here enumerates the outward signs and actions by which a budding affection may be discovered, such as, she cannot look the man in the face, casts side-long glances at him and so on, all of which are quite true to nature.[5] When the outward signs and movements leave no doubt about her love, he should grow less timid gradually, take greater and greater liberties with her without giving any offence[6] and try to gain her over entirely by means of various tricks and devices that recommend themselves to young lovers in every clime. Vātsyāyana takes pains to describe them at some length and at last he again quotes Ghoṭakamukha to warn the young swain that he must be quick to read the signs that betray her passion, because even when love is far advanced success

1 *KS*. pp. 202–203.

2 वर्धमानानुरागां वाख्यानके मनः कुर्वंतोमन्वर्थाभिः कथाभिश्चित्तहारिणीभिश्च रञ्जयेत् । *KS*. p. 203 .

3 उवारवेषश्च स्वयमनुपहतदर्शनश्च स्यात् । युवतयो हि संसृष्टमभीक्ष्णदर्शनं च पुरुषं प्रथमं कामयन्ते । *KS*. p. 203.

4 भावं च कुर्वतीमिङ्गिताकारैः सूचयेत् । *KS*.p. 203.

5 संमुखं न वीक्षते, तं तु वीक्षिता व्रीडां दर्शयति । etc. etc. *KS*. p. 206.

6 दर्शितेङ्गिताकारां कन्यामुपायतोऽभियुञ्जीत । *KS*. p. 208

cannot be achieved with maidens by sloth and despondence and he can never expect a damsel to confess her love.[1]

A maiden has sometimes to look for a Husband

Placed in unfavourable circumstances similar to those from which a young man suffers, a maiden may also have to look for a husband herself and Vātsyāyana takes her case also in hand. When a girl though possessed of excellent qualities, is born in a humble family, or even when well-born, is destitute of wealth and is therefore not sought after by her equals, or has been deprived of her parents and is dependent upon her relatives and if she has come of age *(prāpta-yauvanā)*, then she should stir herself to arrange her marriage herself.[2] Here we are reminded of the rule advocated by Manu himself and supported by other sacred books including the *Mahābhārata*, that a damsel should wait three years after reaching puberty, and after that period she may choose for herself a husband befitting her.[3] Such a maiden should try to gain over a young man of ability possessed of virtues, and of a handsome look, whose affections she had shared in childhood; or, when she feels assured that a man owing to his passion for her would not hesitate to unite with her even against the consent of his parents, then she may win him over by endearing herself to him and by meeting him

1 अन्याभिरपि सह विश्वासनार्थमधिकमधिकं चाभियुञ्जीत न तु वाचा निवदत् । दूरगतभावोऽपि हि कन्यासु न निवदेन सिध्यतीति घोटकमुखः । *KS.* pp. 211–212.

2 मन्दापदेशा गुणवत्यपि कन्या धनहीना कुलीनापि समानैरयाच्यमाना मातापितृवियुक्ता वा ज्ञातिकुलवर्तिनी वा प्राप्तयौवना पाणिग्रहणं स्वयमभीप्सेत । *KS.*p. 213.

3 त्रीणि वर्षाण्युदीक्षेत कुमार्य्यृतुमती सती । ऊर्द्धं न्तु कालादेतस्माद्विन्देत सदृशं पतिम् ॥ *Manu* ix 90. त्रीणि वर्षाण्युदीक्षेत कन्या ऋतुमती सती । चतुर्थेत्वथ सम्प्राप्ते स्वयं भर्तारमर्जयेत् । *Mbt.* XIII. 44, 16.

often.[1] She may show her skill in the arts, and various other devices[2] are recommended by Vātsyāyana, who, however, warns a girl against presenting her suit to a man herself, even when she is deeply in love with him, because such conduct brings ruin unto a damsel, so declare the teachers *(ācāryas)* of the *Kāmaśāstra.*[3] In another connection also he forbids a man to have anything to do with a woman who herself makes overtures of love openly[4]. Vātsyāyana also tries to press upon a girl the sage advice that in choosing a husband, she should look for love and not money ; "It is better," says he, ' to love a husband who is devoted to her though poor, than a rich man, or one endowed with many virtues, when his affections she would have to share with others[5]." When there are several eligible suitors of equal quality, the real suitor is he with whom there is a mutual reciprocation of love[6].

Forms of Marriage resulting from Courtship

Vātsyāyana next proceeds to describe the forms of marriage that would cement the union brought about by courtship between the parties themselves, without the permission of the parents or relatives, and the details furnished by Vātsyāyana are interesting as illustrating the definitions given in the *Gṛhyasūtras* and the *Dharmasūtras.* After

1 सा तु गुणवन्तं शक्तं सुदर्शनं बालप्रीत्याभियोजयेत् । यं वा मन्येत मातापित्रोरसमीक्षया स्वयमप्ययमिन्द्रियदौर्बल्यान्मयि प्रवर्तिष्यत इति प्रियहितोपचारैरभीक्ष्णसन्दर्शनेन च तमावर्जयेत् । *KS.* p. 214.

2 कलाकौशलप्रकाशने वा...। *KS.* p. 214.

3 न चैवातुराऽपि पुरुषं स्वयमभियुञ्जीत, स्वयमभियोगिनी हि युवतिः सौभाग्यं जहातीत्याचार्याः । *KS.* p. 213

4 प्रकाशप्रार्थिनी (अगम्या) ।*KS.* p. 67.

5 वरं वश्यो दरिद्रोऽपि निर्गुणोऽप्यात्मधारणः । गुणैर्युक्तोऽपि न त्वेवं बहुसाधारणः पतिः ॥ *KS.* p. 217.

6 गुणसाम्येऽभियोक्तॄणामेको वरयिता वरः । तत्राभियोक्तरि श्रेष्ठामनुरागात्मको हि सः ॥ *KS.* p. 217.

18

perfect unity of sentiment is established between the parties and all the scruples of the maiden overruled by persuasions, the time and place of meeting should be arranged with the help of friends. When the girl has been brought to a secret place, sacred fire should be brought from the house of a *Śrotriya* Brahmin who maintains a perpetual fire for the performance of his daily sacrificial rites, *kuśa* grass should be spread before it upon the earth, oblations offered in the fire in accordance with the prescriptions of the sacred law (*smṛti*), and then they should thrice go round the fire, and after this is completed, the parents of the girl should be informed[1]; "A marriage performed before fire as witness to the transaction, can never be set aside, this is the rule approved by all teachers" (*ācārya-samaya*), says Vātsyāyana[2]. By and by the relatives on both sides should be informed and be persuaded to confirm the marriage by bestowing the girl upon her lover in the formal way, by representing to them that otherwise the king might punish the bridegroom's side for the violence, and on the other side, the fair name of the girl's family may be tarnished, and then both sides may be reconciled by an exchange of presents. This is the Gāndharva form of marriage[3].

Gāndharva Marriage

Vātsyāyana considers several other cases also : if the girl cannot make up her mind, then the man should, with the help of another lady of good family, have the maiden brought to a secret place on some pretext, and

1 प्रतिपन्नामभिप्रेतावकाशवर्तिनीं नायकः श्रोत्रियागारादग्निमानाय्य कुशानास्तीर्य यथास्मृति हुत्वा च त्रिः परिक्रमेत् । ततो मातरि पितरि च प्रकाशयेत् । *KS.* pp. 219.-220.

2 अग्निसाक्षिका हि विवाहा न निवर्तन्त इत्याचार्यसमयः । *KS.* p. 220.

3 *KS.* p. 220. Thus explains the Commentary. But the text has गान्धर्वेन विवाहेन वा चेष्टेत which seems to show that *Gāndharva* was an alternative form of marriage. However, MM. Durgaprasad's edition (p. 229) gives a variant where "*ca*" is read in the passage in place of '*vā*'.

have the rites performed as before[1]. When the marriage of the girl has been settled with some other person and the date of the nuptial ceremony draws near, then he should by all means turn her mother against the match, by having recounted to her the faults and defects of the prospective bridegroom, and with her consent have the girl brought to a neighbour's house and get the nuptials celebrated ; or he may place the brother of the girl under great obligation to himself, and with his help get the girl brought to a secret place and married to him as described above[2]. All these are supposed to represent the Gāndharva form of marriage.

Then Vātsyāyana gives two illustrations of the Paiśāca form. At public festivities the man may make the daughter of her nurse administer to the girl some intoxicating substance and then have her brought to a secret place when she is senseless under the drug. Afterwards he would inform her relatives of it and persuade them to bestow her on him, or he may do the like when she is asleep[3].

Paiśāca Marriage

Last of all he describes the Rākṣasa form. Coming to know beforehand that the girl would be going on a journey to another village, or to the gardens, the man may lie in ambush with a sufficient number of friends, then frighten away or kill her guards and forcibly carry her off[4].

Rākṣasa Marriage by Capture

1 अप्रतिपद्यमानायामन्तश्चारिणीमन्यां कुलप्रमदां पूर्वसंसृष्टां प्रीयमाणां चोपगृह्य तया सह विषह्यमवकाशमेनामन्यकार्योपदेशेनानाययेत् । ततः श्रोत्रियागारादग्निमिति समानं पूर्वेण । *KS.* p. 220.

2 आसन्ने च विवाहे मातरमस्यास्तदभिमतान्यवरदोषैरनुशयं ग्राहयेत् । ततस्तदनुमतेन प्रातिवेश्याभवने निशि नायकमानाय्य श्रोत्रियागारादग्निमिति समानं पूर्वेण। *KS.* p. 221.

3 अष्टमीचन्द्रिकादिषु धात्रेयिका मदनीयमेनां पाययित्वा किंचिदात्मनः कार्यमुद्दिश्य नायकस्य विषह्यं देशमानयेत् । तत्रैनां मदात्संज्ञामप्रतिपद्यमानां दूषयित्वेति समानं पूर्वेण । सुप्तां चैकचारिणीं धात्रेयिकां वारयित्वा संज्ञामप्रतिपद्यमानां दूषयित्वेति समानं पूर्वेण । *KS.* p. 221-222.

4 ग्रामान्तरमुद्यानं वा गच्छन्तीं विदित्वा सुसंवृतसहायो नायकस्तदा रक्षिणो वित्रास्य हत्वा वा कन्यामपहरेदिति विवाहयोगाः । *KS.* p. 222.

In all these marriages celebrated without the consent of the parents, Vātsyāyana advises, as we have seen, that particular care should be taken to have some nuptial ceremonies performed in sacred fire, so that they may not run the risk of being cancelled. This is to provide against the contingency of the girl's parents overlooking the secret union and bestowing her upon another man, such as is authorised by Baudhāyana and Vasiṣṭha, both of whom prescribe that if a girl has been abducted by force, but the due nuptial rites have not been performed with the recitation of the sacred texts (*mantras*), then she may be lawfully given away with the proper rites, to another person, she is as good as a virgin[1]. Even when the parents agree, it will be necessary to have the marriage ratified, by a formal performance of the rites. Devala declares that in the forms of marriage beginning with the Gāndharva, that is, in the *Gāndharva*, *Paiśāca* and *Rākṣasa* forms, the rites should again be performed by the three higher castes in the regular method, before the fire as witness[2]. There is a difference of opinion among law-givers as to whether this second performance of the rites is in order, Manu declaring against it, as in such cases the girls are no longer virgins[3].

Secret Marriages must be confirmed before Fire

Vātsyāyana has mentioned before[4] four forms of marriage, approved in genteel society, in the order Brāhma, Prājāpatya, Ārṣa and Daiva,

1 बलाच्चेत् प्रहृता कन्या मन्त्रैर्यदि न संस्कृता । अन्यस्मै विधिवद्देया यथा कन्या तथैव सा ॥ *Baudh. Dh. Śāst.* IV. 1, 15; *Vasiṣṭha*, xvii. 73.

2 गान्धर्वेषु विवाहेषु पुनर्वैवाहिको विधिः । कर्त्तव्यश्च त्रिभिर्वर्णैः समयेनाग्निसाक्षिकः ॥ *Devala*, quoted by Kullūkabhaṭṭa on Manu, viii. 226.

3 पाणिग्रहणिका मन्त्राः कन्यास्वेव प्रतिष्ठिताः ।
नाकन्यासु क्वचिन्नृणां लुप्तधर्मक्रिया हि सा ॥
Manu, viii. 226. See Buehler, *SBE*, xxv. p. 291.

4 See *ante* p. 31.

but he has not delineated their distinctive characteristics, taking it for granted perhaps that their connotations were all known to his readers, and he might very well do so, inasmuch as they were exhaustively dealt with in the *Gṛhyasūtras*, the *Dharmaśāstras*, the Great Epic and the *Purāṇas* and similar other literature. Now he describes the G ā n d h a r v a, P a i ś ā c a and R ā k ṣ a s a forms ; of these, the first he mentions by name, and of the last two forms, he only gives the description and leaves the names to be supplied by the reader. However, thus we see that he mentions altogether seven forms, leaving out the Â s u r a marriage in which "the bridegroom receives a maiden, after having given as much wealth as he can afford, to the kinsmen and the bride herself, according to his own will"[1]. It is rather striking that Vātsyāyana does not advise a young man to purchase his bride by money, though he does not shrink from recommending the adoption of meaner and more violent forms like the *Paiśāca* and the *Rākṣasa*. Most probably, it was very much looked down upon in cultured society in his days. Yājñavalkya[2], however, mentions the Âsura marriage along with the other seven. Now, applying Vātsyāyana's dictum that in his list of the seven forms, one that precedes is superior to one that follows, on account of its being more in accordance with *dharma* or the sacred law[3], we arrive at a graded series which is not quite in agreement with the *Dharmaśāstras*. For instance, Manu gives the series thus—Brāhma, Daiva, Prājāpatya, Ârṣa[4]. The other three he has not graded, but taking them

1 Manu, iii. 36. Buehler. SBE XXV. p. 87.

2 *Yāj*. I, 61.

3 पूर्वः पूर्वः प्रधानं स्याद्विवाहो धर्मसंस्थितेः। पुर्वाभावे ततः कार्यो यो य उत्तर उत्तरः। *KS*. p. 222.

4 See *Manu*. iii, 37—38.

in the order in which he enumerates them, they are to be graded as Âsura, Gāndharva, Rākṣasa and Paiśâca the last of which he definitely characterises as the eighth and the worst[1]. Yājñavalkya also agrees with Manu with only the slight difference that he places the *Ārṣa* and the Prâjāpatya in the same category[2]. Kauṭilya also mentions all the eight forms of marriage but what is remarkable, is that he, unlike Manu and others, enumerates the first four forms in exactly the same order as Vātsyāyana,[3] showing here a point of agreement with the latter, as in many other respects. Most of the authors of the law codes differ from Vātsyāyana in condemning the *Paiśāca* as the worst, worse than even the *Rākṣasa*, but the Commentator of Vātsyāyana explains the position of his author by saying that the *Paiśāca*, though not lawful (*adharmya*), yet is better than the *Rākṣasa*, as the latter involves violence[4].

Liberality of Vātsyāyana's Views on Marriage

Summing up the views of Vātsyāyana, it appears that he sanctions a great deal of freedom from ordinary rules and conventions with regard to marriage. We have seen that in the matter of the selection of a bride, he is ready to cast off to the wind all the innumerable checks and tests that hamper the free exercise of choice, non-essential, technical imperfections being never allowed to stand in the way when there is a union of hearts, not even when the consent of the parents is not available on either side. According to him, therefore, the Gāndharva

1 स पापिष्ठो विवाहानां पैशाचश्चाष्टमोऽधमः । *Manu.* iii. 34.

2 *Yāj.* i. 59—60.

3 *Arthaśāstra.* iii. 2.

4 पैशाचोऽधर्म्योऽपि राक्षसात् प्रधानं राक्षसस्य साहसकर्मत्वात् । *KS.* 223.

form of marriage is the most respected (*pūjita*), because, he declares, love is the fruit of all the forms of marriage that can be conceived of, and love is more in evidence here than in any other forms where considerations of birth, money or other qualities are the deciding factors. It brings forth happiness, is not accompanied by all the troubles of a lengthy negotiation and ceremonial, and what is more important, is the result of mutual love[1].

CHAPTER V

SOCIAL LIFE IN ANCIENT INDIA : AS DEPICTED IN VÂTSYÂYANA'S KÂMASŪTRA

III. LIFE OF THE NAGARAKA

Vātsyāyana in his work holds up the ideal of city-life. He wrote the Kāmasūtra as a practical handbook for the guidance of city-bred men of fashion—the Nāgarakas. A whole section of his book is called *Nāgaraka-vṛttam*, wherein he describes the life of a city-man, not of a mere dweller in a city—such a person would only be a *nāgara,*—but of a *nāgaraka,* who, according to Pâṇini, is a city-bred man skilled in the arts and knaveries that specially develop in a big city, one possessing the virtues and vices of "a cockney" : he might be a clever artist or a knave, as the *Kāśikā-vṛitti* so naively explains.[1] Vātsyāyana's book is calculated to benefit such men and women, among them princesses and daughters of high officials (*Mahāmâtras*), who armed with an expert knowledge of the practical directions given by him, would be able to subdue the heart of a husband whose love is shared by a crowded harem of as many as a "thousand" wives.[2] Vātsyāyana recommends the city as the proper place of abode for a person who after finishing his education, thinks of entering the world, the *gṛhasthāśrama,* with the wealth that he may have acquired, either by inheritance or by the pursuit of the profession particularly appertaining to his own caste and

Nāgaraka—the City-bred Man of Fashion.

1 *Kāśikā-Vṛtti* on Pāṇini. Vi. 2 128—"नगरात् कुत्सनप्रावीण्ययोः" - नगरशब्दाद् वुञ्प्रत्ययो भवति शैषिकः, कुत्सने प्रावीण्ये च गम्यमाने।...कुत्सनं निन्दनम्। प्रावीण्यं नैपुण्यम्। 'केनायं मुषितः पन्था गात्रे पक्ष्मालिधूसरः ?' 'इह नगरे मनुष्येण सम्भाव्यत एतन्नागरकेण। चौरा हि नागरका भवन्ति।' 'केनेदं लिखितं चित्रं मनो-नेत्र विकाशि मत् ?'—'इह नगरे मनुष्येण सम्भाव्यत एतन्नागरकेण। प्रवीणा हि नागरका भवन्ति।'

2 योगज्ञा राजपुत्री च महामात्रसुता तथा। सहस्रान्तःपुरमपि स्ववशे कुरुते पतिम्॥—*KS.* p. 41 (*sūtra* 22).

his postion in society;[1] such a man should adopt the life of a *nāgaraka* and fix his habitation in a city—whether small or big, a *nagara*, or a *pattana*, or a *kharvaṭa*, or at least in a resort of many good and noble persons.[2] In the age of Vātsyāyana, apparently everybody who was marked out from the rest by any pre-eminence in intelligence, or learning, or skill in the arts, was attracted to the city, and found his patron in the king, or in a wealthy *nāgaraka*, or found employment at the clubs and assemblies of citizens, or under the guilds of merchants and artisans.

If a person could not afford to live in a city and was forced to shut himself up in a village by the exigencies of earning his livelihood, even then he should, according to Vātsyāyana, look upon civic life as the ideal and by giving to his fellow villagers glowing descriptions of the pleasant life led by the *nāgaraka*, he should inspire those among his own class who show any special cleverness or curiosity, with a desire to imitate the conduct of the city-people and he should give them a taste of the amenities of city-life by starting clubs and social gatherings as in the city, by himself gratifying his friends with his company, by favouring them with his assistance and by introducing the spirit of mutual help and cooperation.[3] A village-wife is spoken of as a simpleton and village-women generally are spoken of as very light and fickle; such rustic women (*carṣaṇis*) are regarded with scant courtesy by Vātsyāyana.[4] The life of a round

1 गृहीतविद्यः प्रतिग्रह-जय-क्रय-निर्वेशाधिगतैरर्थैरन्वयागतैरुभयैर्वा गार्हस्थ्यमधिगम्य नागरकवृत्तं वर्त्तेत ।—*Kāmasūtra*. p. 42 (*sūtra* 1).

2 नगरे पत्तने खर्वटे महति वा सज्जनाश्रये स्थानम् ।—*Ibid*. p. 42 (*sūtra* 2)

3 ग्रामवासी च सजातान्विचक्षणान् कौतुहलिकान् प्रोत्साह्य नागरकजनस्य वृत्तं वर्णयन् श्रद्धां च जनयंस्तदेवानुकुर्वीत गोष्ठींश्च प्रवर्तयेत् सङ्गत्या जनमनुरञ्जयेत् कर्मसु च साहाय्येन चानुगृह्णीयात् उपकारयेच्चेति नागरकवृत्तम् ।—*Ibid*. p. 57 (*sūtra* 49).

4 योषितस्त्विमा अभियोगमात्रसाध्या * * ग्राम्यभार्या—*Ibid*. p. 254 (*sūtra* 52), ग्रामाधिपतेरायुक्तकस्य हलोत्थवृत्तिपुत्रस्य यूनो ग्रामीणयोषितो वचनमात्रसाध्याः, ताश्चर्षण्य इत्याचक्षते विटाः ।...*Ibid*. p. 282 (*sūtra* 5).

of pleasures in the city was naturally very expensive and many ran through their fortunes. Such a *nāgaraka* who had eaten up his fortune (*bhukta-vibhavaḥ*) might, however, if clever, earn a living by placing himself at the service of the clubs and pleasure-houses where he would be respected on account of his skill in the arts, and then he would be called a *viṭa*.[1] Even if a man had no fortune of his own he might enjoy the pleasures of life as a *pīṭhamarda*; he might acquire skill in the arts and go about as an itinerant professor of these at the clubs of citizens and the abodes of *gaṇikās*; such a man was marked by his peculiar seat (*mallikā*) which he hung on his back, by his dyed clothes and by some kind of soap (*phenaka*) which he always carried about in order to keep himself clean.[2] Or he might, if he was skilled in only a few of the arts, attach himself to a wealthy *nāgaraka* as his companion and confidential friend and then he was called a *vidūṣaka* or a *vaihāsika*, a professional jester.[3]

GROWTH OF CITIES IN ANCIENT INDIA

This strong desire for the gay life of the city shows that there must have been a pretty large number of cities at the time when Vātsyāyana's work was written. Cities had grown up in India from very ancient times. The village and its headman,—the *grâma* and

1 भुक्तविभवस्तु गुणवान् सकलत्रो वेशे गोष्ठयां च वहुमतस्तदुपजीवी च विटः।... *Ibid*, p. 56 (*sūtra* 45). We meet with this and the other characters here described, in Bhāsa's *Cārudatta*. The *Viṭa* there is a typical one : he has attached himself to a rich man in power, *Śakāra*, whom however he hates for his grossness for he has still some noble and soft feelings left in himself ; moreover, he speaks Sanskrit, showing that he has received a liberal education and has evidently known better days.

2 अविभवस्तु शरीरमात्रो मल्लिकाफेनकषायमात्रपरिच्छदः पूज्याद्देशादागतः कलासु विचक्षणस्तदुपदेशेन गोष्ठयां वेशोचिते च वृत्ते साधयेदात्मानमिति पीठमर्दः।... *Ibid*, p. 55 (*sūtra* 44).

3 एकदेशविद्यस्तु क्रीडनको विश्वास्यश्च विदूषकः वैहासिको वा।...*Ibid*, p. 55 (*sūtra* 48)

the *grāmaṇī*—are no doubt often met with in the *Ṛgveda*,[1] but the *grāma* sometimes grew into a *mahāgrāma* and people naturally crowded round the settlement of a powerful chieftain, round his *pur* or fortified habitation.[2] In later Vedic literature, cities were very well known; the *Mânava Gṛhyasūtra* mentions the *grāma*, the *nagara* and the *nigama*.[3] The cities were very well known to the compilers of the *Dharmasūtras*, Baudhāyana going so far as to warn people desirous of spiritual growth against residence in cities: he declares that it is hardly possible for a man who resides in a town—"whose body, whose face and eyes are defiled by the impure dust of a city"—to obtain success in his spiritual quest.[4] Pāṇini in the seventh century B.C. knew many towns, as we see from his *sūtras* and some of his *gaṇas*; even the *nâgaraka*, the special product of city-life as we have pointed out, was known to him. Kauṭilya and Megasthenes show that there were some very big cities with elaborate arrangements for civic government and that municipal organisation of the city had developed wonderfully.[5] In the *Jâtakas* and the Buddhist Pali texts we find the description of large and prosperous cities which were seats of government and where trade flourished, where the *gahapati* was a prominent citizen and the *śreṣṭhī* took a leading part.[6] The *Milinda Pañho* gives a splendid description of

1 *Ṛ V.*, i. 44. 10, etc.; see also Macdonell and Keith, *Vedic Index*, vol. i, p. 244.

2 *Ibid*, pp. 245 and 538; *Jaiminīya Upaniṣad Brāhmaṇa*, iii. 13. 4.

3 अत ऊर्द्ध्वं ग्रामचतुष्पथे नगरचतुष्पथे निगमचतुष्पथे वा...बलिमुपहरति।... *Mānava Gṛhyasūtra*. (ed. by Dr. Fr. Knauer), ii. 14. 2. 8 (p. 56).

4 पुररेणुकुण्ठित-शरीरस्तत्परिपूर्णनेत्रवदनश्च। नगरे वसन् सुनियतात्मा सिद्धिमवाप्स्यतीति न तदस्ति।—*Baudhāyana Dharmasūtra*, ii. 3. 53.

5 Vincent A. Smith, *Early History of India* (3rd ed.), pp. 120-29.

6 Rhys Davids, *Buddhist India*, pp. 34-41.

the town of Sākala,[1] and nearer Vātsyāyana's time, we find beautiful descriptions of splendid and prosperous towns given in the *Buddhacarita* and *Lalitavistara*.[2] In Vātsyāyana's time all over India there must have been a large number of cities, great and small, for India was then broken up into innumerable principalities and each prince had his own fortified capital. Besides, cities had grown up at places of pilgrimage—Brahmanic, Buddhist and Jaina—or had sprung up as centres of the growing trade of the country. It was for the dwellers of these cities, where wealth accumulated and where the virtues and vices that wealth brings in its train specially developed, that Vātsyāyana wrote his great work.

ECONOMIC PROSPERITY OF INDIA IN THE AGE OF VÂTSYÂYANA

At the time that Vātsyāyana wrote, India was carrying on an abundant trade, by land and by sea, with China on the one hand and the Roman orient on the other. According to a Chinese book *Funantu-suh-tchuan* written in the third century A.C., Kuntien or Kauṇḍinya founded an Indian Colony in Indo-China about B.C. 53, and it soon grew up into a great centre of foreign trade in that quarter. By way of this Brahmanic colony planted in Indo-China, the Indians carried on an ever-increasing maritime trade with China in the approved Chinese method of sending so-called embassies and making an exchange of presents. We read again and again in the Chinese annals of numerous Indian envoys who presented tribute by way of *Jihnan* (modern Annam and Tonquin).[3] With Asia

1 *The Questions of King Milinda*, *S. B. E.*, xxxv, pp. 2-?.

2 *Buddhacarita*, chaps. i and x; *Lalitavistara*. chap. iii.

3 T. de Lacouperie, *Western Origin of the Chinese Civilisation*, pp. 240-42; see also the *Dawn Magazine*, 1910, Part i. p. 98 and 1911, Part i, pp. 22-28.

Minor and the near West, India had been intimately connected for a long time as we see from Aśoka's inscriptions; and the settlement of the Kushans as a great Indian ruling power in the north-western marches of the country, led to the opening out of trade-routes to the east and the west, and it placed India in a position of vantage with regard to the trade with the civilised world, with the dominions of the "Son of Heaven" on the one hand and the empire of the Cæsars on the other. When in the second century A.C., not very long before Vātsyāyana, a great Kushan emperor adopted the magnificent title of *Mahārāja-Rājātirāja-Devaputra-Kaisara Kaniṣka*—'The great King, the King of Kings, the Son of Heaven, the Cæsar Kaniṣka", we see that in him there was a fusion of the three great civilisations of the time—the Indian, the Chinese and the Roman.[1] The currency of the Kushans shows an equally international character and seems to be designed to facilitate the trade of these dominions with the rest of the world; the coins show a strange and wonderful combination of Greek, Zoroastrian and Indian designs and icons; some of them have Jupiter on one side and Buddha on the other; they have legends in Greek, Iranian or Indian vernaculars and in varied scripts, Greek, Brāhmī or Kharoṣṭhī. There cannot be any doubt that these coins were intended for currency inside as well as outside and they afforded facility of exchange to the Indian merchants trading with the near West. Vātsyāyana also knew coins of copper, silver and gold. He speaks of a *kārṣāpaṇa* of small value and of the *niṣka* or coin of gold; besides, he refers to the art of examining *rūpyas* or coins as one of the sixty-four *kalās*. Moreover, he uses the word *hiraṇya* to mean

1 *Epigraphia Indica*, xiv, p. 143.

money in general including perhaps, gold and silver coins.[1]

Pliny in the first century A.C. and Ptolemy in the second, testify to the great trade that India had with the Roman empire.[2] In the third century when Vātsyāyana lived, this trade must have gone on increasing and we shall not be far mistaken to conjecture that the Brahmanic colonies, that Fa Hien visited in Java, went out about this period. The prosperity that this extensive commerce with the civilised world conferred on India, is fully reflected in the life of the *nāgaraka*, everything about whom, house and furniture, dress and ornaments, sports and pastimes, charity and liberality, bespeak an unstinted expenditure of wealth.

The literature of the period to which Vātsyāyana belongs, amply corroborates the description that he gives of society. But we shall have room only to quote an occasional passage here and there from the works of Bhāsa and from the *Lalitavistara* both of which are supposed to belong to the third century A.C. and, therefore, to have been written about the same time as the *Kāmasūtra* ; we may also draw some illustrations from the works of Aśvaghoṣa who flourished about a century earlier and belongs virtually to the same epoch.[3]

1 See R. D. Banerji, *Prācīna-mudrā*. pp. 81-161, for an account of the Kushan coins. For Vātsyāyana's mention of coins cf. वरं सांशयिकान्निष्कादसांशयिकः कार्षापणः — *Kāmasūtra*, p. 19 (*sūtra* 20) ; रूप्यरत्नपरीक्षा...p. 32 ; and सर्वकार्याणां तन्मूलत्वाद्धिरण्यद इति वात्स्यायनः ।...p. 337 (*sūtra* 6) ; *Jayamaṅgalā* explains, हिरण्यमत्र लोकप्रतीत्या कपर्दकाः.

2 V. A. Smith, *Early History of India* (3rd ed.). pp. 438-44.

3 For the date of the *Lalitavistara* see Winternitz, *Geschichte der indischen Litteratur*, ii, p. 199 For Bhāsa, see D. R. Bhandarkar, *Lectures on the Ancient History of India* (1918), p. 59.

THE HOUSE OF A NÂGARAKA

The house that the *nâgaraka* builds for his residence shows his taste and love of beauty and the simple but choice furniture and decorations that adorn his rooms show his love of art and his many-sided culture. As we have seen before, the *nâgaraka* builds his house in a city. It has to be in close proximity to a supply of water and is divided into two parts, the inner belonging to the ladies and the outer where, as we shall see presently, the master of the house attends to business and receives visitors. There is a number of rooms each set apart for its special purpose, and attached to the house there must be a *vrkṣavâṭikâ* or a garden with wide grounds, if possible, where flowering plants and fruit-trees can grow as well as kitchen vegetables.[1] In the middle of the ground should be excavated either a well, or if there is room enough, a tank or a lake.[2] This garden is attached to the inner court and is looked after by the mistress of the house. It is the duty of a good housewife says Vātsyāyana, to procure the seeds of the common Indian kitchen vegetables and medicinal herbs and plant them each in its season.[3] In neat and clean spots in the garden where the ground has been well dressed, the lady of the house plants beds of green vegetables,—clumps of the tall sugarcane, patches of stunted shrubs of the mustard and similar herbs, and thickets of the dark *tamāla*.[4] The flower-garden

1 तत्र भवनमासन्नोदकं वृक्षवाटिकावद्विभक्तकर्म्मकक्षं द्विवासगृहं कारयेत् ।... *Kāmasūtra*, p. 42 (*sūtra* 4).

2 मध्ये कूपं वापीं दीर्घिकां वा खानयेत् ।—*Ibid*, p. 225 (*sūtra* 8).

3 मूलकालुकपालङ्कीदमनकाम्रातकैर्वारुकत्रपुसवार्ताककूष्माण्डालाबुसूरणशुकनासास्वयंगुप्तातिलपर्णिकाग्निमन्थलशुनपलाण्डुप्रभृतीनां सर्वौषधीनां च बीजग्रहणं काले वापश्च ;— *Ibid*. p 228 (*sūtra* 29).

4 परिपूतेषु च हरितशाकवप्रानिक्षुस्तम्बाञ्जीरकसर्षपाजमोदशतपुष्पातमालगुल्मांश्च कारयेत् ।—*Ibid*, p. 225 (*sūtra* 6).

equally receives her tender care ; she has to see that it is laid out with beds of plants that yield an abundance of flowers—those that regale the nose with their sweet perfume, like the *mallikā*, the *jātī* or the *navamālikā*, as well as those that delight the eye like the *japā* with its crimson glory or the *kuranṭaka* (amaranth) with its unfading yellow splendour, and besides, there should be in this garden, rows of shrubs yielding fragrant leaves or roots, like *bālaka* and *uśīra*. In the gardens there are arbors and sometimes vine-groves where she gets built ***sthaṇḍilas*** or raised platforms with pleasant and comfortable seats for rest or recreation.[1] Flowers should be spread on these seats in these sweet sylvan retreats and a swing be hung at a spot well guarded from the sun by its leafy arbor.[2] An abundance of various flowers should also be arranged with art, here and there over the residential house which must be kept scrupulously clean, the floor should be beautifully smooth and polished so as to soothe the eyes ; besides attending to these duties, the lady of the house should also see that at her abode the morning, noon and evening rites—sacrifices and gifts—are duly observed and the gods worshipped at the sanctuaries of the household ; for she must realise, as an ancient teacher, *Gonardīya*, has observed, that nothing pleases and charms the heart of a householder so much as a well-kept, neat and tidy home where the gods are respected and

1 कुब्जकामलकमल्लिकाजातीकुरण्टकनवमालिकातगरनन्द्यावर्तजपागुल्मानन्यांश्च बहुपुष्पान् वालकोशीरकपातालिकांश्च वृक्षवाटिकायां च स्थण्डिलानि मनोज्ञानि कारयेत् ।—*Ibid*, p. 225 (*sūtra* 7), also वृक्षवाटिकां सृद्धोकामण्डपं ।—*Ibid* p. 284 (*sūtra* 17).

2 स्वास्तीर्णा प्रेङ्खादोला वृक्षवाटिकायां सप्रच्छाया स्थण्डिलपीठिका च सकुसुमेति भवनविन्यासः । —*Ibid*, p. 45 (*sūtra* 15).

the religious duties well observed.[1] The mistress of the house should also see that her kitchen is situated in a quiet and retired spot and is clean and attractive.[2] The proper keeping of the house was thus the particular care of the wife of the *nāgaraka* and the erection of a noble pile of buildings is, according to our author, among the most earnest desires of women.[3]

Large and magnificent houses *harmyas* and *prāsādas*, were known to Vātsyāyana; the *nāgaraka* sometimes might enjoy moonlight on the terrace of a palace and examine the stars and planets with his beloved.[4] The walls of the houses were sometimes beautifully polished so as to reflect the image of a girl, and not infrequently the roof of the house stood on pillars, *stambhas.*[5] The *Buddhacarita* mentions an iron pillar and the *Saundarananda Kāvya* speaks of a pillar of gold and also of a minor support or *upastambha.*[6] The floor of a palace was sometimes decorated with mosaic work, being inlaid with coral or with precious stones. In the palace-gardens there were *samudra-gṛhas* or cool summer-houses surrounded by water, washed as it were, by the sea, and also rooms in the walls of which there were secret

1 वेश्म च शुचि सुसंमृष्टस्थानं विरचितविविधकुसुमं श्लक्ष्णभूमितलं हृद्यदर्शनं त्रिषवणाचरितबलिकर्म पूजितदेवायतनं कुर्यात्। न ह्यतोऽन्यद् गृहस्थानां चित्तग्राहकमस्तीति गोनर्दीयः।—Ibid, p. 224 (*sūtra* 3).

2 महानसं च सुगुप्तं स्याद्दर्शनीयं च।—Ibid, p. 227 (*sūtra* 18).

3 गृहस्योदारस्य करणं महार्हैर्भाण्डैः परिचारकैश्च गृहपरिच्छदस्योज्ज्वलता।—Ibid, p. 341 (*sūtra* 26).

4 हर्म्यतलस्थितयोर्वा चन्द्रिकासेवनार्थमासनम्।—Ibid, p. 174 (*sūtra* 19).

5 आदर्शे कुड्ये सलिले वा प्रयोज्यायाश्छायाचुम्बनमाकारप्रदर्शनार्थमेव कार्यम्।—Ibid, p. 110 (*sūtra* 30) ; तदेव कुड्यसन्दंशेन स्तम्भसन्दंशेन वा स्फुटकमवपीडयेदिति पीडितकम्।—Ibid, p. 96 (*sūtra* 13).

6 स्तम्भमायसम्—*Buddhacarita*, xiv, 12 ; सुवर्णस्तम्भवर्माणः।—*Saundarananda Kāvya*, i. 19 ; उपस्तम्भः पिपतिषोर्दुर्बलस्येव वेश्मनः।—Ibid, xiv, 15.

20

passages for water to circulate and take away the heat.[1] Bhāsa's *Svapna-Vāsavadattam* (Act V) has such a *samudra-gṛha*, and in later dramas also it is not rare; the *Viṣṇu-Smṛti* (V. 117) prescribes punishment for a *samudragṛha-bhedaka.* Secret pleasure-houses standing amidst the waters of garden tanks are referred to by Kālidāsa.[2] Besides the garden, Vātsyāyana has not given much detailed description of the *antaḥpura* or the inner sanctum of the ladies. Bhāsa designates it as the inner court with apartments or houses on four sides (*abhyntara-catuḥśālā*), which suggests the plan of construction of the inner apartments of an Indian house from very ancient times.[3] This plan combined the advantages of seclusion and privacy together with provision for light and air.

Vātsyāyana describes with greater fulness the outer chambers which the master called particularly his own and where he spent by far the greater portion of his day and night. An examination of the furniture and equipments of these chambers will give us an insight into the life of the man of wealth and fashion in the third century after Christ. The articles that Vātsyāyana first draws attention to, in the master's apartment, are two couches with beds, soft and comfortable and spotlessly white, sinking in the middle, and having rests for the head and feet at the top and the bottom. At the head of his bed is a *kūrca-sthāna*, a stand or perhaps a niche for placing an image of the deity that he worships, as the commentary, Jayamaṅgalā explains; besides, at the head there is also an elevated shelf serving the purposes of

1 बहि: प्रवालकुट्टिमं ते दर्शयिष्यामि मणिभूमिकां वृक्षवाटिकां मृद्वीकामण्डपं समुद्रगृहप्रासादान् गूढभित्तिसंचारांश्चित्रकर्माणि ।—*Kāmasūtra*, pp. 283-84 (*sūtra* 17).

2 दीर्घिका: गूढमोहनगृहा: ।—*Raghuvaṃśa*, xix. 9.

3 प्रविश्यतामभ्यन्तरचतु:शालम् ।—Bhāsa, *Cārudatta*, ed. by T.Gaṇapati Śāstrī, Act I. See also *Catuḥśāla* in Bhāsa's *Avimāraka*, Trivandrum Sans. Series, pp. 23, 42, 86.

a table whereon are placed articles necessary for his toilet in the early dawn, namely, fragrant ointments such as sandal-paste, a garland of flowers, small pots containing bees' wax and sweet perfumes, the skin of the *mātuluṅga* or the citron fruit for perfuming the mouth and also betel-leaves prepared with spices and scents. On the floor is a vessel for catching the spittle (*patadgraha*). On the wall, on brackets (elephants' tusks—*nāgadantaka*) are ranged his *vīṇā*, the national instrument of music in ancient India, a casket containing brushes and other requisites for painting, a book—preferably a poetical work—and garlands of the yellow amarnath (*kuranṭaka*), chosen because it does not fade or wither soon and therefore is good for decorating the rooms. Not far from the couch, on the floor, is spread a carpet with cushions for the head, and besides, there are boards for playing at chess and dice. Outside the room is the *nāgaraka*'s aviary where are hung cages of birds for game and sport;[1] we read in the *Buddhacarita* that the birds in such household aviaries in the city of Kapilavastu were disturbed by the hurried movements of ladies hastening to catch a glimpse of the young prince Siddhārtha as he passed along the street.[2] At a somewhat retired spot in the house are places where our *nāgaraka* amuses himself by working at the lathe or the chisel.[3]

THE DAILY LIFE OF THE NĀGARAKA

Vātsyāyana has left us a description of the occupation of the *nāgaraka* during the whole of the day, which though brief,

1 बाह्ये च वासगृहे सुश्लक्ष्णमुभयोपधानं मध्ये विनतं शुक्लोत्तरच्छदं शयनीयं स्यात्, प्रतिशय्यिका च। तस्य शिरोभागे कूर्चस्थानम्। वेदिका च। तत्र रात्रिशेषमनुलेपनं माल्यं सिक्थकरण्डकं सौगन्धिकपुटिका मातुलुङ्गत्वचस्ताम्बूलानि च स्युः। भूमौ पतद्ग्रहः। नागदन्तावसक्ता वीणा, चित्रफलकं, वर्तिकासमुद्गको, यः कश्चित् पुस्तकः, कुरण्टकमाला च। नातिदूरे भूमौ वृत्तास्तरणं समस्तकम्। आकर्षफलकं द्यूतफलकं च। तस्य बहिः क्रीडाशकुनिपञ्जराणि।—*Kāmasūtra*, pp. 43-45 (*sūtras* 5-13).

2 विभ्रामयन्त्यो गृहपक्षिसङ्घानन्योन्यवेगाच्च समाक्षिपन्त्यः।—*Buddhacarita*, iii. 15.

3 एकान्ते च तक्षतक्षणस्थानमन्यासां च क्रीडानाम्।—*Kāmasūtra*, p. 45 (*sūtra* 14).

yet brings up very beautifully the man of fashion of those days before our eyes. Our *nāgaraka* gets up early in the morning and after attending to his morning duties and cleaning his mouth and teeth, proceeds to his toilet. The first article in this toilet is the *anulepana*, a fragrant ointment ordinarily made of fine sandal-wood paste, or of preparations of a variety of sweet-smelling substances.[1] He applies a suitable quantity of this ointment to his person ; it would be considered bad taste if he used too much of this perfume ; he then scents his clothes in the sweet-smelling smoke of incense (*dhūpa*) thrown into the fire and wears a garland on the head, or hangs it round his neck. He applies collyrium made of various substances to his eyes. To his lips, already reddened by the betel he has chewed, he applies *alaktaka* (a red dye made from lac), to impart a deeper crimson to them and then rubs them over with wax to make the dye fast. Then he looks at himself in a glass, chews spiced betel-leaves to perfume his mouth, and proceeds to attend to his business.[2] He attends to his hair and wears rings on his fingers that are sometimes of great value.[3] He generally wears two garments, a *vāsas* or *vastra* and an *uttarīya* or a wrap for the upper part of the body. This upper garment was sometimes very highly scented with rich perfumes or flowers.[4] Bhāsa tells us that the rich fragrance of Cāru-

1 श्लक्ष्णीकृतं चन्दनमन्यद्वानुलेपनं ।—Ibid, p. 173 (*sūtra* 14).

2 स प्रातरुत्थाय कृतनियतकृत्यः, गृहीतदन्तधावनः, मात्रयाऽनुलेपनं धूपं स्रजमिति गृहीत्वा, दत्त्वा सिक्थकमलक्तकं च दृष्ट्वाऽऽदर्शे मुखम्, गृहीतमुखवासताम्बूलः कार्याण्यनुतिष्ठेत् ।—Ibid, pp. 45-46 (*sūtra* 16). Jayamaṅgalā explains—मात्रयेति, प्रभूतानुलेपनादिग्रहणादनागरकः स्यात्, कार्यानुष्ठाने प्रस्तुतत्वात् ।—p. 46.

3 अङ्गुलीयकस्य च निधानम् ।—Ibid, p. 292 (*sūtra* 20) etc. अनेकशतसहस्रमूल्यमङ्गुलीयकम् ।—*Lalita-vistara* (ed. by Lefmann), xiii. 142.

4 See *Kāmasūtra*, pp. 274, 196, etc.; also तत्र महार्हगन्धमुत्तरीयं कुसुमं चात्मीयं स्यादङ्गुलीयकं च तद्धस्तात्ताम्बूलग्रहणं गोष्ठीगमनोद्यतस्य केशहस्तपुष्पयाचनम् ।—Ibid, p. 261 (*sūtra* 21).

datta's wearing apparel assured Vasantasenā that though impoverished, he was not quite unmindful of the amenities of youthful society.[1] At Nanda's house at Kapilavastu when Buddha entered it, some of the maids were preparing the perfumed paste while others were perfuming the clothes.[2] In the *Lalita-vistara* we read that King Śuddhodana ordered that all those who would attend on Māyādevī on her journey to the garden of Lumbinī, should wear clothes, soft and fine, coloured with pleasant dyes and smelling sweet with the best of the scents. Similarly, in another place in the same book, we read of a perfumed garment of the exquisite colour of the *nāgakeśara*.[3]

Sweet scents, we thus see, played a very important part in the toilet of the *nāgaraka*. He made an abundant use of flowers, he rubbed sweet-scented ointments over his body and besides, he used other perfumes—*saugandhikas*—and a box of scents, a *saugandhika-puṭikā*, was kept handy by every *nāgaraka*. He perfumes his mouth with betel-leaves prepared with sweet-scented spices. The fragrant smoke of incense was made to circulate through his rooms and impart a perfume to his clothes. The *Lalita-vistara* corroborates Vātsyāyana about the plentiful use of perfumes. Besides the scented ointment or *anulepana*, the *Lalita-vistara* mentions scented waters of various kinds, perfumed oils and fragrant powders of sandal, flowers or other sweet-smelling things.[4] These objects—flowers, perfumes and betel-leaves

1 गणिका—(प्रावारकं गृहीत्वा सहर्षम्) अणदासीणं जीवणं से पडवासगन्धो सूएदि ।—Bhāsa, *Cārudatta* (Trivandrum Sans. Series), Act I, p. 26.

2 काचित् पिपेषान्तर्विलेपनं हि वासोऽङ्गना काचित् अवासयच्च ।—*Saundarananda-Kāvya*, iv. 26.

3 वरसुरभिसुगन्धां भावरङ्गां विचित्रां ।
वसन मृदु मनोज्ञां प्रावृणोथा उदग्रा: ॥—*Lalita-vistara* (ed. by Lefmann), vii. 80 ; शीघ्रं गृह्णत नागपुष्परुचिरां वस्त्रां सुगन्धां शुभां ।—Ibid, xviii. 282.

4 विविधगन्धोदकपूर्णघटपरिगृहीतै: ।—Ibid, xv. 218. See also ibid, vii. 96 and xiv. 269 ; दिव्यगन्धपरिवासित-तैलपरिगृहीतानि ।- Ibid, vii. 96 ; हंस्नी पुष्पागरु-तगर-चन्दन-चूर्ण-वर्षा ।—Ibid, xxi. 342.

formed the most ordinary gifts exchanged between friends and lovers.[1]

After attending to his business in the morning, the *nāgaraka* takes his bath ; this he does every day but there are other attendant circumstances that are repeated at varying intervals. Every other day he gets his limbs massaged and shampooed (*utsādana*) ; every third day he cleanses his person with soap-like substances that yield a lather with water (*phenaka*). This last was considered an indispensable article for one who aspired to decent life in those days, as we see that even when a man became too poor to maintain himself as a *nāgaraka* and became a *pīṭhamarda*, his *phenaka* or soap marked him out from ordinary men. As regards shaving, the *nāgaraka* was behind the modern man of fashion ; he got his chin and lips cleaned every fourth day and this was probably considered conducive to long life (*āyuṣyam*) and a more thorough tonsorial operation was performed every fifth or every tenth day. This completes the bath.[2] Though he was thus not so fastidious as our modern dandies as regards the hair on his face, he was certainly more careful about his finger nails. They were specially dressed, particularly those of the left hand ; the points of the nails should always be fine and sometimes they were cut into three or more teeth like a saw. The nails must be well-set, smooth, bright, scrupulously clean, not broken, and soft and glossy in appearance. The people of Gauḍa (modern Bengal) had very fine and long nails that imparted a grace to their hands and were very attractive to women, and the southerners (the *Dākṣiṇātyāḥ*) had small nails which were good for work but of which they made very great artistic use, and the people of *Mahārāṣṭra* were midway between the two. The use of the nails was a great art which

1 *Kāmasūtra*, pp. 259, 261, 274, 308, 319.

2 नित्यं स्नानं, द्वितीयकमुत्सादनं, तृतीयक: फेनक:, चतुर्थमायुष्यम्, पञ्चमकं दशमकं वा प्रत्यायुष्यमित्यहीनम् ।—Ibid, p. 46 (*sūtra* 17).

the *nāgaraka* took great pains in acquiring ; with them, he skilfully and without causing pain, affixed on his beloved, marks that might be straight, curved, circular, semicircular like the crescent moon, or which might resemble the tiger's claw, the peacock's foot, the leap of a hare or the leaf of a blue lotus.[1] Similar care was taken of the teeth and artistic use made of them, because, Vātsyāyana says, no other art increases love so much as the clever use of the nails and teeth.[2] Besides attending to the daily ablution and the other things noted above, for keeping his person clean, the *nāgaraka* must always carry a handkerchief (*karpaṭa*) with himself for removing perspiration.[3]

He takes two meals a day, in the forenoon, and the afternoon, but according to *Cārāyaṇa*, and earlier teacher, the last meal had better be taken in the evening.[4] Three kinds of hard or soft food and drinks, *bhakṣya*, *bhojya* and *peya* corresponding to the *khādanīya*, *bhojanīya* and *pāna* of the Buddhist sacred books,[5] have been mentioned by Vātsyāyana. Among his articles of diet we notice rice, wheat, barley, pulses, a large number of vegetables, milk and its preparations including *ghee*, meat and sweets, besides salt and oil. Among the sweets, we have molasses (*guḍa*) and sugar (*śarkarā*) as well as sweetmeats (*khaṇḍa-khādyāni*).[6] Fish is nowhere mentioned by our author as an article of diet. Meat was eaten boiled as soup, and dry or roasted. To desist from eating meat, as prescribed in the law books, was considered to be an act of merit (*dharma*).[7] The *nāgaraka's*

1 Ibid, pp. 112-20 (*sūtras* 1-31).

2 Ibid, pp. 121-30 (*sūtras* 1-42).

3 सातत्याच्च संवृतकक्षास्वेदापनोदः ।—Ibid, p. 47 (*sūtra* 18).

4 पूर्वाह्णापराह्णयोर्भोजनम् । सायं चारायणस्य ।—Ibid, p. 47 (*sūtras* 19 and 20).

5 *Mahāvagga*, vi. 28. 10 and vi. 35. 2.

6 See *Kāmasūtra*, pp. 228-30, 337, 369-71 ; also अन्नानुपानं वा खण्डखाद्य-कमन्यद्वा प्रकृतिसात्म्ययुक्तमुभावप्युपयुञ्जीयाताम् ।—Ibid, p. 174 (*sūtra* 16).

7 प्रवृत्तेभ्यश्च मांसभक्षणादिभ्यः शास्त्रादेव निवारणं धर्मः ।—Ibid, p. 12 (*sūtra* 7).

drinks (*pānakāni*) were also various : besides water and milk, he drank fresh juice, perhaps of the various kinds of palm, extracts of meat, *congey* (or rice gruel), *sherbets*, juice of fruits such as mangoes and citrons mixed with sugar ; of stronger drinks, he used various wines like *surā*, *madhu*, *maireya* and *āsava*,—which he drank from a *chaṣaka*, a vessel of wood or metal, often accompanied by various kinds of sweets, and savouries of bitter and acrid taste in order to impart a relish to drink.[1]

After the midday meal the *nāgaraka* enjoys his siesta, he diverts himself by pleasant talk with his friends, the *pīṭhamarda*, the *viṭa* or the *vidūṣaka*, listens to the talk of parrots, views fights between cocks, quails or rams, or is engaged in various kinds of artistic enjoyments. Besides the animals mentioned above, he also kept for his own amusement a number of cuckoos for their sweet melody and peacocks for their glorious plumage and also monkeys. At the king's palace, besides these animals of sport, lions and tigers were also kept in cages.[2]

In the afternoon, after he has dressed himself, the *nāgaraka* goes out to attend a *goṣṭhī* or a social gathering where he engages, as we shall see below, in pleasant intellectual diversions with his friends and in tests of skill in the various arts. At night-fall, our *nāgaraka* enjoys music, vocal and instrumental, occasionally attended with dances. After music, in his own room which has been made sweet and clean and gay with flowers, and while its fragrant air is charged with

1 अच्छरसकयूषमम्लयवागूं भृष्टमांसोपदंशानि पानकानि चूतफलानि शुष्कमांसं मातुलुङ्गचक्रकाणि सशर्कराणि च यथादेशसात्म्यं च। चषकहस्तः पाययेत्।—Ibid, p. 174 (*sūtras* 17 and 15) ; तत्र मधुमैरेयासवान् विविधलवणफलहरितशाकतिक्तकटुकाम्लोपदंशान् वेश्याः पाययेयुरनुपिबेयुश्च।—Ibid, p. 52 (*sūtra* 38).

2 भोजनानन्तरं शुकसारिकाप्रलापनव्यापाराः लावककुक्कुटमेषयुद्धानि तास्ताश्च कलाक्रीडाः, पीठमर्दविटविदूषकायत्ता व्यापारा, दिवाशय्या च।—Ibid, p. 47 (*sūtra* 21). मेषकुक्कुटलावकशारिका परभृतमयूरवानरमृगाणामवेक्षणम्।—Ibid, p. 229 (*sūtra* 33). क्रीडामृगान् यन्त्राणि शकुनान् व्याघ्रसिंहपञ्जरादीनि च।—Ibid, p. 284 (*sūtra* 17) ; see also p. 307 (*sūtra* 25).

the breath of sweet incense circulating through it, the *nāgaraka* with his associates and friends, awaits there the arrival of his mistress. This completes his daily life.[1]

A word here about the *nāgaraka's* friends whom we meet again and again in the *Kāmasūtra,* will not be out of place. Besides the many artists and craftsmen who served him in his quest of love and pleasure and who are called his *mitras* or companions by Vātsyāyana, the *nāgaraka* appears to have possessed some real, true and devoted friends. Vātsyāyana says that fast and genuine friendship often sprang up among those who had grown up together from infancy tended by the same nurse, who in early boyhood were fellow playmates or were at school together, those who were marked by the same temperament and the same tastes in pleasure and sport, were attached to each other by mutual obligations and whose closest secrets were known to each other. Vātsyāyana regards it particularly fortunate in friendship when the friendship has come down between two families for several generations, has never been tainted by selfishness or greed, nor has been changed by time or by any considerations whatsoever and where the mutual secrets have never been betrayed.[2]

SPORTS AND FESTIVITIES

Besides the various sports and amusements that enlivened the daily life of the *nāgaraka,* there were many high days

1 गृहीतप्रसाधनस्यापराह्णे गोष्ठीविहाराः। प्रदोषे च संगीतकानि। तदन्ते च प्रसाधिते वासगृहे संचारितसुरभिधूपे ससहायस्य शय्यायामभिसारिकाणां प्रतीक्षणं, दूतीनां प्रेषणं, स्वयं वा गमनम्।—Ibid, pp. 47-48 (*sūtras* 22-24). नागरकः सह मित्रजनेन परिचारकैश्च कृतपुष्पोपहारे सञ्चारितसुरभिधूपे रत्यावासे प्रसाधिते वासगृहे etc. सनृत्तमनृत्तं वा गीतं वादित्रं।—Ibid, p. 172 (*sūtras* 1 and 7).

2 सहपांसुक्रीडितमुपकारसंबद्धं समानशीलव्यसनं सहाध्यायिनं यश्चास्य मर्माणि रहस्यानि च विद्यात् यस्य चायं विद्याद्वा धात्रपत्यं सहसंवृद्धं मित्रम्। पितृपैतामहमविसंवादकमदृष्टवैकृतं वश्यं ध्रुवमलोभशील-मपरिहार्यममन्त्रविस्रावीति मित्रसंपत्।—Ibid, pp. 68-69 (*sūtras* 35-36); see also *sūtras* 37 and 38.

and holidays when he made merry with his friends and companions. With regard to all these games and festivities enjoyed in company, Vātsyāyana gives the sage advice that they can be relished best in the company of friends of the same social status, but not with those that are either above or below one, because permanent good relations and mutual understanding can only be established when each party in a sport seeks to afford pleasure to the other and where each is honoured and respected by the other.[1]

Vātsyāyana classifies the occasional festivities into five groups. In the first place he mentions the festivals in connection with the worship of different deities (*samāja, yātrā* and *ghaṭā*), sometimes attended with grand processions ; then come the *goṣṭhīs* or social gatherings of both sexes ; next *āpānakas* or drinking parties and *udyāna-yātrās* or garden-parties, and last of all various social diversions in which many persons take part (*samasyā krīḍā*).[2]

SAMĀJA

At the temple of *Sarasvatī*, the goddess of learning and the fine arts, on a fixed day every fortnight, that is, on the *tithi* or lunar phase specially auspicious to the deity worshipped, a *samāja* or an assemblage of *nāgarakas* was held regularly. They were accompanied by musicians, dancers and other artists permanently employed by them for performances in honour of the deity. Besides, when any itinerant parties of actors, dancers or other such "artists" visited the town, they were afforded an opportunity of showing their

1 समस्याद्याः सहक्रीडा विवाहाः सङ्गतानि च ।
समानैरेव कार्याणि नोत्तमैर्नापि वाऽधमैः ॥
परस्परसुखास्वादा क्रीडा यत्र प्रयुज्यते ।
विशेषयन्ती चान्योन्यं संबन्धः स विधीयते ॥—Ibid, p. 190 (*sūtras* 22 and 25).

2 घटानिबन्धनं, गोष्ठीसमवायः, समापानकम्, उद्यानगमनं, समस्याः क्रीडाश्च प्रवर्तयेत् ।—Ibid, p. 49 (*sūtra* 26).

skill at the temple before the divinity. On the day following the performance the party had to be given their stipulated rewards, and then they might be dismissed or asked to repeat their performances at the pleasure of their patrons. On special occasions, when performances on a grand scale were arranged, parties of actors might co-operate with each other and give a joint performance and it was the duty of the corporation or guild (*gaṇa*), to which the *nāgaraka* belonged, to honour and treat with hospitality the strangers who attended these gatherings. Similar festivities of various kinds were held on a grand scale in honour of different deities according to the customs appertaining to each.[1] On some of these occasions there were processions (*yātrā*) like the procession of images that Fa-Hien saw in Khotan when "they swept and watered the streets inside the city, making a grand display in the lanes and by-ways."[2] In these processions both men and women joined and Vātsyāyana says that they afforded opportunities for meeting one's lady-love.[3] Even a virtuous matron could attend a religious ceremony with the permission of her husband.[4]

GOṢṬHĪ

We now come to the *goṣṭhī* or social gathering where the *nāgaraka* diverts himself in pleasant talk with persons

1 पक्षस्य मासस्य वा प्रज्ञातेऽहनि सरस्वत्या भवने नियुक्तानां नित्यं समाजः। कुशीलवाश्चागन्तवः प्रेक्षणकमेषां दद्युः। द्वितीयेऽहनि तेभ्यः पूजा नियतं लभेरन्। ततो यथाश्रद्धमेषां दर्शनमुत्सर्गो वा। व्यसनोत्सवेषु चैषां परस्परस्यैककार्यता। आगन्तूनां च कृतसमवायानां पूजनमभ्युपपत्तिश्चेति गणधर्मः। एतेन तं तं देवताविशेषमुद्दिश्य संभावितस्थितयोर्विविधा घटा व्याख्याताः। —Ibid, pp. 49-51 (*sūtras* 27-33).

2 Legge, *Fa-Hien*, p. 18.

3 स तु (समागमः) देवताभिगमने यात्रायामुद्यानक्रीडायां जलावतरणे विवाहे यज्ञव्यसनोत्सवेष्व-ग्न्युत्पाते चौरविभ्रमे जनपदस्य चक्रारोहणे प्रेक्षाव्यापारेषु तेषु तेषु च कार्येषु।—*Kāmasūtra*, p. 274 (*sūtra* 41).

4 आवाहे विवाहे यज्ञे गमनं सखीभिः सह गोष्ठीं देवताभिगमनमित्यनुज्ञाता कुर्यात्।—Ibid; p. 226 (*sūtra* 15).

of the same status and position as himself by their education, intelligence, character, wealth and age; there he engages in competitions in making verses or in various other sports of skill and art.[1] Affording, as these *goṣṭhīs* did, opportunities for the *nāgaraka* to exhibit his intellectual accomplishments and mastery of the arts, they were most popular with him, being attended by him every afternoon and they were also held on a comparatively large scale on special occasions. Of the branches of literary art in which competitions were held, we may glean the following from Vātsyāyana's list of the sixty-four arts: there were competitions in the extempore composition of verses, completion of a stanza of which a part only was given, the proper reading of books, with proper intonation and accent, either singly or in groups, the reading of passages in prose or verse that on account of many harsh sounds were hard to pronounce, and the art of composing and expounding passages written in a secret code or cypher. These competitions required knowledge of foreign tongues and provincial dialects, knowledge of lexicons and specical vocabularies, of metres and the figures of rhetoric, the knowledge of dramas and their stories, in short, a very comprehensive litererary and artistic training. One game is described called *pratimālā* in which a number of persons had to recite verses one after another, the condition being that every reciter must repeat a verse commencing with the letter with which the previous speaker's verse ended and any one unable to supply his verse sufficiently quickly had to pay a forfeit. Besides these literary competitions, there were tests of proficiency in the fine arts such as painting, singing, instrumental music and the like and also of manual skill and dexterity in many of the practical arts such

1 वेश्याभवने सभायामन्यतमस्योदवसिते वा समानविद्याबुद्धिशीलवित्तवयसां सह वेश्याभिरनुरूपैरालापैरासनबन्धो गोष्ठी। तत्र चैषां काव्यसमस्या कलासमस्या च।—Ibid, p. 51 (*sūtras* 34 and 35).

as the stringing together of flowers in a garland and so on.[1]

At these gatherings were invited *gaṇikās* or brilliant artists who by their education and knowledge of the arts, could please the *nāgaraka* by meeting him on his own ground, viz., in mental and aesthetic culture, and who were therefore loved and honoured by the people. Sometimes the parties were held at the house of one of the *gaṇikās*, or the *nāgarakas* met at each other's house, or they assembled in the *sabhā*, the public hall of the city or of the *gaṇa* or corporation to which every citizen belonged. Here the citizens came together to discuss politics and philosophy, or to hold competitions in literature or art, or merely to enjoy themselves in convivial parties. This *sabhā* of Vātsyāyana is the direct descendant of the *samiti* or *pariṣad* of the Vedic times, at one of which, viz., that of the *Pañcālas*, Śvetaketu Āruṇeya, who is reputed to be the founder of the science of erotics, was defeated by a Kṣatriya.[2]

At the *goṣṭhīs* were also discussed the sixty-four *Pañcāla* or *kāma-kalās* and Vātsyāyana declares that a person possessing a knowledge of this sixty-four, even though devoid of all the other sciences, leads the talk at the *goṣṭhīs* of men and women; and on the other hand, a person who speaks cleverly on other subjects but knows not the sixty-four, is not much respected in the discussions in the assembly of the learned.[3]

1 मानसी काव्यक्रिया, काव्यसमस्यापूरणम्, पुस्तकवाचनम्, संपाठ्यम्, दुर्वाचकयोगाः, म्लेच्छितविकल्पाः, देशभाषाविज्ञानम्, अभिधानकोषः, छन्दोज्ञानम्, नाटकाख्यायिकादर्शनम्, प्रतिमाला। गीतम्, वाद्यम्, नृत्यम्, आलेख्यम्; माल्यग्रन्थनविकल्पाः, शेखरकापीडयोजनम्, etc.—Ibid, p. 32.

2 तस्यामुज्ज्वला लोककान्ताः पूज्याः प्रीतिसमानाश्चाहारिताः; Ibid, p. 52 (*sūtra* 36). For Śvetaketu, see ibid, p. 5 (*sūtra* 9); also, श्वेतकेतुर्ह वा आरुणेयः पंचालानां परिषदमाजगाम; *Bṛhadāraṇyakopaniṣad* vi. 2. 1, and श्वेतकेतुर्हारुणेयः पंचालानां समितिमियाय; *Chāndogyopaniṣad*, v. 3. 1.

3 ब्रुवन्नप्यन्यशास्त्राणि चतुःषष्टिविवर्जितः।
विद्वत्संसदि नात्यर्थं कथासु परिपूज्यते॥

At the *goṣṭhī* one is neither to speak too much in Sanskrit for he may then be considered a pedant, just as in England two centuries ago to write English in strict accordance with orthography and syntax was considered not necessary for a gentleman ; nor should the *nāgaraka* speak too much in a local dialect, because then he ran the risk of being regarded as uneducated and uncultured ; he should strike a middle course and have full control over both and then he was sure to win great respect.[1] The prevalent language of the period as seen in inscriptions and in the Mahāyāna literature, bears testimony to the fact that the current speech at the time, at least among the cultured classes, was a mixture of Sanskrit and Prakrit. The learned people like Aśvaghoṣa, of course, wrote pure Sanskrit, but the language of conversation among the educated was apparently a mixture of Sanskrit and the provincial dialect (*deśabhāṣā*) as recommended by the author of the *Kāmasūtra*.

There were *goṣṭhīs* for sinister purposes too in the days of Vātsyāyana who warns the *nāgaraka* against frequenting an assembly that is disliked by the people, that is not governed by proper rules and hence is likely to indulge in license or to run beyond the bounds of decency ; nor should he attend a *goṣṭhī* that is intent upon doing mischief to others. A person wins success in life by attending an association that makes the imparting of pleasure to people its sole business and has sport and diversion for its sole object.[2]

वर्जितोऽप्यन्यविद्याभिरेतया यस्त्वलंकृतः ।
स गोष्ठ्यां नरनारीणां कथास्वग्रं विगाहते ॥—*Kāmasūtra*, p.182 (*sūtras* 50-51).

1 नात्यन्तं संस्कृतेनैव नात्यन्तं देशभाषया ।
कथां गोष्ठीषु कथयंल्लोके बहुमतो भवेत् ॥—Ibid, p. 58 (*sūtra* 50).

2 या गोष्ठी लोकविद्विष्टा या च स्वैरविसर्पिणी ।
परहिंसात्मिका या च न तामवतरेद् बुधः ॥
लोकचित्तानुवर्तिन्या क्रीडामात्रैककार्यया ।
गोष्ठ्या सह चरन् विद्वांल्लोके सिद्धिं नियच्छति ॥—Ibid, p. 58 (*sūtras* 51-2).

The *goṣṭhī* on account of its association with art, refinement and culture, was much appreciated by the people in Vātsyāyana's times. A *nāgaraka* was expected to be liberal in spending on *goṣṭhīs* and his success in courtship and love depended in no small measure on his power to shine in the sports and festivities including the *goṣṭhī* and *samāja*.[1] In Bhāsa's dramas we meet with many references to *goṣṭhī*; his ***Avimāraka*** mourns the supposed loss of his friend who was humorous at goṣṭhīs.[2]

Women also met together in *goṣṭhīs* or social assemblies among themselves. For an unmarried girl it was considered a qualification that she was fond of *goṣṭhīs* and *kalās*. Married ladies also sometimes, with the permission of their husbands, instituted among their own friends *goṣṭhīs* or social gatherings where they discussed artistic and literary matters. But a married woman who was too fond of instituting *goṣṭhīs* was looked upon with suspicion, specially one who arranged such gatherings in the house of a youthful neighbour.[3] In Bhāsa's *Avimāraka* (Act V) the maids invite the *Vidūṣaka* to recount a story which they would listen to among their *goṣṭhījanas* in the inner court.[4]

ĀPĀNAKA

Besides the *goṣṭhīs* the *nāgarakas* also met at each other's house to hold drinking parties where they drank various kinds of liquors with sauces of various tastes and flavours, but

1 कविराख्यानकुशलो—विविधशिल्पज्ञो—घटागोष्ठीप्रेक्षणकसमाजसमस्याक्रीडनशीलो — श्रमसह इति नायकगुणाः ।—Ibid, p. 302 (*sūtra* 12).

2 गोष्ठीषु हास्यः, Trivandrum Series, p. 69.

3 गोष्ठीकलाप्रिया चेति नायिकागुणाः—*Kāmasūtra*, p. 303 (*sūtra* 13); सखीभिः सह गोष्ठीं ।—p. 226 (*sūtra* 15); तरुणप्रातिवेश्यगृहे गोष्ठीयोजिनी ।—p. 254 (*sūtra* 52).

4 इमं गच्छिय चउस्सालं पविसिय गोट्ठीजणेन सह वुत्तन्तं सुणामि, Trivandrum Series, p. 86 मूढ़ बह्मण चउस्साले उवविसिय गोट्ठीजणेन सह सुणामि, p. 87.

abstention from wine was considered a special qualification in a *nāgaraka.*[1]

GARDEN PARTIES

Next we come to another diversion which was very dear to the soul of the *nāgaraka*, viz, *udyāna-yātrā* or picnics in gardens. Every great city in those days was surrounded by extensive gardens where the residents of the city could find some relief from the congested streets of the town. Round Kapilavastu, says the *Lalitavistara,* five hnudred gardens sprang up for the diversions of Bodhisattva, and prince Siddhārtha went out through the gates of the city for enjoying himself in the gardens outside.[2] In the *Kāmasūtra* also we find that these gardens were outside the town and a whole day was spent in the picnic there. Early in the morning a party of well-dressed *nāgarakas* would go out of the town mounted on horses accompanied by *gaṇikās* and followed by servants ; there they would arrange for their daily meal and pass the time in pleasant games of chance or in diverting themselves with the fights of cocks, quails or rams or in any other way that they pleased, in the afternoon they would return wearing some token of remembrance of the picnic such as a bunch of flowers or a twig from a garden-tree. Similar parties were enjoyed in connection with sports in water, which took place in artificial lakes or tanks from which all mischievous water-animals had first been removed.[3] Picnicking in the

1 See footnote 1, p. 160 and footnote 1, p. 167.

2 पञ्च चोद्यानशतानि समन्तान्नगरस्य प्रादुर्बभूवुर्बोधिसत्त्वस्य परिभोगाय ।—*Lalita-vistara*, (ed. by Lefmann), vii. 95 ; बोधिसत्त्वस्य पूर्वेण नगरद्वारेणोद्यानभूमिमभिनिष्क्रामतो महता व्यूहेन etc. Ibid, xiv. 183-191.

3 पूर्वाह्ण एव स्वलंकृतास्तुरगाधिरूढा वेश्याभिः सह परिचारिकानुगता गच्छेयुर्दैवसिकीं च यात्रां तत्रानुभूय कुक्कुटलावकमेषयुद्धद्यूतैः प्रेक्षाभिरनुकूलैश्च चेष्टितैः कालं गमयित्वाऽपराह्णे गृहीततदुद्यानोपभोगचिह्नास्तथैव प्रत्याव्रजेयुः । एतेन रचितोद्ग्राहोदकानां ग्रीष्मे जलक्रीडागमनं व्याख्यातम् ।—*Kāmasūtra*, p. 53 (*sūtras* 40-41).

gardens outside the city was very popular in the days of Vātsyāyana who again and again speaks of it. His description of *udyānayātrā* agrees in every particular with that given in *mṛcchakaṭika*, the only difference being that in the drama, Cārudatta goes out in a bullock-cart instead of on horseback. A *nāgaraka's* liberality was often tested by his readiness to spend on these garden picnics and dramatic performances. A king who has many wives is advised by Vātsyāyana to please every one of them by such shows and garden-parties.[1] Unmarried girls, and even married women, sometimes went to these picnics; a virgin on her way to a garden-party was sometimes snatched away from her friends and guardians for the purposes of marriage.[2] Ladies perhaps went on such picnics in parties of their own sex, because Vātsyāyana says that *udyāna-yātrās* afforded opportunities for meeting and making offers of love to them.[3] But picnics arranged by married women appear to be rather rare. It was only a *punarbhū*, that is, a widow who had attached herself to a second husband, that induced her adopted lover to institute these picnics and convivial assemblies at which she herself took part.[4]

SAMASYĀ-KRĪḌĀ

Last of all we come to the sports that Vātsyāyana calls *samasyā-krīḍā* or *saṃbhūya-krīḍā*, that is social diversions in which a number of persons took part. He says that they varied with each country and province. Of about a score of them he has given only the names from which their character may sometimes be surmised. Some of them are well-known

1 प्रेक्षोद्यानत्यागशील: ।—Ibid, p. 253 (*sūtra* 50); उद्यानगमनैः—एकैकामनुरञ्जयेत् ।—Ibid, p. 245 (*sūtra* 89).

2 ग्रामान्तरमुद्यानं वा गच्छन्तीं विदित्वा सुसंभृतसहायो नायकस्तदा रक्षिणो वित्रास्य हत्वा वा कन्यामपहरेदिति विवाहयोगाः ।—Ibid, p. 222 (*sūtra* 27).

3 Ibid, p. 258 (*sūtra* 6); also p. 274 (*sūtra* 41).

4 Ibid, p. 239 (*sūtra* 44); also p. 240 (*sūtra* 59).

22

up to the present day, at least in parts of India, such as *Kaumudī-jāgara*, in which the whole night of the full moon in the month of Āśvina is passed without sleep by playing at dice or similar other amusements, and the *Holākā* or *Holi* on the day of the vernal full moon in the month of Phālguna; such is also the *Ālola-caturthī* or *Hindolotsava* in the month of Śrāvaṇa. The *Hallīsaka*, accompanied by dancing and music and supposed to be similar to the *Rāsotsava* described in the *Bhāgavata-Purāṇa*, is referred to by Vātsyāyana and a form of it is still current in Kāthiāwāḍ. The festival of *Suvasantaka* reminds us of the *Dule-vasaṃtiyā* of the Sitabenga Cave-Inscription which tells us that at this "swing-festival of the vernal full-moon, frolic and music abound and people tie around their necks garlands thick with jasmine flowers."[1] We are also reminded of the *Kāmadevānuyāna* of Bhāsa's *Cārudatta* (Act I) and of the *Madanodyāna-yātrā* of Bhavabhūti's *Mālatī-Mādhava* (Act I). It appears that persons of both sexes took part in many of these festivities. At such festivals as *Kaumudī-jāgara*, *Suvasantaka* and *Aṣṭamī Candraka*, the women of the cities and towns entered the harem of the king and sported with the royal ladies there.[2]

SPORTS OF GIRLS

Some of the sports of girls have been described by Vātsyāyana, as well as some of their playthings. The girls took delight in making garlands of flowers, building small houses of earth, of wood, playing with dolls, or in cooking imaginary food with such materials as earth etc. They sometimes played games of chance with dice or cards, or other games

1 Dr. T. Bloch, "Rāmgarh Cave Inscriptions," *Report of the Arch. Sur. of India* (1903-1904), pp. 124-25.

2 See *Kāmasūtra*, p. 54 (*sūtra* 42) and p. 283 (*sūtra* 11); for *Hallīsaka* cf. हल्लीसकक्रीडनकैर्गायनैर्नाट्यरासकैः ।—p. 175 (*sūtra* 25) and see *East and West*, i, pp. 748ff. (May, 1902).

like "odd and even," the game of "close fists" and so on; or they might play the game of finding out the middle finger or the sport with six pebbles; sometimes a number of girls played together at games involving some exercise of the limbs (*Kṣveḍitakāni*) such as hide and seek, spinning round holding each other's out-stretched arms, blindman's buff, games with salt or heaps of wheat.[1] We see from this list that many of these sports and games are much the same as those in vogue at the present day among Indian girls and boys.

The games and festivities of the *nāgaraka* are, as we see from the description given above, the diversions of a seeker after pleasure and amusement—of one that had plenty of leisure to enjoy and an ample fortune to provide the means of enjoyment. Among manly sports, wrestling matches were known to Vātsyāyana, but the *nāgaraka* appears to have been rather a spectator at these games than one who took an active part in them; the *Kāmasūtra* also speaks of hunting as a pastime that becomes a source of pleasure by practice, when one has acquired some skill in it and this seems to be the one manly sport that the *nāgaraka* knows of.[2]

1 *Kāmasūtra*, p. 201 (*sūtras* 5-7).

2 मल्लयोर्युद्धं—Ibid, p. 84 (*sūtra* 57); प्रीतिः साभ्यासिकी ज्ञेया मृगयादिषु कर्मसु।—Ibid, p. 90 (*sūtra* 2).

THE POSITION OF WOMEN

THE NĀGARAKA'S WIFE

While the life of a *nāgaraka* has been painted by Vātsyāyana as a round of pleasures, that of his wife presents a striking contrast and is a round of duties. The picture presented by him of a wife is in no way inferior to the ideal held up in the *Dharmaśāstras* and in many respects he gives greater details.[1] She attends on her husband with all the love and devotion a devotee shows to the deity he worships. She ministers to his personal needs, looks after his food and drink, as well as his toilet and his amusements; she tries to appreciate his likes and dislikes, welcomes his friends with proper presents, respects and loves his parents and relatives and is liberal to his servants; when she finds that he is coming home, she hastens to meet him and waits upon him herself; in his games and sports she follows him; even when offended, she does not speak too bitterly to him. She may attend a festive assembly only with his permission and in the company of her friends. She does not even give away anything without his knowledge. She should do nothing that might rouse his suspicion against her fidelity; she should avoid the company of women of questionable character such as female ascetics, actresses,

1 For the section of the *Kāmasūtra* dealing with the character of the virtuous wife see pp. 224-46. This section has not been dealt with here in detail as the whole of it has been translated by Prof. P. Peterson in his paper on "Vātsyāyana on the Duties of a Hindu Wife," read before the Anthropological Society of Bombay (16th December, 1891) and published in the *Journal of the Anthro. Soc. of Bom.* 1892, pp. 459-66. The same learned Professor has written upon "Courtship in Ancient India," as given in the section of the *Kāmasūtra* dealing with it (*Jour. Bom. Br. R.A.S.* xviii), and hence, we have omitted a consideration of that section including the rules of marriage.

fortune-tellers, or women given to the practice of black art (*mūlakārikā*), nor should she loiter about in solitary parts of the house. She might take lessons in the *Kāmasūtra* or in the subsidiary arts, if her husband so wishes, and he may occasionally himself give these lessons.[1] One is here reminded of Bhāsa's *Udayana* who calls his beloved queen "his dear disciple,"[2] and of the beautiful line of Kālidāsa (with whom our author has so many points of contact) where Aja mourns the loss of Indumatī, his "beloved pupil in the fine arts."[3]

There is an atmosphere of control and restraint about her. In her talk she is moderate and never speaks or laughs aloud; she does not return an answer when reproved by her husband's parents. She does not give herself airs when she enjoys great good fortune. In her dress she practises moderation: when going out on festive occasions, she wears a few ornaments and only a few garments of fine and soft texture, uses perfumes and ointments very moderately and adorns herself only with white flowers. But when she is going to meet her husband, she takes the greatest care with her toilet; then she makes herself tidy, sweet and clean, she puts on many ornaments, wears flowers of various hues and smells, uses perfumes and in every way makes herself attractive. Flowers were worn in garlands hanging from the neck (*sraj*), or in chaplets (*āpīḍa*) on the head, or were simply put in the hair,[4] or in elaborate ornaments for the ears (*karṇapūra* or *karṇapatra*). Another item of a woman's toilet was the paint or the dots and patches on the forehead and cheeks,

1 *Kāmasūtra*, p. 28 (*sūtras* 2 and 3); p. 197 (*sūtra* 36), and चतुःषष्ट्यां शिष्यत्वम् । p. 310 (*sūtra* 9).

2 Bhāsa's *Svapnavāsavadattam*, Act V, हा प्रिये, हा प्रियशिष्ये etc.

3 प्रियशिष्या ललिते कलाविधौ ।—*Raghuvaṃśa*, viii. 57.

4 प्रकीर्यमाणकेशकुसुमा—*Kāmasūtra*, p.152 (*sūtra* 3); केशेषु कुसुमन्यासैः Bhāsa, *Cārudatta*, Act I,

put on in various designs (*viśeṣaka*). Sometimes leaves of such plants as *tamāla* were used with it, as we find in the *Saundarananda-Kāvya*.[1] Vātsyāyana advises a wife never to present herself before her husband without some ornaments on her person even when alone with him.[2] This idea is found in Indian literature as early as the time of Yāska, who says, "to the man who understands her meaning, the Veda shows herself as a loving wife shows herself to her husband in all her rich apparel." As Yāska here is quoting a verse of the *Ṛgveda* where it occurs at least four times, the idea belongs to the very earliest period of Indian thought.[3] But when the husband is away from home the wife goes, as it were, into mourning; she puts away all her ornaments and finery with the exception of those that mark her married condition, such as the bangles of shells, only one on each wrist.[4] At that time she also practises fasts and austerities in honour of the gods and does not go to visit even the near relatives except in very urgent cases when they are in some danger, or when there are some festivities there, and even then, she must not change her quiet dress indicating the separation (*pravāsa-veṣa*); and she should never go there but in the company of her husband's people and must not stay there long. When the husband returns home she goes to meet him as she is, then she worships the gods, specially Kāmadeva, the god of love, and offers gifts of food to men and birds.

1 *Kāmasūtra*, p. 124 (*sūtra* 19); p. 206 (*sūtra* 32); also *Saundarananda Kāvya*, chap. iv.

2 नायकस्य च न विमुक्ताभूषणं विजने संदर्शने तिष्ठेत् ।—*Kāmasūtra*, p.226 (*sūtra* 13)

3 Quoted by Prof. Peterson in *Journal of the Anth. Soc. of Bom.*, 1891, p. 463. The Vedic passage is जायेव पत्य उशती सुवासाः, *Ṛv.* i. 124. 7; see also iv. 3. 2; x. 71. 4 and x. 91. 13. Cf. also जाया पतिमिव वाससा *Av.* xviii. 2. 51.

4 *Kāmasūtra*, p. 231 (*sūtra* 43), also एकं शङ्खवलयं वा धारयेत्, pp. 315-16 (*sūtra* 44).

Ordinarily also it is the wife who looks after the performance of the daily worship of gods at the household temple and the due performance of rites and the offering of gifts at the three fixed periods in the day—morning, mid-day and evening. She takes upon herself the observance of the vows and fasts that fall to the share of her husband. Sometimes the lady vowed gifts and offerings to the gods, and when her lord acquired some wealth, or obtained success in any venture, or regained his health after some illness, she carried out her vow.[1] To institute the worship of some deity was one of the dear desires of the women.[2] The qualities enumerated by Śuddhodana as requisite for a bride for the young Siddhārtha[3] are very much the same as those in the picture given above by Vātsyāyana of a virtuous and devoted wife.

With the permission of her husband the wife takes upon herself the whole care and management of the family. She prepares a budget for the whole year and regulates the expenditure in proportion with the annual income. She must also know how to keep the daily accounts and total up the daily receipts and expenditure ; Manu also lays down that the husband should appoint the wife to receive and spend the wealth, by keeping accounts, as Medhātithi explains.[4] When the husband is inclined to spend beyond his means, or to run into improper expenditure, she remonstrates with him in secret. She lays in a stock of all articles necessary for consumption and replenishes her stores at the proper season. She knows how to calculate and pay the wages and

1 तस्यार्थाधिगमेऽभिप्रेतसिद्धौ शरीरोपचये वा पूर्वसंभावित इष्टदेवतोपहारः ।—Ibid, p. 311 (*sūtra* 20).

2 देवतानां पूजोपहारप्रवर्त्तनम् ।—Ibid, p. 340 (*sūtra* 25).

3 *Lalita-vistara*, chap. xii, 138ff.

4 सांवत्सरिकं आयं संख्याय तदनुरूपं व्ययं कुर्यात् । दैवसिकायव्ययपिण्डीकरणमिति च विद्यात्—*Kāmasūtra*, p. 229 (*sūtras* 32-33) ; अर्थस्य संग्रहे चैनां व्यये चैव नियोजयेत् ।—*Manu* x. 11 where Medhātithi explains संग्रहः, संख्यादिना परिच्छिद्य रक्षार्थं वेश्मनि निधानम् ।

salaries of the servants, has to look after agriculture and cattle, and also to take care of the animals and birds kept for sport by the master of the house. We have seen that the garden also is a special charge of the lady of the house. When the husband is absent from home she also looks after his affairs and tries to administer them carefully so that they may not suffer by his absence; on such occasions she endeavours to minimise the expenditure to the best of her power and to increase the resources of the family by sales and purchases carried on through trusty servants. She has to attend to the kitchen, and besides, she employs her leisure in spinning cotton and also in doing some weaving.

POOR WOMEN

Many of the poorer women,—widows, helpless women, or those who had adopted the ascetic's vow (*pravrajitā*), earned a living by spinning and weaving as at the time of Kauṭilya, and got their wages from a government officer, the *Sūtrādhyakṣa*, "the Superintendent of Yarn," and the sales and purchases were made with the *Paṇyādhyakṣa*, "the Superintendent of Manufactures." In the villages, the peasant women did various kinds of work under the control of the government officer (*Āyuktaka*) in charge of the village or the headman who lived upon a share of the agricultural produce. Under his orders these women perform unpaid work (*viṣṭi*) for him, they fill up his granaries, take things in or out of his house, clean and decorate his residence, or work in his fields; they also take from him cotton, wool, flax or hemp for spinning yarn and the bark of trees, or thread, for preparing wearing apparel; moreover, they made with him transactions of sale, purchase or exchange of various articles. Similarly the women in dairy settlements (*vrajas*) transacted business with the *gavādhyakṣa*, "the Superintendent of Cattle."[1]

1 *Kāmasūtra*, pp. 282-83 (*sūtras* 5-10).

THE JOINT-FAMILY

The joint family system seems to have obtained in Vātsyāyana's age. The wife of the householder has to wait upon his parents and to obey them implicitly as we have already seen, and moreover, she has to show proper regard to all senior relations (*gurus*) and to his sisters as well as to their husbands. But nowhere are her duties to his brothers mentioned, though a woman with many younger brothers of her husband is referred to in one place[1] showing probably that sometimes the brothers lived together, but more often they established separate households when they got married, as it was prescribed in some of the *Dharma-śāstras*, in Manu for example, that after the death of the parents the brothers might live jointly or they might separate for the sake of increasing the *dharma*, for, if they lived separate, their spiritual merit would increase and hence separation was sanctioned by *dharma*: the meaning is that if they lived apart "each of them had to kindle the sacred fire, to offer separately the *agnihotra*, to perform the five great sacrifices and so forth, and hence each gains merit separately." This principle had been recognised from very early times as we have it clearly laid down by *Gautama*, the author of the earliest of the extant *Dharmasūtras*.[2]

POLYGAMY

Polygamy appears to have been prevalent in Vātsyāyana's days among the wealthy. Kings generally considered it a privilege to have a crowded harem, a harem "with a thousand spouses" is spoken of by Vātsyāyana.[3] This is in line with what

1 ज्येष्ठभार्या बहुदेवरिका—Ibid, p. 254 (*sūtra* 52).

2 Note by Prof. Bühler on *Manu* ix. 111, *S.B.E.* xxv, p. 347. Cf. also सर्वे वा पूर्वजस्येतरान् बिभृयात् पितृवत् । विभागे तु धर्मवृद्धिः ।—*Gautama*, xxviii. 3 and 4.

3 *Kāmasūtra*, p. 41 (*sūtra* 22); also pp. 289-98.

the *Lalita-vistara* says about Māyādevī that she was the best and greatest of the thousands of women of Śuddhodana. The *Buddhacarita* mentions the same fact though not in such extravagant terms.[1] Princes, high officials and the rich also married more than one wife. Vātsyāyana says that the wealthy people had ganerally a plurality of spouses who, outwardly no doubt, appeared to enjoy many objects of pleasure, but in reality, were very miserable indeed, as the husband was but one and the claimants to his affection were many; and he gives the sage advice that it is better to have a poor husband even though he may not have many qualities to recommend him than to have a clever man whose favours have to be shared with many.[2] A single wife for a wealthy man, however, was not unknown: we read in Vātsyāyana of a *nāgaraka* who may be devoted to one wife (*ekacārin*).[3] Prince Nanda of the *Saundarananda-Kāvya* was such a person. The majority of the people appeared to have only one wife; but if she had no child, or if she bore only daughters and the continuity of the family was in danger, then the husband might marry again. In case of barrenness, Vātsyāyana counsels the wife herself to induce the husband to marry again and look upon the newly married bride as a younger sister.[4] He advises a man with many wives not to be partial, neither to show any disregard towards any one in particular, nor to allow any offence on the part of any one of them to pass unnoticed.[5]

ANTAḤPURA

We have already seen that every house had an *antaḥpura*, or inner suite of apartments where the ladies resided in seclusion, guarded against intrusion from any stranger; not even

1 शुद्धोदनस्य प्रमदा प्रधाना नारीसहस्रेष साग्रप्राप्ता—*Lalita-vistara* (ed. by Lefmann) 328. समयदेवीनिवहायदेवी बभूव मायापगतेव माया ।—*Buddhacarita*, i. 15.

2 *Kāmasūtra*, p. 217 (*sūtras* 55, 56).

3 Ibid, p. 55 (*sūtra* 43).

4 Ibid, pp. 233-4 (*sūtras* 1-5).

5 Ibid, p. 245 (*sūtras* 85-89).

women except those of approved character, were admitted within.[1] Bhāsa's *Vasantasenā* complains that she had the misfortune of not being entitled to enter into the inner courtyard of Cārudatta's house.[2] It was not considered decent for the wife of a *nāgaraka* to stand at the door and look out or to observe people in the street from her windows; even when she hastens to meet her husband coming home, she does not go out into the street or to the door but waits for him inside the house.[3] Nevertheless, on the occasion of religious festivities and processions, she could accompany the images of the gods with the permission of her husband. The inability of women to protect themselves against temptations as compared with men, is recognised by Vātsyāyana and he like Manu, condemns the absence of a restraining guardian (*niraṅkuśatva*) for a woman.[4]

The kings having a large number of wives took greater care than the ordinary *nāgaraka* in confining them in seraglios guarded by officers of proved honesty and purity. No man was allowed to enter into the royal harem except relatives and servants and in some provinces, artisans; Brāhmaṇas were allowed to get into the harem for supplying flowers to the ladies, with whom they conversed separated by a screen. There were in the harem female officers, the *kañcukīyā* and the *mahattarikā* who carried presents of garlands, perfumes and garments from the ladies to the king who also sent gifts in return. In the afternoon, the king paid a visit to the harem and met all the ladies assembled together and con-

1 Ibid, p. 244 (*sūtra* 83).

2 अभाइणी अहं अब्भन्तरप्पवेसस्स।—Bhāsa, (Trivandrum Sanskrit series), Act I, p. 26.

3 *Kāmasūtra,* p. 227 (*sūtra* 22); and p. 226 (*sūtra* 12); also द्वारदेशावस्थायिनी प्रासादाद्राजमार्गावलोकिनी।—p. 254 (*sūtra* 52).

4 Ibid, p. 249 (*sūtras* 10 and 13); also pp. 296-97 (*sūtras* 43-52); cf. *Manu*, v. 147-149 and ix. 2 and 3.

versed with them in accordance with their rank and position.[1]

EDUCATION OF WOMEN

The fact that the mistress of the house was expected to keep the daily accounts, to prepare the annual budget of receipts and expenditure, and supervise in general over the purse, proves, beyond a doubt, that women ordinarily were literate. Besides, from what Vātsyāyana says, it is apparent that an ordinary woman could receive and reply to love letters smuggled into ear ornaments, chaplets or garlands made of flowers carried by female messengers (*patrahārīdūtī*). Such love letters not infrequently contained verses and songs having special reference to the beloved and replies were obtained from her.[2] Unless women had some education, this would be without meaning.

Higher education (*śāstragrahaṇa*), however, was not so common among them, as Vātsyāyana himself says that women did not ordinarily get any education in the *śāstras*, but our author avers that the daughters of kings and nobles, as also the *gaṇikās*, were highly educated and "had their intelligence trained and sharpened by the *śāstras*," and he advises that a woman might learn either the whole or a part of the work (*śāstra*) composed by himself from a person who by character and attainments could be trusted.[3] The sixty-four subsidiary sciences that had to be studied along with the *Kāmasūtra*, included many that required, as we have seen, no inconsiderable proficiency in *belles lettres*, in the humanities in general. Such accomplishments as extempore compo-

1 Ibid, pp. 289-298 and pp. 242-44.

2 Ibid, p. 274 (*sūtras* 38-40) ; p. 276 (*sūtra* 51) : p. 279 (*sūtra* 60); also यत्र संपातोऽस्यास्तत्र···द्यर्थानां गीतवस्तुकानां···च निधानम्। प्रत्युत्तरं तया दत्तं प्रपश्येत्।—p. 292, (*sūtras* 20, 21).

3 Ibid, pp. 28-30.

sition of verses (*mānasī-kāvyakriyā*) and the completion of fragmentary verses (*kāvyasamasyāpūraṇam*) required a ready facility in versification that could be acquired only by a highly educated girl ; and such sports as *pratimālā* required the memorising of a large mass of verses and good literature. In Vātsyāyana's opinion a knowledge of the *Kāmasūtra* with its subsidiary sciences would be useful to all women, both high and low, rich and poor. A poor woman who on account of the absence of her husband, finds herself in great distress and difficulty, might earn a decent living even in a foreign country by means of the knowledge of these sciences. A woman whose husband has been away from home without making provision for her, is advised by Manu also to live by the arts, by such *śilpas* as have nothing reprehensible in them. On the other hand, Vātsyāyana affirms that, a daughter of wealthy parents, if accomplished in the arts, might win the affection of her husband even if he happens to have a large number of wives. We see, moreover, from Vātsyāyana's work, as well as from contemporary literature, that a knowledge of the arts was considered necessary for all women.[1] The bride for Prince Siddhārtha was required, according to his father, to be "versed in the sacred literature (*śāstra*) and skilled in the arts, even like a Gaṇikā."[2] The *carama-buddha* could be born only of a mother "versed in many sciences," and Māyādevī satisfied this requirement ; besides, she was well skilled in the arts.[3]

WIDOW RE-MARRIAGE

The position of a widow who wished for a second husband, has been clearly defined by Vātsyāyana. There was no regular marriage for a widow ; but if a woman who had lost

1 Ibid, pp. 32-41, cf. प्रोषितेत्वविधायैव जीवेच्छिल्पैरगर्हितैः ।—*Manu*, ix. 75.

2 शास्त्रे विधिज्ञ कुशला गणिका यथैव ।—*Lalitavistara* (ed. by Lefmann), xii. 139.

3 बहुश्रुतायाः पण्डितायाः ।—Ibid, iii. 25, कलाविचक्षणा ।—iii. 27.

her husband, was of weak character and was unable to restrain her desires, she might ally herself for a second time to a man who was a seeker after pleasures (*bhogin*) and was desirable on account of his excellent qualities as a lover, and such a woman was called a *punarbhū*. Vātsyāyana quotes the opinions of several teachers as to how far, in the selection of her second master, the *punarbhū* should be swayed by the excellence of the qualities of the man of her choice or by the chances of participating in the joys of life, and he concludes that in his opinion it was best for her to follow the natural inclinations of her own heart. The connection with her was of a loose character and she enjoyed a degree of independence unknown to the wife wedded according to sacramental rites. When the *punarahū* seeks her lover's house, she assumes the role of a mistress, patronises his wives, is generous to his servants and treats his friends with familiarity ; she chides the lover herself if he gives any cause for quarrel. She shows greater knowledge of the arts than his wedded wives and seeks to please the lover with the sixty-four *Kāmakalās*. She takes part in sports and festivities, drinking parties, garden picnics, and other games and amusements. She might leave her lover (*nāyaka*), but if she did so of her own accord, she had to restore to him all presents given by him, except the tokens of love, mutually exchanged between them ; if she is driven out, she does not give back any thing.[1]

The position of the *punarbhū* is therefore quite distinct from that of the wedded wife who participated with her husband in all religious observances and had to live with decency in the *antaḥpura* ; the position of the *punarbhū* approaches nearer to that of a mistress than that of a wedded

1 *Kamasūtra*, pp. 238-40 (*sūtras* 39-59). विधवा त्विन्द्रियदौर्बल्यादातुरा भोगिनं गुणसंपन्नं च या पुनर्विन्देत सा पुनर्भूः (*sūtra* 39) ; सौख्यार्थिनी सा किलान्यं पुनर्विन्देत (*sūtra* 41) ; सा प्रभविष्णुरिव तस्य भवनमाप्नुयात् (*sūtra* 48) ; समाजापानकोद्यानयात्राविहारशीलता चेति पुनर्भूवृत्तम् (*sūtra* 59), etc.

wife. In the king's harem where there were separate quarters and suites of chambers for the various types of women, the *punarbhūs* occupied a position midway between the *devīs* or queens who were quartered in the innermost apartments, and the *gaṇikās* and actresses in the outermost, and this exactly indicates also the position occupied by them in society. Vātsyāyana indicates this in another place where he places the *punarbhū* between the virgin (*kanyā*) and the courtesan (*veśyā*)[1] and says that the establishment of sexual relations with either the courtesans or the *punarbhūs* was not considered as right, neither was it absolutely condemned, because pleasure was the guiding motive in all such connections.[2] It is clear that in Vātsyāyana'a opinion there could not be any second marriage of the widow. Manu, whose code must have received its present from about that time, declares in unmistakable terms that in the sacred toxts concerning marriage, the re-marriage of widows was nowhere prescribed.[3] Vātsyāyana's attitude towards the question of widow-remarriage shows that in his days, public opinion allowed the widow to live with the man of her choice as his mistress, just as public opinion was not particularly nice or fastidious about making love to courtesans, but she could never receive the same regard, nor acquire the same position, as the married wife.

About the question of marriage in general, Vātsyāyana gives it as his considered opinion that for a man of any of the four *varṇas* or castes, *kāma* or desire should be provided its scope in the acceptance, according to the prescriptions of the holy writ, of a maiden who belongs to the same caste as himself and who had no contact with any one before, and this, he says, leads to progeny and to fame and is also sanctioned by popular usage ; and again, he affirms, in another connection,

1 Ibid, p. 243, (*sūtra* 78) ; and तत्र नायिकास्तिस्रः, कन्या पुनर्भूर्वेश्या च—p. 60 (*sūtra* 4).

2 वेश्यासु पुनर्भूषु च न शिष्टो न प्रतिषिद्धः सुखार्थत्वात् ।—Ibid, p. 59 (*sūtra* 3).

3 न विवाहविधावुक्तं विधवावेदनं पुनः ।—*Manu*, ix. 65.

that when a maiden of the same caste, not given to any one before, is married in accordance with the prescriptions of the holy writ, then one secures *dharma* and *artha*, affspring, high connection, an increase of friends and partisans, and also genuine, untarnished love. He further adds definitely that the contrary procedure of marrying girls of higher castes or of those who had previously been accepted by others, was absolutely prohibited, but that public opinion was indifferent with regard to connection with women of the lower castes (if not actually outside the pale of Aryan society), as also with widows and courtesans, for such relatians were not considered as amounting to marriage at all, but entered into merely for pleasure for its own sake.[1]

ANUMARAṆA

Vātsyāyana once refers to the *anumaraṇa*[2] of a woman upon the death of her lover; perhaps it has a reference to the practice of *sahamaraṇa* or dying with the husband, that is, burning herself on the same funeral pyre, but we cannot be sure about it upon such meagre evidence.

FEMALE ASCETICS

Some women also took the monastic vow like men and lived upon the charity of the people. Nuns of the three main religions of India at that time are referred to in the *Kāmasūtra*. We have the Buddhist nun *śramaṇā*, and her Jaina sister, *kṣapaṇā* or *kṣapaṇikā*; and associated with them we find the *tāpasī* whom I take to be the woman who belonging to the Brahmanic faith, has renounced the world. Besides, we read of women who had their heads shaven (*muṇḍāḥ*). All of them are generally spoken of as *pravrajitās* or *bhikṣukīs*, *i.e.*, female ascetics or mendicants. It appears, from

1 *Kāmasūtra*, p. 59 (*sūtras* 1-3); and p. 184 (*sūtra* 1).

2 सक्तस्य चानुमरणं ब्रूयात् ।—Ibid, p. 316 (*sūtra* 53).

[illegible]at Vātsyāyana says, that these female mendicant o[illegible] did not enjoy a high reputation for morality: they are included among those who are declared to be company unfit for decent married ladies.[1] Some of the mendicant women were proficient in the arts and their help was often sought by the *nāgaraka* in affairs of love; the house of the *bhikṣukī* often formed the rendezvous for lovers; she was often employed to carry messages of love and was regarded as a go-between who could easily create confidence and succeed in her mission.[2] Vātsyāyana, however, positively asserts that the love of the female ascetic was never to be sought for by a *nāgaraka*, though a former teacher had expressed a contrary view.[3] All this does not imply that female ascetics were in general considered as depraved but that some of them abused the confidence of the public and thus forfeited the respect with which they had previously been regarded, just like some of the male ascetics and mendicants who erred from the right path,[4] and we learn from Kauṭilya that the respect which the *parivrājikā* or *bhikṣukī* commanded in society was made use of in order to fish out political secrets.[5] In Bhavabhūti's *Mālatīmādhava* we find the *parivrājikā*, Kāmandakī, represented as a highly respectable lady who took great interest in the love affair between the hero and the heroine and worked hard for its fruition. This drama is an illustration, as it were, of the *Kāmasūtra*, and Bhavabhūti in this drama shows himself very well-versed in Vātsyāyana's writings.[6]

1 भिक्षुकश्रमणाक्षपणाकुलटाकुहकेक्षणिकोमूलकारिकाभिर्न संसृज्येत ।—Ibid, p. 225 (*sūtra* 9); सखीभिक्षुकीक्षपणिकातापसीभवनेषु सुखोपाय: (समागम:)—p. 274 (*sūtra* 42), etc.

2 Ibid, p. 57 (*sūtra* 48); p. 274 (*sūtra* 42); p. 364 (*sūtra* 15); p.285 (*sūtra* 25); and p. 280 (*sūtra* 62).

3 Ibid, p. 65 (*sūtra* 23); p. 67 (*sūtra* 32).

4 *Bhikṣukāḥ*, ibid, p. 300 (*sūtra* 9); *liṅgin*, p. 301 (*sūtra* 10), p. 351 (*sūtra* 28).

5 Kauṭilya, *Arthaśāstra*, i, chaps. 11 and 12.

6 Cf. भौवत्यमायोजितकामसूत्रम् ।—*Mālatīmādhava*, *Prologue*, Act i.

ARTS AND CRAFTS

The age of Vātsyāyana being characterised by very refined tastes and æsthetic perceptions, as we have seen above, there was joy and consequently beauty in life, and it was necessarily an age when the arts flourished and the crafts prospered. Vātsyāyana's *nāgaraka* is a man of varied culture and from the picture that we have obtained of his life and surrounding, of his home and friends, and of his sports and amusements, there can be no doubt that he was a great patron of the arts; in fact, it is evident that every one who aspired to be a member of cultured society, had to acquire some proficiency in poetry and music, painting and sculpture and to possess some knowledge of a host of minor arts, the twice sixty-four *kalās*[1] enumerated by our author. This knowledge of the arts was evidently an essential part of his education and without this modicum of practical acquaintance with them he would not be respected, as Vātsyāyana says, in the assemblies of the cultured and educated people.[2] The ideal *nāgaraka*, according to Vātsyāyana, was he who possessed, in addition to a healthy physique, good birth and independent means of livelihood, a knowledge of the various arts, who was learned and eloquent and was moreover, a poet, well skilled in telling stories, who was fond of all the literary and artistic competitions and festivities including *goṣṭhīs* and dramatic performances and above all, a person whose character was marked by largeness of heart and liberality, by affection and love. Skill in the sixty-four arts subsidiary to

1 The sixty-four *śilpa-kalās* and the sixty-four *pāñcālikā* or *sāmprayogika-kalās* enumerated in the *Kāmasūtra*, pp. 92-183. The former are called *karma-kalās* and the latter *kāma-kalās* in the *Lalitavistara* (Chaps. xii and xxi).

2 *Kāmasūtra*, p. 182 (*sūtras* 50-51), also p. 41 (*sūtras* 24-25).

the *Kāmasūtra* as well as a knowledge of the *Sūtras* themselves was an essential part of the qualification of every cultured man and woman.[1] To win a girl in marriage called for an exercise of many of the arts. A maiden had to be propitiated by rare and curious objects of art, by nicely recited romances and by sweet songs; if she showed a partiality for feats of "magic," her favour was to be won by performing various tricks of legerdemain; if she manifested a curiosity for the arts (*kalās*), her lover must demonstrate before her his skill in them; the art of gathering flowers in bouquets, or weaving them into chaplets and garlands was specially to be cultivated.[2] Tournaments in which a charming and rarely accomplished girl like Gopā was the prize of the victor (*jaya-patākā*),[3] appear to have been held in cities ruled by a semi-republican government like that of the Śākyakula. If a man was uncultured and ignorant of the arts it would be a source of great sorrow to his wife who, Vātsyāyana suggests, might herself be more proficient in them than he.[4] In the *Lalitavistara* we find that unless Siddhārtha showed his skill in some of the arts (*śilpas*), Daṇḍapāṇi Śākya refused to give his girl in marriage to him, prince though he was.[5] It may easily be imagined that art in all its forms was likely to develop and prosper in a society where men and women were inspired by such ideals, and that at the same time the sciences that analysed and minis-

1 विद्वान् कविराख्यानकुशलो वाग्मी विविधशिल्पज्ञो महोत्साहस्त्यागी मित्रवत्सलो घटागोष्टीप्रेक्षणक. समाजसमस्य: क्रीडनशीलो नीरुजोऽव्यङ्गशरीर: प्राणवानमद्यप: etc. इति नायकगुणा:—p. 302 (*sūtra* 12); also कामसूत्रे कौशलं तदङ्गविद्यासु चेति साधारणगुणा: ।—p. 303 (*sūtra* 14).

2 Ibid, pp. 202-203 (*sūtras* 11-18).

3 दण्डपाणेश्च शाक्यस्य दुहिता गोपा नाम शाक्यकन्या जयपताका स्थापिताऽभूत्—*Lalita-vistara*, xii, 144.

4 *Kāmasūtra*, p. 254 (*sūtra* 52).

5 अस्माकञ्चायं कुलधर्म: शिल्पज्ञस्य कन्या दातव्या नाशिल्पज्ञस्येति । कुमारश्च न शिल्पज्ञ......तत् कथमशिल्पज्ञायाहं दुहितरं दास्यामि ।—*Lalitavistara*, xii, 143.

tered to the manifold forms of artistic expression of this highly intellectual and cultured community also grew and were assiduously pursued. Not only erotics, to which Vātsyāyana devoted himself, but also the sciences of æsthetics and poetics received a great impetus during this period. Bharata's *Nāṭyaśāstra* appears to be a product of this age of æsthetic culture which reached its culmination in the great Kālidāsa, the most careful student of Bharata and Vātsyāyana.

LITERARY ART

We have already had evidence of the *nāgaraka's* good taste in house-building and architecture and also of his fondness for poetry and romance. He always had a poetical work on a table in his room, and we have seen from his skill at the *gosṭhīs* where *kāvya-samasyās* or competitions in poetic skill were held every evening, that readiness in versification and a wide reading of poetical literature in general, formed the essential accomplishment of every one of the class to which he belonged. While wooing the maiden of his choice, he was expected to recite sweetly agreeable stories that would just apply to his case, or the romances of *Śakuntalā* and *Avimāraka* and of the heroes and heroines of literature who had prospered in their loves. One skilled in reciting these stories and romances had, according to Vātsyāyana, the best chance of success in love-making.[1]

PAINTING

The Pictorial art, *ālekhyaṃ*, was one of the foremost of the sixty-four *kalās* cultivated during this period. Every cultured man had in his house a drawing board, *citraphalaka*, and a vessel (*samudgaka*) for holding brushes and other requisites of painting.[2] Pictures, *citrakarma*, appear to have

1 *Kāmasūtra*, p. 203 *sūtra* 17) ; p. 218 (*sūtra* 5); p. 252 (*sūtra* 50); p. 269 (*sūtra* 2) ; p. 271 (*sūtra* 14) ; p. 302 (*sūtra* 12).

2 Ibid, p. 32 and p. 44 (*sūtra* 10).

been drawn, as the commentator of Vātsyāyana explains, both on the walls (*bhitti*) as well as on panels or boards (*phalaka*); Vātsyāyana advises a lover who wants to attract the attention of the lady whose charms have captivated him, to put in places frequented by her, paintings (probably representing himself) done on panels[1]; in another place we read of a kiss imprinted on a picture (*citrakarma*),[2] most probably on a wall. For *citrakarma* or painting, the surface of the wall appears to have been most ordinarily used in ancient India, as appears from a passage in the *Mudrārākṣasa* where the futility of the earnest efforts of a statesman is compared to "the composition of a picture (*citrakarma*) without the wall."[3] The same idea is found in the *Lalitavistara* where the daughters of Māra declare that it was easier to paint pictures on the sky than to tempt Bodhisattva.[4] Bharata clearly refers to fresco-painting by the phrase *citrakarma*; he says that the walls of the theatre-hall were to be decorated with *citrakarma* after they had been carefully plastered, coated with lime and nicely polished, the paintings consisting of the representation of male and female figures, of creeper-patterns and a record of great deeds.[5] It is fortunate that in our country where we have so few pictorial records of the past, the caves at Ajanta have preserved a

1 यत्र संपातोऽस्यास्तत्र चित्रकर्मणः···निधानम् ।—Ibid, p. 292 (*sūtra* 20).

2 Ibid, p. 111 (*sūtra* 31).

3 सैवेयं मम चित्रकर्मरचना भित्तिं विना वर्त्तते ।—*Mudrārākṣasa*, Act ii.

4 शक्य तात अन्तरीक्षे लेख्यचित्र चित्रितुं, न बोधिसत्त्व शक्य तात बोधिमण्डि चालितुम् ।—*Lalitavistara*, xxi, 312.

5 भित्तिष्वथ विलिप्तासु परिमृष्टासु सर्वतः ।
समासु जातशोभासु चित्रकर्म प्रयोजयेत् ॥
चित्रकर्मणि चालेख्याः पुरुषाः स्त्रीजनस्तथा ।
लताबन्धाश्च कर्तव्याश्चरितं चात्मभोगजम् ॥

Bhāratīya Nāṭyaśāstram (Nirṇaya-sāgara Press), Chap. ii, verses 72-74.

few frescoes, the solitary survivals of this age of prolific artistic production.

Vātsyāyana speaks also of the *ākhyānaka-paṭa*[1] which is evidently a roll of canvas containing the representation of a short story in several scenes like the *yamapaṭa* which was spread by a spy of Cāṇakya before the people in Candanadāsa's house and was exhibited by him with songs;[2] we may add that the direct descendant of this *yamapaṭa* may still be seen in the villages of Bengal. Balls with various designs painted on them in a variety of colours, as also water jugs of various elegant shapes with many paintings, are mentioned by Vātsyāyana as welcome presents to a maiden whose favours one is courting.[3] The *Lalitavistara* mentions a similar plaything for children, viz., jugs beautifully painted on the outside but containing valueless things within.[4]

According to Vātsyāyana a welcome object of presentation to maidens was a colour-box (*paṭolikā*) containing the following colours:—*alaktaka* (the red dye obtained from lac), *manaḥśilā* (red arsenic), *haritāla* (yellow orpiment), *hiṅgula* (vermillion) and *śyāmavarṇaka*; the last named appears to be a vegetable dye, black, blue or green because the word *śyāma* is used to signify all these colours. The commentator says that it means a powder used in painting, of *rājāvarta*, a mineral substance.[5] A painter surrounded by many cups (*mallakas*) of wet colours is referred to in Bhāsa's Cārudatta.[6] Jayamaṅgalā quotes a beautiful verse

1 *Kāmasūtra*, p. 269 (*sūtra* 2).

2 तहिं जमपडं पसारिअ पउत्तह्मि गीदाइं गाइदुम् ।—*Mudrārākṣasa*, Act i.

3 कन्दुकमनेकभक्तिचित्रं संदर्शयेत् ।—*Kāmasūtra*, p. 202 (*sūtra* 13). विचित्राकृतिसंयुक्तानां जलभाजनानाञ्च दानं ।—Ibid, p. 203 (*sūtra* 14).

4 इह ते बाला रज्यन्ते चित्रघटेष्विवामेध्यपरिपूर्णेष्वविद्वांसः ।—*Lalitavistara*, xv, 207.

5 पट्टोलिकानामलक्तकमनःशिलाहरितालहिङ्गुलकश्यामवर्णकादीनां दानं। *Kāmasūtra*, p. 203

6 चित्तअरो विअ बहुमल्लएहि परिवुदो ।—Bhāsa, *Cārudatta* (Trivandrum Sanskrit Series), Act ix, p. 7.

apparently from a *śilpaśāstra* about the six great requisites of painting, viz., "knowledge of appearances, correct perception, measure and structure of forms, action of feelings on forms, infusion of grace or artistic representation, similitude and artistic manner of using the brush and colours."[1] Bharata speaks of the pictorial representation of the feelings or rather sentiments, the *rasas*, by different colours, the erotic or amatory sentiment is represented by the *śyāma* or dark colour spoken of above, the sentiment of mirth by white; the piteous sentiment is grey (*kapota*) and the choleric is red, the heroic is yellowish white (*gaura*) and the terrible, black; the repulsive is blue and the amazing, yellow.[2]

SCULPTURE

Sculpture flourished as much as painting in the age of Vātsyāyana as is fully borne out by the numerous sculptural records that have come down to our time from that period. Vātsyāyana himself bears ample testimony to it: *takṣaṇa*, carving on wood or stone was one of the sixty-four arts and every *nāgaraka* had in his house implements for working at it; similarly in every house there was a lathe and other arrangements for turning which, likewise, had its place among the sixty-four kalās. Vātsyāyana does not expressly mention an image of a god, but from what he says

1 रूपभेदा: प्रमाणानि भावलावण्ययोजनम् ।
साद्दश्यं वर्णिकाभङ्ग इति चित्रं षडङ्गकमिति ॥

Kāmasūtra p. 33. The translation is by Mr. Abanindranath Tagore, the founder of the modern Bengal school of painting, who has discussed this verse in the *Modern Review*, xv, (1914), pp. 581-2.

2 श्यामो भवति शृङ्गार: सितो हास्य: प्रकीर्त्तित: ।
कपोत: करुणश्चैव रक्तो रौद्र: प्रकीर्त्तित: ॥
गौरो वीरस्तु विज्ञेय: कृष्णश्चैव भयानक: ।
नीलवर्णस्तु वीभत्स: पीतश्चैवाद्भुत: स्मृत: ॥

Nāṭyaśāstra, ch. vi, 42-43 (p. 63).

to the household temple where the gods were worshipped, of the worship offered and the gifts made to the deity to whom one was particularly devoted,[1] it is apparent that such images were familiar objects in his days. The *Lalitavistara* speaks of the numerous images of the gods that came down from their pedestals to do obeisance to the child Buddha when he made his appearance in the *Devakula*, the quarter of the palace occupied by the gods.[2] Besides these images for worship, representations in wood and stone of human beings, both male and female, *puruṣapratimā* and *strīpratimā*—were used by the class for whom Vātsyāyana wrote, for decoration and as appertenances of love. Stands for placing images, or *piṇḍoḷikās*, are mentioned by Vātsyāyana, and life-size statues in wood or stone evidently stood on them in every *nāgaraka's* house, as Vātsyāyana speaks of very familiar uses made of them by lovers who often gave an indication of their passion for a lady by slyly kissing or embracing a statue in her sight. Similar other uses of portrait-statues in the harems of kings have been indicated by Vātsyāyana.[3] In Bhāsa's *Pratimā-nāṭaka* (Act III) we read of the life-like representations of past kings ranged round a room as in a museum.

The demand for beautiful dolls and play-things of which the girls in Vātsyāyana's age appear to have been very fond, offered a vast field for the exercise of the plastic art. Vātsyāyana advises a young man trying to win the affection of a maiden to present her with dolls (*duhitṛkā*) made of wood, horn, ivory, cloth, wax, plaster or earth. Erotic pairs of human figures made of wood might also be presented; such erotic pairs (*mithunam*) cut of the leaves of trees were also sent by

1 See *Kāmasūtra*, p. 224 (*sūtra* 3) ; इष्टदेवतोपहार:—p. 311 (*sūtra* 20); देवतानां पूजोपहारप्रवर्तनम् etc.—p. 340 (*sūtra* 25).

2 अचेतन्यो देवप्रतिमा etc.—*Lalitavistara*, viii, 119.

3 *Kāmasūtra*, p. 289 (*sūtra* 3) ; p. 290 (*sūtra* 5) ; p. 203 (*sūtra* 14); also चित्रकर्मणः प्रतिमायाश्च चुम्बं संक्रान्तकमालिङ्गनं च ।—p. 111 (*sūtra* 31).

sweethearts to each other. Playthings liked by girls are miniature cooking utensils, small temples of the gods (*deva-kula-gṛhaka*), toy animals like goats or rams and playthings made of earth, split bamboo or wood, such as cages of birds. Small *vīṇās*, stands for images, ear ornaments made of wax or whatever other objects of art might be demanded by the girl of his choice, must be presented by the man courting her either openly or in secret.[1]

MUSIC

Three *kalās* appertaining to music, singing (*gīta*), playing on instruments (*vādya*) and dancing (*nṛtya*) have been given by our author the first place in the list of arts; besides, there are more—*udakavādya* or playing on cups filled with water in varying proportions and *vīṇāḍamarukavādyāni*, that is, playing on string instruments of which the chief was the *vīṇā* and also on percussion instruments represented by the *ḍamaru.*[2] This last most probably represents the earliest from which in course of time had evolved the *mṛdaṅga*, which has lately been proved by one of our eminent scientists to be the most scientifically constructed percussion instrument ever used.[3] The *mṛdaṅga* was already known to the *Mahā-vagga* and Aśvaghoṣa speaks of songs sung to the accompaniment of the *mṛdaṅga* and of music produced on *mṛdaṅgas* struck by the fingers of women, and the *Lalitavistara* mentions it again and again with other varieties of drums.[4]

1 Ibid, pp. 202-3 (*sūtras* 12-14); p. 208 (*sūtra* 4).

2 Ibid, p. 32 (*sūtra* 16).

3 Prof. C. V. Raman "The Acoustic Knowledge of Ancient Hindus," *Central Hindu College Magazine* (Benares), January, 1920, pp. 9-12.

4 भञ्जिस्सा कच्छे वीणं भञ्जिस्सा कण्ठे मुतिङ्गम्—*Mahāvagga*, i, 7, 1-2; मृदङ्गगीतैः *Buddhacarita*, i, 45; नारीकराग्राभिहतैर्मृदङ्गैः—Ibid, ii, 30, भेरीमृदङ्गपणवतूणववीणावेणु-वल्लकीसंपताडप्रभृतयस्तूर्यभाण्डाः—*Lalitavistara*, v, 40.

25

I am inclined to think that Vātsyāyana's *ḍamaruka* stands here for percussion instruments in general. The *vīṇā* even then formed the most popular of the musical instruments in India, as is apparent from the fact that it formed a necessary piece of furniture in the rooms of every *nāgaraka* on which, as we have seen, he played almost every evening. Such a *vīṇā* in the room of Nanda reminds the bereaved Sundarī of her dear absent husband,[1] and Bhāsa's Cārudatta is overwhelmed by its merits and is enthusiastic in its praises.[2] Of wind instruments, the flute made of a bamboo reed (*vaṃśa*) is mentioned by Vātsyāyana who praises it as capable of winning the heart of any girl when used in the way he prescribes.[3] In the *Buddhacarita* and *Lalitavistara* it is called *veṇu* and is generally associated with the *vīṇā*; and women play upon it.[4] We have seen that music with or without dances was enjoyed by our *nāgaraka* every evening. The *nāgaraka's* sons received lessons in music at the *gāndharvaśālā* or college of music belonging perhaps to the city or to the *gaṇa* or corporation to which he belonged. Sweet and ravishing songs delighting the ear, form, according to Vātsyāyana, the readiest means of gaining the love of a man or a woman, and sometimes songs were specially composed containing a mention of the name and the family of the lover.[5] Concerts (*tūryya*) are mentioned by Vātsyāyana, in which a party of musicians of both sexes sang and played

1 वीणाप्रभृतिश्च लीड़ा:—*Saudarananda Kāvya*, vi, 32.

2 वीणा नानासमुद्रोत्थितं रत्नम् ।—*Cārudatta* (Trivandrum Sanskrit Series), Act iii, p. 49.

3 वंशं वादयतो या शब्दं शृणोति सा वश्या भवति ।—*Kāmasūtra*, p. 379 (*sūtra* 43).

4 करलग्नवेणु—*Buddhacarita*, v, 49 ; वीणावेणु वल्लकी, etc.—*Lalitavistara*, v, 40 ; xxi, 301, etc. ; also भार्या मुदितमना: प्रसन्नचित्ता वेणुभ्यो मधुरमनोरमं रमन्ते ।—Ibid, xiii, 163.

5 *Kāmasūtra*, p. 364 (*sūtra* 15) ; p. 203 (*sūtra* 18) ; p. 312 (*sūtra* 22) ; p. 314 (*sūtra* 32).

together on various instruments. A party of such players was sometimes strengthened by its head (*raṅgopajīvin*) giving his daughter in marriage to a clever artist who could help in the concert. An actress (*ikṣaṇikā*) is mentioned by Vātsyāyana as a very good carrier of love messages,[1] because, as Cārudatta says, a person making a living by the *kalās*, like her, must be very clever at all sorts of tricks.[2] Bharata says that sometimes on the stage the female parts were acted by men and an actress sometimes acted that of a man.[3] Some actresses were maintained by the king and suitable quarters in the palace were set apart for them.[4]

CRAFTS

In a society where both men and women wore ornaments, it was quite natural that the crafts of the jewller (*maṇikāra*) and goldsmith (*sauvarṇika* or *suvarṇakāra*) should prosper. The *nāgaraka*, when going to his club or to his garden picnic, wore ornaments and the king did so on his formal visit to the queens every afternoon.[5] The statues that have come down from this age bear this out. It was, however, the demands of the ladies, who could not appear before their husbands without having ornaments on, that furnished the amplest occupation to the goldsmith and the jeweller. Some of the ladies decorated their whole person with ornaments. Those who could not afford to have pure gold ornaments had to be satisfied with those made of an inferior kind of gold alloyed with an inferior metal. Beyond a general mention of the *alaṃkāras* Vātsyāyana does not name other ornaments

1 Ibid, p. 280 (*sūtra* 62) ; p. 366 (*sūtras* 23-24).

2 *Cārudatta*, Act iii, p. 64.

3 स्त्री पुंसः प्रकृतिं कुर्यात् स्त्रीभावं पुरुषोऽपि वा etc.—Bharata, *Nāṭyaśāstra*, Chap. xii, 166ff.

4 *Kāmasūtra*, p. 243 (*sūtras* 78-79).

5 Ibid, p, 53 (*sūtra* 40) ; p. 243 (*sūtra* 75).

than rings which are very frequently referred to as tokens of love presented by lovers to each other.[1] The *Lalitavistara* mentions a ring worth several lacs and a pearl necklace that was worth many times that sum. Cārudatta's wife also had a pearl necklace given to her by her parents worth a lac.[2] The testing of jewels and coins (*rupya-ratna-parīkṣā*) was a useful art in this community and Vātsyāyana knows a *Vaikaṭika*, a diamond-cutter, whose craft was to purify or refine precious stones.[3] Plates and other vessels made of the precious metals, gold and silver, are mentioned by Vātsyāyana and were evidently often used in the houses of the rich while those made of the baser metals, copper, bell-metal or iron, were used by ordinary people ; moreover, vessels made of earth, split-bamboo, wood and skins were in very general use.[4]

Besides the jeweller, the goldsmith and the diamond-cutter, the dyer of clothes (*rañjaka*) also was an artisan who appears to have access to the inner apartments of the *nāgaraka's* house and to take orders from the ladies direct. Blue and orange (colour of the *kusumbha* flower) seem to be the dyes most fashionable ; the dyer is by preference called the *nīlīkusumbharañjaka*. The yellow dye was also perhaps generally used, though the dye obtained from turmeric (*haridrā*) provides a proverbial expression for denoting fickle, impermanent affection.[5] Sundarī, Nanda's beloved wife, is

1 सार्वाङ्गिकोऽलङ्कारयोगो, p. 341 (*sūtra* 26); मणिरत्नमालालंकरणम् ।—Ibid, p. 341 (*sūtra* 27). About rings see ibid, p. 244 (*sūtra* 80) ; p 261 (*sūtra* 21) ; p. 274 (*sūtra* 35) ; p. 292 (*sūtra* 20), etc.

2 अनेकशतसहस्रमूल्यमङ्गुलीयकम् ।—*Lalitavistara*, xii, 142 ; कोटिशतसहस्रमूल्येन च मुक्ताहारेण ।—Ibid, vii, 83ff. *Cārudatta*, p. 32.

3 *Kāmasūtra*, p. 32 (*sūtra* 16) ; p. 259 (*sūtra* 12).

4 Ibid, p. 337 (*sūtra* 7) ; p. 228 (*sūtra* 27).

5 नीलीकुसुम्भरञ्जकादिषु, etc.—Ibid, p. 259 (*sūtra* 12). हरिद्रारागो वा ।—Ibid, p. 330 (*sūtra* 17).

described as weaving a garment of the colour of the ruby (*padmarāga*) which is no doubt the same as the *kusumbha* colour of Vātsyāyana, and in the *Buddhacarita* a lady is represented as wearing a blue dress.[1] Earlier still, these very same dyes appear to have been in favour. The noble Licchavi youths who went out of Vesāli to pay their respects to the great Buddha are described in the *Mahāvagga* as wearing blue, red and yellow robes besides white ones; the same work enumerates a number of other colours being used by people living in the enjoyments of the world, though even there the blue, yellow and red are given the first place.[2] The economic housewife is described by Vātsyāyana as getting the rejected clothes of her husband cleaned and redyed and then presenting them to the servants.[3]

A number of artisans are mentioned by Vātsyāyana as helping the *nāgaraka* in the decoration of his person and thus in his quest of love, and are spoken of by Vātsyāyana as his friends: among them we find in the first place, the florist who looks after his flowerbeds, who makes garlands for his neck and chaplets for his head, and who helps him in preparing floral decorations for presentation to his beloved.[4] Next comes the perfumer (*saugandhika*) whom, as we have seen, he patronised very liberally. Then we have the goldsmith, the betel-leaf-seller, as also the washerman, the barber and the wine-seller. The women folk of these artisans were also regarded by him as his friends (*mitrāṇī*).[5] This establishment of friendly relations between the wealthy *nāgaraka* and the craftsman appears to indicate a great respect for the

1 पद्मरागं वसनं वसाना।—*Saundarananda Kāvya*, vi, 26; नीलांशुका—*Buddhacarita*, iv, 33; नीलकम्बलवासिनी—Ibid, xii, 107.

2 *Mahāvagga*, vi, 30, 3 and viii, 29.

3 *Kāmasūtra*, p. 230 (*sūtra* 34).

4 पुष्पास्तरणम्, माल्यग्रथनविकल्पाः, शेखरकापीडयोजनम्, कर्णपत्रभङ्गाः etc.—Ibid, p. 32.

5 See p. 69 (*sūtras* 37 and 38); p. 300 (*sūtra* 9).

crafts which are nowhere in Vātsyāyana spoken of as implying any inferior rank or position.

THE POSITION OF THE GAṆIKĀS

In the age of Vātsyāyana, the *Gaṇikā*, or the educated and accomplished woman about the town, occupied a peculiar position. Though belonging to the class of "public women," still she appears to have been treated with special consideration. But it was not every courtesan that received this appellation: it was only when a woman of this class was marked out by high intellectual attainments, and striking pre-eminence in the arts that she won the coveted title of *gaṇikā*. She must have her mind cultivated and trained by a thorough education (*śāstraprahatabuddhiḥ*) and Vātsyāyana lays down that it is only when a courtesan is versed in both the series of sixty-four arts or *kalās* enumerated by him and is endowed with an amiable disposition, personal charms and other winning qualities, that she acquires the designation of a *gaṇikā* and receives a seat of honour in the assemblies of men. She is always honoured by the king and is highly lauded by men qualified to appreciate merit; her favours and company are sought for, and she becomes, in fact, the observed of all observers, a model and pattern for all.[1] In the *Lalitavistara*, king Śuddhodana desires for the young Siddhārtha a bride who was as much learned in the *śāstras* and as accomplished in the arts as a *gaṇikā*.[2] Bharata's *Nāṭyaśāstra*, which is a work of the same period, speaks equally, if not more, enthusiastically, about the excellences of the *gaṇikā*. Bharata describes her as one who knows

1 आभिरभ्युच्छ्रिता वेश्या शीलरूपगुणान्विता ।
लभते गणिकाशब्दं स्थानं च जनसंसदि ॥
पूजिता सा सदा राज्ञा गुणवद्भिश्च संस्तुता ।
प्रार्थनीयाऽभिगम्या च लक्ष्यभूता च जायते ॥—Ibid, p. 40 (*sūtras* 20-21).

2 शास्त्रे विधिज्ञकुशला गणिका यथैव ; *Lalitavistara*, xii, 139.

the practical application of various arts, who possesses a deep knowledge of many of the sciences (*śāstras*), who is skilled in the sixty-four *kalās* and in dancing to the accompaniment of music, whose conduct is marked by respect towards superiors, by graceful and engaging manners, by charming gestures and sweet blandishments; who possessed strength and firmness of mind and at the same time modesty and a sweetness of temper; who is free from the characteristic defects of women; who speaks gracefully and clearly; who is clever in work and does not get tired—a woman possessed of all these rare qualities and accomplishments would be called a *gaṇikā*.[1] That she was regarded by Bharata as a woman of great education and culture appears from the fact that the *gaṇikā*, when introduced as a character in a drama, is, according to him, to speak Sanskrit.[2] The uses to which the *gaṇikā* puts her money are also characterised by a desire for public good and her charity shows the noble tendencies of her cultured mind. The *gaṇikās* of the highest class, says Vātsyāyana, consider it as the highest gain to themselves when they receive sufficient money to spend on the building of temples, excavation of tanks, planting of gardens, erection of bridges and of houses for sacrifice and ceremonies or the institution of permanent arrangements for the worship of the gods. They valued very highly any chance of giving away cows to Brāhmaṇas, of course through a third person, because no Brāhmaṇa would accept anything from a courtesan.[3]

The *gaṇikā* literally appears to mean a woman who is the member of a *gaṇa* or corporation, whose charms are the

1 *Bhāratīya Nāṭyaśāstra*—(Nirṇaya-Sāgara Press ed.), Chap. xxiv, 109-113.

2 राज्ञ्य गणिकायाश्च शिल्पकार्यास्तथैव च। कालावस्थान्तरकृतं योज्यं पाठ्यं तु संस्कृतम्॥—Ibid, Chap. xvii, 37-38.

3 *Kāmasūtra*, p. 340 (*sūtra* 25).

common poetry of the whole body of men associated together by a common bond, economic or political. Manu associates the *gaṇa* and the *gaṇikā* in one verse saying that the food offered by both were equally to be refused by a Brahmin.[1] The *gaṇa* might be a corporation of citizens, the *nāgaraka-jana-samavāya* of Vātsyāyana, like the one to which our *nāgaraka* belonged, or it might be a political body like that of the Licchavis of Vaiśālī whose *gaṇikā*, Ambapālikā, was a glory of their capital and was credited with all the virtues and qualities contemplated by Vātsyāyana and Bharata, thus testifying that their definitions were not fanciful and imaginary. We read in the *Mahāvagga* that she was charming, attractive, graceful, possessed of a fine and tender complexion, generous, and proficient in dancing, song and music. The wealth and power that the *gaṇikā* of Vaiśālī possessed and the position that she occupied, were in no way inferior to those of the best of the proud Licchavis ; her train was as numerous and as sumptuously decorated, her carriages were as magnificent as those of the Licchavis against whom she drove up axle to axle, wheel to wheel, and yoke to yoke. Her presence made the city of Vaiśālī shine forth in great splendour and glory. She constituted, as it were, a valued institution of the city, the high model of beauty and art thus set up by the *gaṇikā* of Vesālī roused a merchant of the rival city of Rājagaha to induce king Bimbisāra to have this institution of *gaṇikā* in his own capital which suffered in this respect in comparison with the chief city of the *gaṇarājya* or republic of the Licchavis.[2] It shows that in those early times *gaṇikās* were not so numerous as they became in Vātsyāyana's days. But we observe that in the days of Kātyāyana, the author of the *Vārttika-sūtras* of the grammatical school of Pāṇini, there were already guilds of *gaṇikās* (*gāṇikyam*), as

1 गणान्नं गणिकान्नञ्च विदुषा च जुगुप्सितम् ।—*Manu*, iv, 209.

2 *Mahāvagga*, vi. 30 and viii. 1.

explained in the *Mahābhāṣya*, just as we read of the *gaṇikā-saṅgha* in Vātsyāyana.[1]

We may also note the fact that Buddha excludes from his fold the eunuch and the hermaphrodite, but not the *gaṇikā*, who does not appear to have been looked upon as a moral outcaste past redemption. The Buddhist religious books have hardly anything to say against Ambapālikā, the courtesan of Vaiśālī, nor do they suggest that there was anything peculiar or out of the way in the favour that Buddha showed towards her. Reading the *Vinaya-Piṭaka* we are indeed astonished to see how careful and anxious the Buddha was in order not to offend public opinion and to give a decent and respectable appearance to his congregation. He thought it disreputable and exceedingly revolting to the sense of common decency of the people to harbour sinners like the parricide or the matricide, but apparently he experienced no difficulty in ordaining a courtesan who had reformed herself; he could take her in without causing a shock to the moral susceptibilities of the people and in fact some of the noble sisters (*therīs*), whose inspired songs have been compiled in the *Therīgāthā*, had reformed their life which before ordination was not quite above reproach.

The position that the *gaṇikā* enjoyed may be explained by the fact that in a society characterised by æsthetic refinement as was that of the age of Vātsyāyana, women who possessed special proficiency in the arts were respected for the value of their art, and their company was sought for by all lovers of art; the long training and education needed for the acquisition of such literary and artistic accomplishments as the *gaṇikā* possessed, could not be obtained by a girl who was married and had to manage a household, especially as she was married rather early, though Vātsyāyana's chapter on courtship shows

1 केदाराद्यञ्च।—*Pāṇini*, iv, 2, 40. गणिकायाश्च (*Vārttika*) गणिकायाश्चेति वक्तव्यम्। गणिकानां समूहो गाणिक्यम्। *Mahābhāṣya* of Patañjali. Cf. पूजिता गणिकासंघैर्नन्दिनी को न पूजयेत्—*Kāmasūtra*, p. 182 (*sūtra* 52).

that many of them remained unmarried even after puberty. Moreover, it was certainly not considered decent for such a girl to attend the public schools of art or *gāndharva śālās*, where the daughters of the *gaṇikās* received lessons in the arts, and formed, as Vātsyāyana says, acquaintance with the sons of the wealthy citizens;[1] nor could any but very wealthy parents afford to give their daughters such education at home. Where the parents were very rich, as in the case of the daughters of princes and high officials, they did receive, as we have seen before, a thorough education in the arts and sciences. Gopā was as learned and clever as any *gaṇikā*, as the *Lalitavistara* says. Then again, the wedded wife, on account of her manifold duties in the household, could not cultivate the arts as thoroughly as she would like to; besides, the great regard for purity in the married woman and the strict and rigid rules that guided her conduct even in the age of Vātsyāyana, prohibited, as we have seen above, her receiving lessons in the arts except from her own husband. We see, therefore, that the *gaṇikās*, like the Hetæræ in the Athens of Pericles, were generally more educated and better skilled in the arts than the married women, and the *nāgarakas*, though they had devoted wives at home, as the ideal of a wife drawn by Vātsyāyana shows, were attracted by the intellectual and artistic qualities of the educated *gaṇikā*. Such a noble soul as Bhāsa's Cārudatta, though he had a devoted wife at home, who was ready to sacrifice the last bit of her personal property for his sake and for whom he himself had a great regard, had no scruple in falling in love with the actress Vasantasenā, and the *Mṛcchakaṭika* makes him even marry her.[2] With such ideals of the

1 तेषां कलाग्रहणे गान्धर्वशालायां......सन्दर्शनयोगाः ।—Ibid, p. 364 (*sūtra* 15).

2 *Cārudatta*, Act iii, pp. 63 ff. Vātsyāyana also refers to the marriage with a courtesan, though it was fully binding only for one year, after which period, the husband still retained some, but not

devoted wife as we have in Vātsyāyana and in Bhāsa's Cārudatta, it cannot be said with any sound reason that the *nāgaraka* sought the company of the *gaṇikā* because his life at home was miserable or unbearable, but evidently he was drawn by her accomplishments. Even the general public, though they despised her for the life she led, tolerated her on account of her high artistic qualifications which they found many occasions to enjoy and appreciate at the *prekṣaṇakas* or performances at the festive assemblies (*samājas*) such as we have described above.

exclusive, claim to her affections :—पाणिग्रहश्च संवत्सरमव्यभिचार्यभर्ता यथा कामिनी स्यात् ऊर्ध्वमपि संवत्सरात् etc.—*Kāmasūtra*, p. 365 (*sūtras* 20-22).

CONCLUSION

We havs thus seen that the *nāgaraka* was a man of considerable intellectual culture and æsthetic refinement, but at the same time he was not very scrupulous with regard to sexual morality. He is the product of an age when wealth and riches were flowing into India through an extensive commerce with the east and the west and the picture that the *Kāmasūtra* furnishes of his life also shows the virtues and vices characteristic of such an age. In the first place we observe that this materialistic prosperity had led to the formation in the country of materialistic ideals that made more of the comforts of the world than of *dharma* or the life of discipline. There are people, says Vātsyāyana, who hold that the *dharmas* should not be practised, in as much as the fruits of such practice,—the rewards for these austerities, are only prospective, and moreover they are doubtful and uncertain at the best ; who but a fool would give away to others, what he has in his own hands, in the hope of some future gain ? Better a dove to-day than a peacock to-morrow. Better a copper token (*kārṣāpaṇa*) that is certain than a piece of sterling gold—a *niṣka*—the acquisition of which is doubtful. Vātsyāyana, of course, combats these ideas, but it shows that the materialistic ideals of pleasure are there in the country, though limited only to a small section of the people, mostly to the Laukāyatikas or materialists.[1]

It must not be imagined, however, that the age in which Vātsyāyana lived was as a whole an age of gross materialism or that the whole of Indian society at the time bore this

1 न धर्मांश्चरेत्। एष्यत्फलत्वात्। सांशयिकत्वाच्च। कोह्यबालिशो हस्तगतं परगतं कुर्यात्। वरमद्य कपोतः श्वो मयूरात्, वरं सांशयिकान्निष्कादसांशयिकः कार्षापण इति लौकायतिकाः।—Ibid, p. 19 (*sūtras* 25-30).

character ; it will be a mistake to suppose that the *nāgaraka's* easy morality was even a main feature of the character of the majority of the people. In the first place, Vātsyāyana paints in his *nāgaraka* the picture of a particular and limited section of the dwellers in cities. A *nāgaraka* is a wealthy person who has received a liberal education in youth and has already earned a competence by inheritance or by personal endeavour, so that he can afford to lead the life of comfort and pleasure in a city. The class which he represents has lived in all ages and in all countries wherever economic prosperity has enabled a section of the people to command and enjoy the good things of the earth. His counterpart is not wanting in our modern days in countries which are rich in material wealth and where the people "enjoy life." He can be traced with but few changes, and these only in details, in the salons of Paris and Vienna, of London and Berlin. In India itself, his successors, though not absolutely extinct, are but few, for the good reason that the abundance of material riches and the consequent joys of life out of which the *nāgaraka* could grow, have departed from this country.

Then, again, we observe that the character of the matron was marked by firmness and purity, modesty and restraint, showing that the general ideals of society as regards sexual purity had not been lowered since the age of the *Dharmasūtras.* In fact it is apparent from what Vātsyāyana says, that the main current of social life had not undergone much transformation and that the ideals set up in the *Dharma*-codes still controlled society. He asserts that the whole structure of society is upheld and maintained by the observance of the principle of the division of the people into *varṇas* or classes and into *āśramas* or stages of life. In this society a man does not marry until he has finished his education ; after marrying he lives the life of a good citizen and brings up a family, and in advanced years, retires from worldly activities and devotes himself exclusively to matters spiritual. The Brāhmaṇas among the four classes were highly respected, their blessings being considered as conducive to long life and glory.[1] Respect for the *Vedas* and the other Holy scriptures is insisted upon ; it is declared that there is no room for doubting the validity of their teachings : in matters relating to life in this world, which can produce visible effects, one has to guide oneself in accordance with the ordinances of the Sacred Codes, and in matters relating to the life beyond and producing effects beyond the physical vision of man, one is also guided by the prescriptions of Holy Writ such as the performance of sacrifices and similar other observances. It is declared that the authority of the sacred scriptures is binding with regard to *dharma* or the principles of right conduct which have to be learned from *Śruti*, or the *Vedas*, and also from the assembly of men proficient in them.[2]

Vedic sacrifices still appear to have constituted an important feature of the religious exercises of the people ; along with other common occurrences of life sacrifices are mentioned by Vātsyāyana as occasions which permitted a gathering of people of both sexes and we are told that even the virtuous matron could attend such assemblies with the permission of her husband. The erection of sacrificial altars and houses, formed one of the most earnest desires of women, nay even of the courtesans. Sacrifices formed an indispensable part of the ceremony of marriage, which, if once performed in the presence of fire, i. e., with sacrifices, could never be repudiated ; this is declared as the rule upheld by all teachers and throughout his chapter on courtship and marriage,

1 ब्राह्मणानां प्रशस्तानामाशिषः (यशस्यमायुष्यम्)।— Ibid, p. 380 (*sūtra* 51) ; also p. 170 (*sūtra* 36). Cf. वर्णाश्रमाचारस्थितिलक्षणत्वाच्च लोकयात्रायाः etc.— Ibid, p. 20 (*sūtra* 31) ; ब्रह्मचर्यमेव त्वाविद्याग्रहणात्।—p. 12 (*sūtra* 6) ; बाल्ये विद्याग्रहणादीनर्थान्। कामं च यौवने। स्थाविरे धर्मं मोक्षं च।—pp. 11-12 (*sūtras* 2-4).

2 ·····अलौकिकत्वाददृष्टार्थत्वादप्रवृत्तानां यज्ञादीनां शास्त्रात् प्रवर्तनम्, लौकिकत्वाद दृष्टार्थत्वाच्च प्रवृत्तेभ्यश्च मांसभक्षणादिभ्यः शास्त्रादेव निवारणं धर्मः। श्रुतेर्धर्मज्ञसमवायाच्च प्रतिपद्येत।— Ibid, pp. 12-13 (*sūtras* 7-8).

Vātsyāyana advises a young lover, again and again, to ratify his marriage with the maiden of his love with sacrifices in the fire brought from the house of a *śrotriya*, i. e. a man who keeps up the sacrificial fire constantly burning in his house and daily offers oblations in it. A person initiated for sacrifice (*dīkṣita*) is also mentioned along with persons who have taken certain vows or have assumed the marks of certain sects of ascetics.[1] This makes it abundantly clear that the sacrifices laid down in the *gṛhya-sūtras* still held a prominent place in the life of the period when Vātsyāyana lived and here he is corroborated by epigraphic evidence. The inscriptions in Western India of the early centuries of the Christian era show that sacrifices on a large scale were performed at the time and munificent gifts were made to Bhikṣus and Brāhmaṇas even by persons of foreign extraction like Uṣabhadāta. Vātsyāyana speaks of a thousand cows given away to Brāhmaṇas. Moreover the daily performance of *bali-karma* at the *nāgaraka's* under the supervision of his wife shows the unabated influence of the *gṛhyasūtras.*[2] Then again, the *nāgaraka*, though a pleasure-seeker, was a worshipper of the gods. We have already referred to the niche at the head of his bed for holding an image of the *iṣṭa-devatā* or the deity to whom he was particularly

1 प्रतिपन्नामभिप्रेतावकाशवर्तिनीं नायकः श्रोत्रियागारादग्निमानाय्य कुशानास्तीर्य यथास्मृति हुत्वा च त्रिः परिक्रमेत्। अग्निसाक्षिका हि विवाहा न निवर्तन्त इत्याचार्यसमयः।—Ibid, pp. 219-220 (*sūtras* 11 and 13). See also pp. 220-222 (*sūtras* 14-27) ; and आवाहे विवाहे यज्ञे गमनं सखीभिः सह गोष्ठीं देवताभिगमनमित्यनुज्ञाता कुर्यात्।—Ibid, p. 226 (*sūtra* 15). विवाहे यज्ञव्यसनोत्सवेषु etc.—Ibid, p. 274 (*sūtra* 41) ; स्थलीनामग्निचैत्यानां निबन्धनं etc.—Ibid, p. 340 (*sūtra* 25) ; श्रोत्रियस्य ब्रह्मचारिणो दीक्षितस्य व्रतिनो लिङ्गिनो वा etc.—Ibid, p. 351 (*sūtra* 28).

2 For the epigraphic evidence see *Epigrahia Indica*, vol. viii, pp. 59-96, etc. ; also *Report of the Arch. Sur. of Western India*, vols. iv and v. गोसहस्राणां पात्रान्तरितं ब्राह्मणेभ्यो दानं।—*Kāmasūtra*, p. 340 (*sūtra* 25) ; and त्रिषवणाचरितबलिकर्म—Ibid, p. 224 (*sūtra* 3).

devoted and also to the daily worship of the gods at the household temple. Moreover, he, and specially his wife, took part in fasts and observances whose number was apparently not insignificant. Besides, we have seen, how at regular, as well as irregular, intervals the public took part in grand religious festivals (*ghaṭā*) often accompanied by processions of images and attended by men and women in large numbers. Even a courtesan considered it as the greatest happiness of her life (*lābhātiśaya*) to institute arrangements for the worship of the gods.[1] All these facts go to prove that religious observances played a great part in the life of the people in Vātsyāyana's time, and that the Code of Manu had at the time acquired its full authority over the public mind as is shown by Vātsyāyana who speaks of *Svāyambhuva Manu* as the person who had taken up the *Dharma* section of Prajāpati's all-embracing encyclopædia and dealt with it in a separate treatise. Besides, Yājñavalkya's great code, second in importance to Manu alone, is supposed to have been composed about the time when Vātsyāyana lived.[2]

It was in this period, again, that Mahāyāna Buddhism grew and spread, and it must be admitted that the literature of the Mahāyāna school bears on its face the impress of this age of æsthetic refinement and culture. Its great preacher, Aśvaghoṣa, sought to popularise his faith by writing dramas and magnificent poetical works instead of works on dry dialectics and abstruse theology. The few fragments that we possess of Aśvaghoṣa's dramas, *Śāriputraprakaraṇa* and others, show that in at least one of them the *gaṇikā* played almost as important a part as in Bhāsa's *Cārudatta*, and that

1 Ibid, p. 43 (*sūtra* 6); p. 224 (*sūtra* 3); p. 228 (*sūtra* 26); pp. 49-51; p. 226 (*sūtra* 15); p. 311 (*sūtra* 20); p. 340 (*sūtra* 25).

2 प्रजापतिर्हि प्रजाः सृष्ट्वा तासां स्थितिनिबन्धनं त्रिवर्गस्य साधनमध्यायानां शतसहस्रेणाग्रे प्रोवाच। तस्यैकदेशं स्वायंभुवो मनुर्धर्माधिकारिकं पृथक् चकार।—Ibid, p. 4 (*sūtras* 5-6). For Yājñavalkya, see Weber, *History of Indian Literature* (Eng. Trans.), p. 281.

too in a work where Buddha himself makes his appearance with some of his dearest disciples. Aśvaghoṣa was in the first place a theologian and a dialectician as his *Vajrasūcī* would go to prove, but in an age of great æsthetic culture, he had to adapt himself to the refined tastes of his audience and so he sweetened the tasteless doses of his dry theological doctrines with the honey of poetry and music, and he knew how to mix the ingredients with all the skill of a master. The *Lalitavistara* also has succeeded eminently in combining intense love and reverence for the Master with poetic skill and grace. The *Dīvyāvadāna* and the *Mahāvastu* also appear to have received, at least, some additions in this era of *kathās* and *ākhyānas* of which we find a frequent mention in Vātsyāyana.[1]

In the next place, we gather from the philosophical literature of the age in which Vātsyāyana lived, that it was one of intense philosophical speculation. Nāgārjuna in the second century A. D. had established his *Śūnyavāda* or Philosophic Nihilism and he was followed by a string of great logicians of his school. His success roused to activity all the orthodox schools of philosophy the representatives of which proceeded to compose new works, to write extensive commentaries on the already existing texts, or at any rate to bring their systems up to date by fresh additions calculated to combat successfully the new school that was gradually acquiring strength and volume. Whether we do or do not accept the conclusion of Prof. Jacobi that the *Nyāyadarśana* and the *Brahmasūtra* were originally composed between 200 and 450 A.D., we have less reason to doubt him when he assigns to this period the old commentators, Vātsyāyana, Upavarṣa and Baudhāyana (the *Vṛttikāra*) who were all working to bring their respective systems in line with the new ideas

1 For Aśvaghoṣa's Dramas, see Lüders, *Königliche preuss. Turfan Exp., Kleinere Sanskrit Texte,* Heft I and *Das Śāriputraprakaraṇa* (*Sitz. der K. preuss. Akad. d. Wiss.*), 1911.

27

originated by Buddhist thinkers. Even the author oft he *Kāmasūtra* has shown the prevailing tendency of the time by defining his general concepts and discussing the current theories about them in the approved philosophical method, and he has approached his subject with the detatchment of a scientific observer and the analytic skill of a subtle logician. Moreover, we must not forget that in the period embraced by the first four centuries of the Christian era, the Mahābhārata was receiving the final form in which we possess it now.[1]

There can be no doubt, then, that this age of great philosophical discovery and analysis, the age that produced the *Lalitavistara* and the code of Yājñavalkya, could not have been marked by a general low tone in moral life. The age to be studied as a whole requires a study of all sides of the Indian civilisation of the time based on a far ampler stock of materials than only Vātsyāyana can supply. Vātsyāyana's work deals with only one aspect of it and shows that his was an age of great intellectual activity in all directions. and the great thinker makes an analysis of the erotic feelings and of the elementary relations between the sexes in a right scientific spirit : in doing so he naturally turned for illustration to the class that had cultivated this side of the humanistics for centuries, at least since the time of Pāṇini, to whom as we have seen, the *nāgaraka* was a familiar character. Vātsyāyana does not cast a charm over illicit love, nor does he invest it with the halo of romance. He merely gives a frank and matter of fact account of the social sore, proceeds to a masterly analysis of the psychology of the man who seeks

1 For Prof. Jacobi's views see *Journal of the American Oriental Society*, 1911, p. 29. For Vātsyāyana's philosophical discussions see *Kāmasūtra*, pp. 11-25. For the date of the *Mahābhārgta*, see E. W. Hopkins, *The Great Epic of India*, pp. 397-98 and Winternitz, *Geschichte der Indischen Litteratur*, i, p. 403.

such love—the jealousy, anger, hatred, passion, greed, selfishness that working within the brain of the human animal, cloud his judgment and pervert his tastes. He points out categorically that a scientific work (*śāstra*), dealing with a subject as a whole, must be exhaustive, but that is no reason why a particular practice described in it should be carried into effect; for example, the taste, the properties and the digestive qualities of dog's flesh are given in medical works, but that is no reason why it should be adopted as an article of diet by sober men.[1] He winds up his thesis by saying, "whenever, on account of the character of the subject dealt with, I had to speak about things that might smack of lust and desire, I have taken care immediately afterwards to censure and condemn them", and he adds that, he himself had followed the strictly pure life of a *brahmacārin* and had been deeply immersed in contemplation (*samādhi*) while composing the work for the benefit of the world and not for feeding the flames of desire. The ideal of life that he holds up, is that of harmonious blending of the three elements—*dharma, artha* and *kama*—which sum up according to Indian ideas all human motives of action for the people of the world. He enjoins that a rightminded person should occupy himself with such actions as, while giving pleasure (*kāma*), do not stand in the way of the acquisition of the good things of the earth (*artha*), and at the same time do not disregard the behests of *dharma*, that is, as he explains, do not afford any ground for the fear of their being followed by evil effects hereafter. This is the same as the teaching of the *Bhagavadgītā* that God dwells in such desires as do not violate *dharma*. Vātsyāyana thus emphasises the working out of the threefold functions of man

1 For Vātsyāyana's analysis of illicit love see *Kāmasūtra*, pp. 60-65 (*sutras* 5-22), and his *Pāradārika* section, pp. 247-298. Cf. also न शास्त्रमस्तीत्येतावत् प्रयोगे कारणं भवेत्। शास्त्रार्थान् व्यापिनो विद्यात् प्रयोगांस्त्वेकदेशिकान्। रसवीर्यविपाका हि श्वमांसस्यापि वैद्यके। कीर्तिता इति तत् किं स्याद्भक्षणीयं विचक्षणैः।—Ibid, p. 170 (*sūtras* 37-38).

(*trivarga*) in such a way that there may be no conflict among these three, while he is not unmindful of the fourth or final good of mankind, *viz.*, *mokṣa*,[1] the ultimate release from the limitations that curb the eternal growth of his soul.

1 अधिकारवशादुक्ता ये चित्रा रागवर्धनाः। तदनन्तरमत्रैव ते यत्नाद्विनिवारिताः॥ तदेतद्ब्रह्मचर्येण परेण च समाधिना। विहितं लोकयात्रार्थं न रागार्थोऽस्य संविधिः॥ रक्षन् धर्मार्थकामानां स्थितिं स्वां लोकवर्तिनीम्। अस्य शास्त्रस्य तत्त्वज्ञो भवत्येव जितेन्द्रियः।—Ibid, pp. 381-382 (*sūtras* 54, 57 and 58). किं स्यात्परत्रेत्याशङ्का कार्ये यस्मिन्न जायते। न चार्थघ्नं सुखं चेति शिष्टास्तत्र व्यवस्थिताः॥ त्रिवर्गसाधकं यत्स्याद्द्वयोरेकस्य वा पुनः। कार्यं तदपि कुर्वीत न त्वेकार्थं द्विबाधकम्।—Ibid. p. 26 (*sūtras* 50-51). Cf. धर्माविरुद्धो भूतेषु कामोऽस्मि भरतर्षभ।—*Bhagavadgītā*, viii, 11 see also स्थाविरे धर्मं मोक्षं च।—*Kāmasūtra*, p. 12 (*sūtra* 4).